BISHNOIS AND THE BLACKBUCK
CAN DHARMA SAVE THE ENVIRONMENT?

ANU LALL

Vitasta

Thank you for choosing a Vitasta book. For years we've been committed to publishing books that inform, inspire, and endure. Reach out to us for bulk purchases. Discover more titles at www.vitastapublishing.com
Renu Kaul Verma
Managing Director
Vitasta Publishing Pvt Ltd
4348/4C, Ansari Road, Daryaganj
New Delhi-110 002
info@vitastapublishing.com

ISBN: 978-93-47098-83-3

© Anu Lall
First Edition 2025
MRP ₹ 695

All Rights Reserved.
No part of this publication may be reproduced, stored in a retrieval system, or transmitted in any form, or by any means—electronic, mechanical, photocopying, recording or otherwise—without the prior permission of the publisher. Opinions expressed in this book are the author's own. The publisher is in no way responsible for these.

Edited by Cora Bhatia
Typeset by Rohit Gautam
Cover Design by Bhaskar J Borah and Rohit Gautam
Images by Anu Lall
Printed by Vikas Computer and Printers, New Delhi

For
Mummy and Papa

What We Were Afraid to Place on the Cover

In my study of the Bishnoi community, a poignant moment that stopped me in my tracks was witnessing a woman breast-feeding a baby deer alongside their own child. It was not a performance, not dramatic, simply an act of care that dissolved the boundary between human and animal, between 'us and them'. Such sightings are not rare. Images and videos are available online, in archives and as stories in oral history.

Yet, when I wanted to capture this on the book cover it was deemed inappropriate. Online marketplaces flag breast-feeding pictures as inappropriate. So, I turned to artificial intelligence hoping to recreate the emotion, without an explicit documentary photograph. But there too, the door was closed. Artificial Intelligence has been trained to flag breast feeding as 'obscenity, inappropriate and against community guidelines.'

Whose moral code of conduct is humanity living with? How did our machines learn that the source of life must be hidden? Our advanced technologies, algorithms, and platforms, our loud proclamations of progress, cannot appreciate this first act of tenderness a baby, whether human or animal, receives.

After much deliberation I decided to reproduce few images here under permissible use, drawn from Wiki Commons license, individual contributors and the Jambhani Sahitya Akademi. The idea is not to provoke, but to remember that compassion needs no approval. Nurturing life can never be obscene.

Let's teach machines to be human. And maybe learn to be human ourselves.

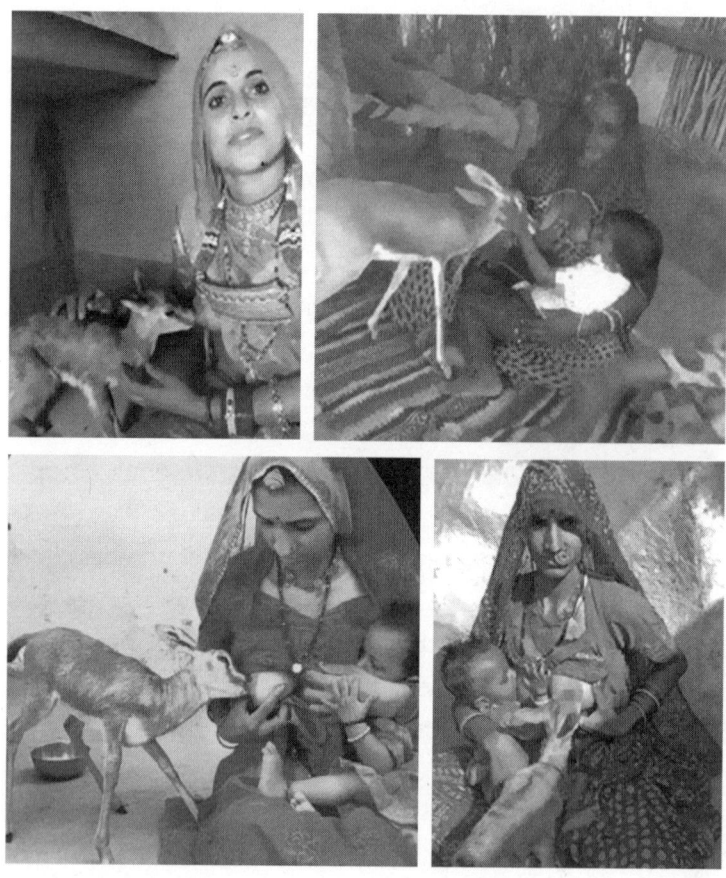

What We Were Afraid to Place on the Cover | vii

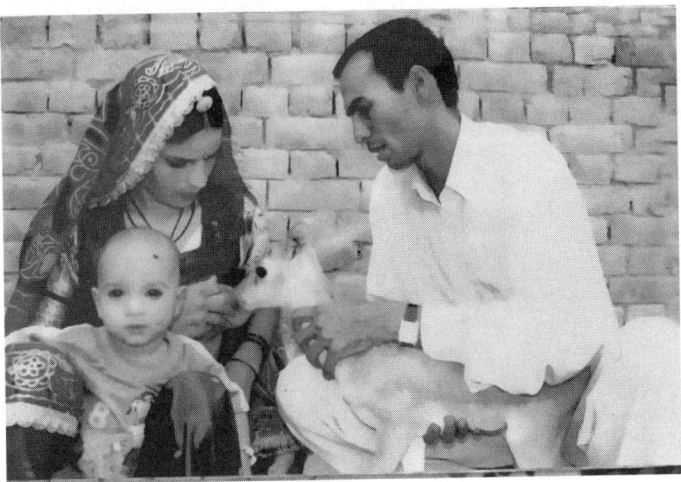

Image Source: Smt Vijay Lakshmi and Shri Vijay Pal Sahu Bishnoi

Advance Praise

In the book, *Bishnois and the Blackbuck: Can Dharma Save the Environment*, Anu Lall lays out a thesis at the very centre of Indian culture—the integration of nature as a way of life. This well-researched book not only highlights the environmental practices of the Bishnoi community, but also presents a dharmic, civilisational approach that supports the protection and preservation of nature. It is time for India to create a new modernity rooted in this cultural strength—one that can also offer a healing balm to a world facing an unprecedented environmental crisis. This innovative book invites further discussion and reflection.

Shashank Mani
Member of Parliament, Lok Sabha, Deoria
Founder Jagriti Movement

Dharma teaches us that we are a part of nature; we can take from nature what we need for our sustenance but not to satisfy our greed. We are inheritors and protectors of our environment to ensure we pass it on to future generations whole, flourishing and safe. At a time when planet Earth, our only home, faces a crisis due to over exploitation and destruction, all humans must look within to understand the reality of our existence and protect our only home to make it sustainable. *Dharma* ensures we discharge our duty to nature and its creations and answers the critical question of Who owns our Earth? All creations of nature do. We are mere Trustees. Anu Lall brings alive the spirit of trusteeship from the Bishnoi principles and Bishnoi way of life, with insight and compassion in her book – *Bishnois and the Blackbuck: Can Dharma Save the Environment.*

T V Mohandas Pai
Chairman, Aarin Capital Partners

Bishnois and the Blackbuck: Can Religion Save the Environment? is a powerful and authentic presentation of the Bishnoi community's spiritual philosophy, life values, and more than five centuries of ancient ecological commitment.

The depth with which Anu Lall has researched the history of the Bishnoi community, and the intellectual and cultural sensitivity with which it is presented, is truly admirable. The skill with which the author has connected our ancient traditions to the contemporary environmental discourse is praiseworthy, showing how relevant this philosophy is in today's world, where stability and environmental conservation are more necessary than ever before.

The work also presents the cultural and philosophical foundation that defines this community's identity. It reminds the world that religious communities like ours have lived for centuries—without external pressure or propaganda—in harmony with nature, guided by spiritual duty.

This is not merely a book; it gives voice to a community that has lived environmental conservation for the past 500 years—something the world has only recently begun to understand. This book does not just tell a story; it revives a civilisational memory.

We wish this book great success. We hope it will inspire scholars and environmentalists alike to also look toward religious traditions for environmental conservation. Anu Lall has contributed to preserving a sacred heritage, and for this we are deeply grateful to her.

Vinod Jambhadas
General Secretary
Jambhani Sahitya Akademi
Bikaner

Contents

Foreword		*xv*
Acknowledgements		*xix*
Introduction		*xxiii*
Chapter 1	: Who Owns the Earth?	1
Chapter 2	: Blackbuck Poaching: Breaking a Sacred Bond	11
Chapter 3	: Why were the Bishnois So Relentless?	25
Chapter 4	: Shaheed Scroll: Martyrs for 'Hirans'	35
Chapter 5	: Khejarli Massacre: Sacrificing Heads for Trees	55
Chapter 6	: Desert *Dharma:* Philosophy of Spirituality and Sustainability	73
Chapter 7	: Festivals, Traditions and Rituals	101
Chapter 8	: Are Bishnois Hindus or Muslims?	113
Chapter 9	: The Bishnoi Effect	127

Chapter 10	:	When Faith Becomes Forest	141
Chapter 11	:	Portraits of Devotion	161
Chapter 12	:	From Protest to Policy: The Art of Environmental Advocacy	179
Chapter 13	:	Badopal Wildlife Habitat Case: How Activism Helps	197
Chapter 14	:	Religious Roots of Ecological Crisis	213
Chapter 15	:	Can Dharma Save the Environment?	229

Appendix	*251*
363 Martyrs of Khejarli	*259*
Census of Marwar 1891	*271*
References	*273*
Index	*295*
About the Author	*303*

Foreword

Among developing countries, India stands out as particularly supportive of nature conservation. We are mainly vegetarian, regard life sacrosanct and hold many animals, trees and places sacred. However, we are "passive" conservationists. We may not kill or cut, but we don't prevent others from doing so. There are a few communities who are an exception, the foremost being the Bishnois of Rajasthan and Haryana.

Blackbuck and Chinkara were once the most numerous and commonly seen animals in India. Living in open, inhabited tracts, outside protected forests, they suffered the most drastic decline of all after independence. The Bishnoi areas become their only havens of survival. When driving through Marwar if one came upon their clusters, one could safely presume that a Bishnoi settlement was closeby. Jamboji, Mukam, Khejarli, Abohar, Doli, Lohawat, Guda Bishnoia and Tal Chhapar became the showpieces of Rajasthan and of the sanctity of living creatures.

A very respected former Principal of Mayo College, Ajmer, an Englishman, told me that he shot a blackbuck in a Bishnoi area, whereupon the Bishnoi womenfolk of a nearby *"Dhani"* broke his rifle and almost beat him to death. I never forget that and in the chapter on 'Religious Sentiment and Wildlife' in my book *Beyond the Tiger*, wrote the following: "I have seen chinkara gazelle that I wished to photograph streak off as soon as I stopped the vehicle and go stand close by the huts of Bishnoi encampments, from which sallied out the Bishnoi women in their colourful costumes, shouting and waiving staves. Unless accompanied by a Bishnoi guide who could vouchsafe my bonafides, I had always taken the precaution to keep the engine of the vehicle running whilst stopping to take pictures in a Bishnoi area!"

Anu Lall has done signal service by recounting the contribution and sacrifices of the Bishnois, which hopefully, would inspire others. Since the name of Sobha Ram of Doli does not appear in the roll of honour in this book, I take the liberty of recounting his tale and quote from my chapter on him. In the late 1960s, India was plagued by severe, serial droughts. The Bishnois of Doli as with others elsewhere, pooled their meagre resources to bring water-tankers for the antelope and even bored a tubewell, presided over by Sobha Ram, "a combination of priest, patriarch and blackbuck guardian angel", who I am privileged to call my friend. "At the height of summer—the blackbuck hovered around the village well to lick the droplets that fell off the bodies of bathing women to accumulate on the masonry floor. In the worst period, Sobha Ram did not waste even the water with which he washed the cooking utensils. He left the vessels outside his hut with the dirty water in them and the blackbuck came and licked them. Then in June, two blackbuck died. Sobha Ram vowed that he too would die, that he would not drink till the Patron Deity relented and sent rain. On the second night of the fast it rained, an occurrence to which the villagers also bore testimony".

When I drafted the Wildlife (Protection) Act of 1972, we had to take cognisance of our hunting past and I put "Game Reserves" which then existed, as a third protected area after parks and sanctuaries. Two decades later, with experience gained and with the 'Orans' of the Bishnois as a role model, I dropped the Game Reserves and included Community Reserves and Conservation Reserves in the Act.

I wish the book *Bishnois and the Blackbuck* all the success it deserves and hope it will inspire others to emulate.

Dr M K Ranjitsinh
'Krishnasar'
New Delhi

Dr MK Ranjitsinh IAS (Retd) | Former Director of Wildlife Preservation India | Forest Secretary MP | Senior Regional Advisor Asia Pacific United Nations Environment Program (UNEP) | Author

Acknowledgements

This book owes its *spanda* or pulsation to the spirit of the Bishnoi community, whose wisdom and unwavering dedication to the environment have inspired every page. Thank you for opening your world to me, for sharing your homes and spaces, for allowing me to share your legacy and philosophy with others. It's a rare privilege to weave together the voices of those who live by a philosophy that has an unwavering reverence for nature.

To echo the words of Maya Angelou—*I come as one, but I stand as many*—those who have stood behind me, encouraged and helped me along the way.

My first applause goes to Papa, who first told us tales of the Bishnoi community, stories that sounded like fables, long before the world had heard of them.

My special gratitude to leaders from the Bishnoi community, especially—Acharya Dr Govardhan Ram Ji, Swami Bhagwandas Ji (Mahant Aguni Jaanga Jambha), Acharya Bhagirthdas Ji Jajiwal Dhora, Swami Ramananad Ji (Mukkam Peethadheeshwar) and Acharya Dr Sachchidanand Ji (Mahant Lalasar Saathri) for their blessings and valuable time, making the philosophy so accessible to me, and sharing their knowledge in such a simple way.

I am indebted to Vinod Jambhadas Ji (whom I now call *bhai sa*) General Secretary, Jambhani Sahitya Akademi, for helping me find treasure troves of information and helping me appreciate the finer nuances of *Jambho Darshan*.

I am grateful to Arunina Bishnoi, Advocate at the Jaipur High Court, for painstakingly compiling the chronology of the blackbuck poaching cases, presented in the annexure.

My sincere thanks to the countless members of the Bishnoi community who generously shared their time, insights and expertise, especially Khamu Ram Bishnoi Ji, who helped me at every step of the way, Late Radheshyam Pemani Bishnoi, Parineeti Bishnoi, Peera Ram Bishnoi, Ranaram Bishnoi Ji, Vishek Bishnoi and Shiv Pratap Bishnoi.

I am deeply thankful to Rampal Bhavad Ji and Vinod Karwasara Ji for taking me along their modern-day legal advocacy in the policy arena.

A warm thank you to Mom for painstakingly reading so many unfinished drafts and not breaking my heart when they were not good enough, maintaining a constant supply of sumptuous food and endless *chai*, an addiction I promise to give up very soon. Endless love and gratitude for Bibi, whose hugs, radiant smiles, and warm *champis* offer the greatest comfort.

My heartfelt appreciation goes to Anil Sir, whose tireless work in translating every draft into Hindi, often on short notice, made the monumental feat of the simultaneous release of both the English and Hindi versions possible. Thank you for beautifully preserving the *'bhaav'* of my writing.

I am blessed to have Lipika Bhushan for her encouragement, laughs and gentle nudges to attend events I usually shy away from.

Many thanks to Punit Modhgil for his valuable ideas. I

thank Vanaja Kodungallur for generously sharing her wealth of knowledge and inspiring discussions.

A big thank you, to my family, friends and online community, your encouragement and belief in me is my strength that keeps me going. Especially my Gita class students, for your patience as I wrecked this year's teaching schedule. I shall commence teaching classes very soon.

I extend my thanks to Renu Kaul Verma, the team at Vitasta, editors and designers, Saumya, Cora, Reena, Rohit and Shubhpreet for shaping my manuscript with such care and giving it the beautiful form it now holds.

Finally, thank you, dear reader, for embarking on this journey. May these pages move and inspire you as deeply as this journey has inspired me.

Image ©Anu Lall Bishnois and the Blackbuck

Introduction

For most Indians, the word *'Bishnoi'* evokes two stark images—the blackbuck poaching case involving superstar Salman Khan and, more recently, the Lawrence Bishnoi stand-off with him. Unfortunately, neither of these emanates the positive recall that the community deserves. As the legal battle unfolded and dragged on for over twenty-six years and still counting, the nation watched in disbelief as an entire community rose to defend a few animals.

In a country where human lives don't matter as much, the country was astonished to witness a community stand resolute in seeking justice for a few animals. The case became a rare moment when modern justice systems intersected with a five-hundred-year-old philosophy that views the protection of nature as a spiritual duty—a *dharma*.

My journey with this book began with childhood tales of Bishnoi women nursing orphaned deer fawns. Growing up with roots in Haryana, these anecdotes felt like distant folklore from another land, far away from me. In my fast-paced life, I failed to realise many Bishnoi villages were, quite literally, in my own backyard. That's how distant the *dharmic* life is for most of us, in the modern world. It's still there—in the background, wherever we are—waiting to be rediscovered beneath the haze of modernity we have built around ourselves. Dharma demands conscious effort.

In the India I grew up, particularly among modern educated circles, the word *dharma* was taboo, and still is in many ways. It was fashionable to say—*I am spiritual, but not religious.* In this mindset, we imported ecological frameworks and sustainability goals from the West—but ironically, we ignored the deep ecological wisdom hidden in our own traditions. Hiding in every nook and corner of our *dharmic* texts is deep ecological wisdom and insight that are waiting to be dusted off and revisited.

Our history books didn't teach us anything much that made us proud of our cultural heritage. Nowhere in my curriculum, at least in my generation was the Bishnoi community mentioned as protectors of nature, or as torchbearers of an ancient ecological consciousness. As I immersed myself into the Bishnoi way of life, I realised how this philosophy and way of life refuses to see nature as separate from the self, but as an extension of it. As the events turned, I felt compelled to write a book—a tribute to the Bishnoi spirit and devotion to the environment that could serve as a blueprint for a more sustainable future for the entire world.

The Bishnois are sometimes called the *first eco-warriors*, defenders of the Earth protecting the environment as their spiritual duty. In truth, they are the last, standing fiercely resolute, where others have long abandoned their sacred duty. *Sanatan Dharma* regards human beings as the custodians of *Bhu Devi,* the Earth, sustaining the environment, and ecology. While most *dharmic sampradayas* and *panths* have strayed away from this sacred responsibility, the Bishnoi's remain unshaken, literally the last standing eco-warriors, not just protectors of nature, but also as warriors of *dharma*, in an age of apathy.

Bishnoi stories are not echoes of the past; they are a call to action, in today's bleak environment. Their legacy is one intense and unwavering devotion which is also unabashedly intense, where life itself is willingly sacrificed to protect the land, the trees, and the creatures that share it with us. The Bishnoi's message to the world on the brink of destruction is this: it is still possible to fight for nature, and if need be, to lay down one's life in her defence. The Bishnois show us the way.

The question is: are we listening?

Across the world, ancient bonds with nature have been severed. Europe has forgotten its pre-pagan roots. Indigenous communities have been erased. Aboriginal cultures erased, and great civilisations have crumbled. Bharat, that is India, is a civilisation that is still fighting to survive—lifting its head, holding onto faint memories of its own distant *dharmic* thought leadership, struggling but refusing to let go, trying to return to its spiritual core.

Sanatan Dharma has a close relationship with the environment. A human being pays five important debts in their lifetime, one of them being the *Bhuta-rin*, reminding us of our responsibilities beyond ourselves, guiding us towards a life of gratitude and responsibility. *Bhuta-rin* transforms environmental care from a ritual into a sacred duty, telling us that ecological responsibility is not optional but a spiritual obligation. The five elements of *prakriti* or nature guide all aspects of life.

In *Sanatan Dharma,* nature was never a passive backdrop—it was the centre of the human experience. Forests were living entities with distinct personalities. In the *Ramayana*, Valmiki Ji paints vivid portraits of hundreds of tree species and forest types, making it a treasure trove for nature lovers, and a guidebook for ecologists, as much as a sacred treatise.

The *Vana Parva* in the *Mahabharata* and the *Aranya Kanda* unfold amidst the wilderness, where nature moulds destinies and transforms characters.

Indian lands—its forests, mountains and rivers—were sacred, largely managed by informal, yet tight knit communities rather than state authorities. Across India, thousands of sacred groves thrive under the protection of local communities, upheld as living, divine entities. Even today, Indian forestry has a separate legal classification for sacred groves and forests. They stand as silent witnesses to an ecological consciousness embedded in our traditions, unfortunately being run down every day, first by colonial greed, now by modernity fuelled by capitalist greed, and our lost connection with our own spiritual roots.

As citizens of this planet, it is time we confront a few profound and long-neglected questions—questions that are rarely voiced but are long overdue.

Who owns the Earth?
Is it Kings and Governments? Is it Capitalists? Or is it indigenous communities who have lived on the land and protected it for generations?

The short answer is: no one.

The Earth cannot be owned—forests, rivers and nature can't be owned; only shared by those who understand its rhythms.

This question lies at the heart of this book, and we will revisit it several times. Across the country, different communities, tribes, *dharmic panths* and *sampradayas* have revered the Earth in their own ways, with a deep spiritual connection with nature, treating animals, mountains, rivers and forests as sacred.

Going beyond the question of mere ownership, another pertinent question this book explores is a relatively unexplored one.

Can *Dharma* save the environment?

Modern environmentalism focuses on metrics such as carbon footprints and ESG (Environmental, Social, and Governance) goals, measuring sustainability in numbers and implementing it through laws and policies. But perhaps what we have overlooked is something deeper: *sacred devotion*—a spiritual, moral, and mystical duty to protect what sustains us. Where nature is revered rather than exploited.

This book shines a spotlight on local Indian communities, *sampradayas* and *panths*—who live close to the land, with their own rules of engagement, built into their *dharma* of protecting nature. These communities instinctively understand that they are mere guardians of the Earth, entrusted with the *dharmic* duty of passing it on, not as a depleted resource, but as a thriving sanctuary for future generations.

The academic conversation around religion and ecology took a pivotal turn in the late sixties, when historian Lynn White Jr argued that Christianity and other Western religions are a major cause of the global environmental crisis. His paper was short and terse, and ironically the rebuttals and commentaries on his concise write-up have been much larger and wider in reach. Sometimes I think, had Lynn White's paper just remained buried, this field of study would probably never have even evolved.

Lynn single-handedly brought the spotlight on religion and ecology, sparking a firestorm of debates and shaping a field of study that might never have gained prominence otherwise.

While western scholars rushed to defend Christianity against Lynn's thesis; Indian thought leaders of that time, rarely used Lynn's thesis to uncover our own native spiritual practices that have been intrinsic to our civilisation, which put nature and environment centre stage. India's own ecological consciousness with its *dharmic* backdrop remain largely unexplored in public discourse.

Until recently, Indian thought remained absent from modern environmental discourse. The connection between religiosity and environmental behaviour was barely acknowledged in academic frameworks, and popular culture. It was as if Indian society had collective amnesia about the strong relationship between humans and nature, enshrined in *Sanatan Dharma*. Academic frameworks seldom acknowledge the role of *dharmic wisdom* in shaping ecological values or creating modern frameworks. This glaring omission of *Sanatan Dharma*, side lines one of the world's last surviving ancient civilisations that has sustained a harmonious relationship with nature for millennia.

Why have we let this wisdom fade into obscurity?
Can reconnecting with it help us save the environment?

Voices like Dr Vandana Shiva have championed the preservation of and engagement with indigenous knowledge, including its Hindu roots to some extent. In more recent times, scholars like Christopher Chapple studied Hinduism and Ecology, exploring sacred forests and sacred rivers.

Late Dr O P Dwivedi worked on *Dharma Ecology* and Hindu spiritual and cultural beliefs intertwined with environment. Platforms like the Yale Forum on Religion and Ecology have opened avenues for more discussions, and David Haberman's research examine Hindu ecological philosophy to some extent.

Yet one of the most powerful living embodiments of Indian environmentalism with roots in *dharma*, remains with the Bishnoi community of Rajasthan—a Hindu *Vaishnavite panth* founded by Guru Jambheshwar Ji, fondly called Jambho Ji. A mystic, yogi, and reformer Jambho Ji laid down 29 principles that have woven ecology into everyday life.

For over five centuries, the Bishnois have followed an ecological code as a sacred duty, fiercely safeguarding wildlife and trees, at the cost of their own lives. They have made unimaginable sacrifices and their reverence for nature is woven into the very fabric of their existence.

I am acutely aware of the perils of writing about a community, *panth* or *sampradaya* which can inevitably lead to generalisations. It goes without saying that there are always a few people in every community, who are 'born into' the community, and may not necessarily live the philosophy. However, in a world struggling to save the environment, the Bishnoi principles and commitment can teach us a lot. They have lived in harmony with nature, following a strict ecological code, for over five centuries. These fierce eco-warriors regard it as their spiritual duty, their *dharma* to protect the environment, animals and trees. All of humanity can emulate this conduct.

Even secular laws beseech us to protect forests, lakes, rivers, and wildlife and to have compassion for living creatures. Article 51A(g) of the Indian Constitution makes it a fundamental duty to protect and improve the environment.

Article 48A of the Directive Principle of State Policy directs the state to protect and safeguard the environment, forests and wildlife. Whether or not you are a Bishnoi, the Indian Constitution enshrines environmental compassion into the domain of policy and activism.

The focus of this book is the Bishnoi philosophy and their principles—enshrined within the larger context of *Sanatan Dharma* which regards humans as guardians of nature, not owners, of nature.

This book is an invitation to view ancient wisdom, not as a nostalgic relic of the past, but as a living philosophy, even today. It can serve as a guiding light for a sustainable future.

This book is a call to rediscover the ecological consciousness inherent in *Sanatan Dharma*, through the Bishnoi lens, to integrate this wisdom into modern environmental efforts, and to recognise how communities continue to embody these values against all odds.

We have forgotten that ecology is not just a science; it is a spiritual orientation. When nature is sacred, protection becomes instinctive. When nature is reduced to metrics, care becomes optional. The commodification of nature mirrors the commodification of life itself.

In writing this book, I have chosen to maintain an academic backdrop while staying close to the spirit of eco-spiritualism. I balance scholarly research while integrating my personal experiences and travels to Bishnoi villages, which I believe, are a window to their world.

I hope this book inspires young academicians and researchers to look beyond Western conservation models alone and evaluate the possibility of using the *dharma* framework as an academic theory of environmental conservation.

I hope that one day *Sanatan Dharma* can be a new paradigm to explain human behaviour. Just like researchers use theories of Value-Belief-Norm (VBN), Precautionary Principle *et al*, someday they can use the theory of *Sanatan Dharma* in academia, the principle that explains it all.

I hope filmmakers and storytellers bring the Bishnoi legacy—and other indigenous *dharmic* communities—into cultural mainstream narratives.

I hope these stories find a place in our collective consciousness, shaping the way we approach sustainability.

Above all, I hope academia, society and humanity realise, that we must reclaim this ancient wisdom—not just for nostalgia's sake, but for the survival of our planet.

I know it is a big ask, but let's dare to dream.

I dare!

Signing off, as the Bishnois say—*Nivan Pranam!*

Anu Lall
Mysore, India
January 2026

Image ©Anu Lall Bishnois and the Blackbuck

Chapter 1

Who Owns the Earth?

सत्यं बृहदृतमुग्रं दीक्षा तपो ब्रह्म यज्ञः पृथिवीं धारयन्ति
*Satyam Brhad-Rtam-Ugram Diikssaa Tapo Brahma
Yajnyah Prthiviim Dhaarayanti*
Truth, extensive, powerful universal law, dedication,
penances and spiritual acts sustain the Earth
—Bhumi Suktam, *Atharva Veda,* 12.1.1

On August 2022, an unexpected cinematic phenomenon swept across India. *Kantara*, a small budget Kannada film with no grand promotions or star-studded campaigns, captured the nation's imagination, transcending linguistic and regional barriers. What began as a locally rooted tale was soon dubbed in multiple languages, and emerged as one of the year's highest-grossing films. Beyond its success at the box office, *Kantara* struck a deep chord with Indians, especially at a time, when India is on a path of re-discovering its roots, heritage and uncovering history beyond inaccurate textbooks.

Kantara celebrated indigenous knowledge and critiqued exploitative development through its portrayal of traditional rituals and beliefs (Kumar, S C 2024).[1]

The story is set in 1847, amidst the lush forests of coastal Karnataka. A benevolent king gifts a portion of the forest to the local tribes in exchange for the blessings of their deity, Panjurli; a divine boar spirit believed to be the guardian of land and people.

The legend was deeply woven into the spiritual fabric of the region.

According to ancient lore, Goddess Parvati had taken an orphaned wild boar under her care. But as he grew up, he wreaked havoc in Lord Shiva's celestial garden, who banished him to Earth, as the divine *Panjurli Daiva*, with the duty of protecting the land and people.

Over time, Panjurli became synonymous with *Varaha*, Vishnu's boar incarnation, a symbol of nature's dual forces: destroyer and protector, feared yet revered. The forest dwellers worship Panjurli, and treat the forest as a sacred living entity. They take only what is necessary, allowing nature to thrive alongside them.

As time passed, greed crept in. The king's descendants sought to reclaim their land, challenging this delicate equilibrium. Local landlords desired ownership of the forests, eager to exploit their wealth. By now, India had gained independence, and forest officials also had a say in forest management.

One of *Kantara's* most hard-hitting scenes captures this conflict vividly. A tribal man ventures into the forest gathering herbal roots for medicine. Before he can harvest the plant, a forest officer intercepts him, slaps him across the face, and asks:

'Do you think this forest is your ancestral property?'

Ironically, these are the original inhabitants, who have co-existed in the forest since generations. With new laws, they have lost access to it. At the centre of this conflict is the hero of the film: a lost rebellious, tribal man, who disbelieves his own traditions and hunts endangered wild boars for mindless pleasure and merry making, in the sacred forest. The forest officials often intercept him, but each hunt haunts him. Paradoxically, the more he kills mindlessly, the more the wild boar scares him in his dreams.

The film explores layered themes: land ownership, faith, tradition, and our relationship with nature.

Kantara is roughly the story of every indigenous community and tribe in India, guarding nature for the sake of *dharma,* and the difficulty of doing so with changing laws and modern capitalism.

With many layers of spirituality, governance, and traditions as citizens of the Earth, all humans need to ask a few pertinent, fundamental questions. Questions that have been long brewing but seldom found a voice.

Who owns the Earth?

Do kings and governments own it? Do capitalists? Or is it the indigenous communities who live in rhythm with the land?

The short answer is—No one.

Forests, rivers and nature are not possessions. They are to be shared by those who understand its rhythms.

This question lies at the heart of this book. Across India, different communities, tribes, *dharmic panths* and *sampradayas* have revered the Earth in their own ways, with a deep spiritual connection with nature, treating animals, mountains, rivers and forests as sacred.

Beyond mere ownership, this book explores another question that remains largely unexamined.

Can *Dharma* save the environment?

In modern environmental frameworks we have overlooked something that runs very deep.

Are our discarded, long forgotten *dharmic* practices and devotion the key to rekindling our zeal for environmental protection in the modern world?

Dharma means the path of righteousness, duty, virtue, justice, law, the natural function or characteristic of anything, cosmic order and the moral law. Individuals follow their respective *swa-dharma,* or their duties and obligations. *Dharma* comes from the root word *'dhṛ'* (धृ) which is to hold, sustain, bear and support. It supports everything, from the individual to the cosmos. As the saying goes: *yatha pinde tatha brahmande,* as in the microcosm, so in the macrocosm.

Dharma recognises the divine in nature—the spiritual, mystical and moral duty to protect nature that sustains us. It calls for reverence not exploitation. Perhaps the key to environmental preservation is not numbers and metrics, but *dharma*.

Environmentalist Vandana Shiva describes *dharma* in the context of environment, as the principle of unity between humans and nature, born of interconnectedness. *Dharma* is care for all humans and all species alike. Its opposite *adharma* is what violates the ecological balance. Whatever separates us from nature and each other, every action that leads to the disintegration of societies and ecosystems is *adharma* (Vandana Shiva, 2015).[2]

***

India is rich with traditions that honour nature. Panjurli Daiva of *Kantara,* is just one example. Across India, thousands of sacred groves still thrive under the protection of local communities, upheld as living, divine entities. Lands, mountains and rivers are largely managed by many such informal, yet tight-knit communities. These communities have their own local rules, built into their *dharma* of protecting nature. The

Chenchus of Andhra, Telengana, Karnataka and Odisha, revere many animals as both deity and kin. The Todas of Tamil Nadu honour buffaloes as sacred, and ensure their well-being through sustainable rituals. In Arunachal Pradesh, the Galos have rituals celebrating ecological harmony. The Dangs of Gujarat, untouched by British colonisation, have preserved their unique way of life in the forests.

In the arid deserts of Rajasthan, the Bishnois have lived in harmony with nature for centuries—ensuring conservation, protecting flora and fauna, with a devotion rooted in their *dharma*.

The entry of the British wrecked the delicate balance of these ecosystems. As Ramchandra Guha writes in *Speaking with Nature: The Origins of Indian Environmentalism*, 2024:

> Prior to the British conquest of India, the forests of the subcontinent had largely been under the control of peasant and tribal communities. The British rule brought a radical departure, when the colonisers took over large tracts of forests and designated them as state reserves. The British interest in Indian forests was commercial and strategic. The timber from forests was critical for building railways. The forests of India provided a steady stream of revenue to the imperial exchequer. On the other hand, for Indian villagers in forests, access to the forest was vital. To regulate and check over-exploitation villages had informal systems of management in place (Guha 2024).[3]

With the takeover of the forests by the British, everything changed. Forest officials were trained to treat peasants and tribals as enemies of the forest. A series of peasant and tribal rebellions erupted in the late nineteenth and early twentieth century (Guha, Gadgil, 1989).[4]

Unfortunately, even after Independence, India retained the colonial administrative framework, and their system of governance over forests remained intact. The government took control of these lands, enforcing conservation laws and appointing officers who were *burra sahibs,* detached from the indigenous way of life and local ways of thinking. They inherited the colonial mind-set, and saw things through the British lens, viewing local communities not as custodians and guardians of the land, but as encroachers.

Communities that once protected these ecosystems for centuries, as their *dharmic,* spiritual and sacred duty, were now treated as outsiders in their own homes. As laws tightened, and capitalism expanded, modern conservation laws threatened indigenous traditions, their access to land, and also their way of life.

Capitalism drove the environmental decimation of the planet. The environment was seen as a free good, while the consequences of dirty industrial and agricultural processes were seen as external to the firm. Public policies largely allowed this to happen, with a preference for short-term economic growth, job creation and higher living standards over the natural environment (Jones, 2022).[5]

India stands between two forestry paradigms: one life-enhancing and the other life-destroying. The former is the indigenous and the ecological approach; the latter is the colonialist approach. The ecological approach is derived from 'the feminine principle' and the latter is reductionistic, exploitative, and patriarchal (Shiva, Vandana, 1994).[6]

Governments claim dominion through decrees and taxes, policed by officers and guns, often, play a dubious role. While championing conservation, they also approve unsustainable projects for 'development'.

For indigenous communities, the forests, mountains and rivers were not commodities to be traded or even treated as a resource. It is their home, their identity, and their way of life; living entities that sustained generations. Modern civilisation has strayed far from this understanding, caught in an endless pursuit of ownership and control. *Sanatan Dharma,* the philosophy that once tied everything together, recognised this interconnectedness, but it is now no longer a framework to live by.

Dharma saw nature as divine, not as property. It offered a framework where heightened consciousness guided human actions, ensuring harmony rather than destruction. But as we moved away from these principles, our world spiralled into chaos.

The result? We have a crisis of disconnection.

Crisis of Disconnection
Modern society's disconnection from nature manifests in every facet of our lives—our cities, our health, and our collective well-being, or the lack thereof.

In modern-day life, everything is just a commodity, and nothing matters except shareholder value and the relentless pursuit of profit. Wastelands are seen merely as mineral deposits to be extracted, rivers must be diverted, bottled and sold under glossy labels. Mountains once revered as majestic sanctuaries of biodiversity, are reduced to mere heaps of ore, waiting to be blasted and crushed. Oceans are treated not as living ecosystems, but as limitless troves to be overfished and bottomless bins for our waste.

Soil is no longer regarded as the sacred womb of life, but as a chemically saturated platform for monocropping and genetically modified crops. Animals are no longer sentient beings; they are processed meat and hides, optimised for efficiency. Forests hold no value, until they are felled and converted into a stack of timber. Trees are not seen as natural healers but standing timber waiting to be monetised. Wetlands are viewed not as sanctuaries for migratory birds but as undeveloped real estate perfect for shopping malls and technology parks. Even deserts with their fragile ecosystems, are dismissed as barren spaces to be covered with solar panels.

This deep disengagement from nature has led to a crisis of purpose—a pervasive inner conflict and fear that resides at the heart of modern society's conflict, where individuals are increasingly alienated from their own minds, bodies and mother nature. We are living in a state of shrunken consciousness, deteriorating health, and diminished awareness—of ourselves and of the natural world around us.

This rupture is not merely environmental; it is spiritual and civilizational. To heal it, we must return to an older understanding, one in which the Earth was never owned, but revered. The way out of this chaos, is to retrace our steps and re-establish our relationship with nature.

In Sanātana Dharma, this relationship is expressed with profound clarity. When the Earth sinks under the weight of disorder, it is Varāha, the incarnation of Viṣhṇu, who descends to rescue Bhūdevī, not to conquer her, but to restore balance. The divine power manifests to remind us of our eternal duty, that safeguarding the Earth is inseparable from sustaining cosmic order.

The Bhūmi Sūktam of the Atharva Veda gives voice to this sacred vision. Earth is praised not as inert ground, but as divine mother. The Bhūmi Sūktam reaches beyond sustenance into cosmic depth. Bhūdevī is aligned with Ṛta, the universal law that governs truth, movement, and harmony. She supports spiritual practice, penance, and initiation, extending from the highest heavens to the deepest realms below.

Above all, the Bhūmi Sūktam speaks of interconnectedness. Humanity is not separate from nature, nor nature from the divine. Every act upon the Earth reverberates through the web of life. To reconnect with the Earth, is not a modern invention, it is a remembrance.

> *May the Earth, our mother, give us strength,*
> *And may we, her children, take only what we need,*
> *Leaving her bounty undiminished for future generations.*

Image ©Anu Lall Bishnois and the Blackbuck

Chapter 2

Blackbuck Poaching
Breaking a Sacred Bond

यो नो द्वेषत्पृथिवी यः पृतन्याद्योऽभिदासान्मनसा यो वधेन
तं नो भूमे रन्धय पूर्वकृत्वरि

He who hates us, O earth, he who attacks us or mentally considers us as enemies, or strikes us, Mother Earth, subdue him, as you have done since earliest times.
—Bhumi Suktam, *Atharva Veda*, 12.1.14

As the winter of 1998 settled over India, newspapers blared a sensational story from villages near Jodhpur: endangered blackbuck had been killed. The finger of accusation pointed directly at Bollywood superstar Salman Khan. Many people would have nonchalantly flipped the pages of the newspaper, dismissing it as just another scandal involving a celebrity. Many others questioned the fuss. The story gripped the national headlines back then—and continues to do so with every new litigation date and every court appearance made by Salman Khan.

What's the big deal about a deer?

In a country where human life is often undervalued, the hullabaloo over killing a wild animal appeared trivial to many. Yet, this wasn't just about any animal; it was about the blackbuck, a species protected by a little-known community in western Rajasthan, the Bishnois. Villagers who claimed to have witnessed the incident immediately reported it to the authorities, triggering legal cases that would span over decades.

The Salman Khan Case

In 1998, the deserts of Rajasthan played host not only to the camera crew of a major Bollywood production, *Hum Saath-Saath Hain*, but also to an unfolding legal saga that would span more than two decades—and still continues. The cast of *Hum Saath-Saath Hain*, a quintessential family drama, found themselves enmeshed in a legal drama of a very different kind, one that would test the limits of wildlife law enforcement, evidentiary standards, and celebrity justice in India. At the centre of it all was Salman Khan, then one of Bollywood's most bankable stars. Accused alongside him were actors Saif Ali Khan, Sonali Bendre, Tabu, Neelam Kothari, and Satish Shah. At its core were allegations under the Wildlife Protection Act, 1972: Illegal hunting of blackbuck and chinkaras, both protected wildlife species.

In total, four First Information Reports (FIRs) were filed—three for poaching, and one under the Arms Act for the possession of expired firearm licenses.

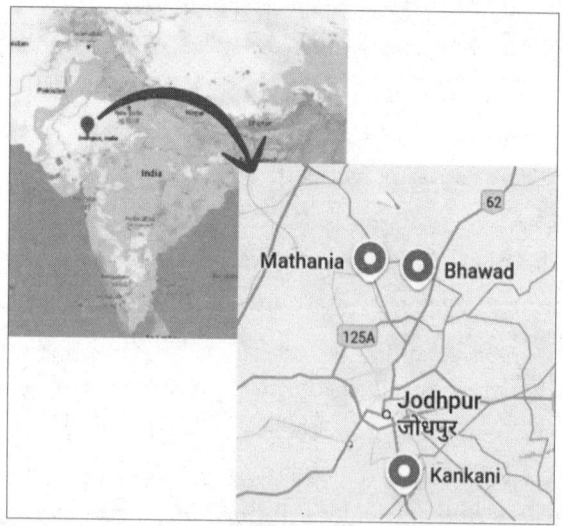

Poaching Incidents

These cases would come to be known collectively, and somewhat misleadingly, as the 'Salman Khan Blackbuck Case'—a reflection of the media's celebrity fixation and the public's oversimplified understanding of the law. In reality, each case was distinct, involving different incidents, animals, and at times, different co-accused.

- The first case alleged killing of two chinkaras at village Bhavad. (FIR No.162/1998, registered on 11.10.1998, at police station Mathania, Jodhpur).
- The second case alleged killing of one chinkara at Ghoda Farms (FIR No.163/1998 registered on 11.10.1998, at the police station of Mathania Jodhpur).
- The third poaching case alleged killing of two blackbuck (FIR No.93(26)/1998) registered on 02.10.1998 with the Forest Department.

All the evidence was collected during the investigation of the third case, which related to the hunting of a total of five animals—two blackbuck and three chinkaras. This same evidence was used across the proceedings of all three cases. Below is a summary of the legal journey of each case. The details are reproduced from the FIRs and the Court judgements. The chronology, court orders and appeals are provided as an annexure.

The Bhavad Chinkara Case (FIR No. 162/1998)
The earliest reported incident, occurred on the night of 26 September 1998, near Bhavad village. According to the prosecution, Salman Khan, accompanied by Satish Shah and others, drove a Gypsy into the desert. Harish Dulani, a driver assigned to the unit, alleged that Salman fired three shots—missing twice before fatally hitting a deer. What followed

according to the allegations was even more chilling. Salman Khan is said to have stepped out of the vehicle and slit the deer's throat with a knife. A second deer was allegedly killed in the same manner later that night—shot and throat slit. The bodies were allegedly loaded into the Gypsy and taken to the home of one Bhanwar Singh, who reportedly refused to butcher the deer at his house. They were then allegedly transported to Hotel Ashirwad, where the killed deer were unloaded, and the vehicle was washed and cleaned the following morning.

However, as the case proceeded, many of these claims made in the FIR could not be substantiated. Many prosecution witnesses, hotel staff and the key witness including Harish Dulani and Bhanwar Singh turned hostile.

Dulani disappeared during the trial and was never cross-examined. Though his statement under Section 164 of the Criminal Procedure Code (CrPC), was vivid and detailed, it could not be admitted as substantive evidence without in-court testimony. The case relied heavily on circumstantial evidence.

Nevertheless, the Trial Court convicted Salman Khan under Section 51 of the Wildlife Protection Act, 1972, sentencing him to one year of simple imprisonment and a fine of Rs 5,000. The co-accused Satish Shah, was acquitted.

The case went into appeal and in 2016, the Rajasthan High Court overturned the conviction citing procedural lapses and unreliable evidence.

The Court judgement was scathing, not against the accused, but the investigation itself. The Court pointed towards a botched up, hurried investigation and many lapses in evidence. The judgement pointed to procedural lapses, delayed forensic testing, and poor custody of physical evidence. The chain of custody for the Gypsy was not proven. Bloodstains found in the vehicle could not be linked to the date of the alleged crime. The FSL (Forensic) Report, confirmed the bloodstains found in the Gypsy were of a deer, but there was no conclusive evidence of the hunt. The prosecution failed to prove that the bloodstains were of the deer hunted on the said date. The recovered pellets could not be conclusively matched to any firearm recovered. Weapons seized from the accused were not firearms capable of killing a deer and it could not be proved they were used in the hunt. The bodies of the deer weren't found, and the blood stains at the hotel were discovered only seventeen days after the incident. The vehicle allegedly used for the hunt, was sent for forensic examination almost a month after the incident.

Ultimately, the legal burden of proof—beyond reasonable doubt—was not met. The High Court concluded that the prosecution failed to establish guilt beyond a reasonable doubt, and acquitted Salman Khan and the co-accused.

The Ghoda Farm Chinkara Case (FIR No. 163/1998)

Two days later, on 28 September 1998, another alleged incident occurred at Ghoda Farms, again implicating Salman Khan. This time, the prosecution claimed that a single Chinkara had been killed. The evidence followed a similar pattern—largely circumstantial, with little direct proof. Nevertheless, in 2006, the Trial Court convicted Salman Khan under the Wildlife Protection Act, this time sentencing him to five years of simple imprisonment and imposing a fine of Rs 25,000.

Salman Khan appealed, and although the Sessions Court upheld the conviction, the High Court admitted his revision petition.

In a noteworthy turn in 2011, the travel ban imposed on Salman as a bail condition was lifted. When his UK visa application was rejected due to the conviction, he sought and obtained a suspension of the conviction itself, an extraordinary remedy, on the ground that it was hampering his professional life and there were no moral turpitude or corruption charges against him.

The Blackbuck Case at Kankani (FIR No. 93(26)/1998)
The most prominent of the three cases involved the killing of two blackbucks on the intervening night of October first and second, on the outskirts of Kankani village. Local villagers claimed to have seen a group of actors, including Salman Khan, Saif Ali Khan, Tabu, Sonali Bendre, and Neelam Kothari, chasing and killing the animals during a late-night safari. According to prosecution witnesses, the sound of gunfire and the headlights of the vehicle alerted the villagers and drew them to the scene, where they identified the actors as the occupants of the vehicle. Local Bishnoi community members became key complainants. Salman Khan was the primary accused in this case, along with others as the co-accused. This case attracted the most media attention and saw significant courtroom drama.

The Trial Court again convicted Salman Khan, sentencing him to five years' imprisonment and imposing a fine of Rs 10,000. However, the co-accused were acquitted due to lack of direct evidence against them. The case is currently under appeal, with the Rajasthan High Court having assumed jurisdiction over all related appeals to ensure a holistic approach. The saga continues, now shaped as much by the courtroom as by the media's lens.

As with the previous cases, the court observed many lacunae in the investigation of this case as well. Forensic delays, procedural gaps, and inconsistent witness testimonies plagued the investigation.

Crucially, no investigation was conducted to establish where the blackbuck carcasses were taken after the alleged hunting, nor what happened to them thereafter—a critical link in the chain of evidence left entirely unexamined.

The forensic findings were ambiguous and could not provide proof. The Forensic Science Laboratory (FSL) could not provide a definitive opinion on whether the hair and tail samples recovered from the vehicle or site belonged to a blackbuck or another animal. This lack of conclusive identification struck at the heart of the case, which rested on proving that a protected species had been killed.

Further complications arose from delayed and contaminated vehicle tyre impression matchings. Tyre moulds collected from the alleged scene—twelve days after the incident were matched against the accused's vehicle. But the delay, coupled with the site's location in a military area frequented by several military vehicles, rendered the evidence unreliable. Even after the delayed collection, the tyre impressions were not sent for FSL examination until nearly one and a half months later, making evidentiary dilution almost certain.

Across all three judgements, the courts repeatedly identified a consistent pattern of investigation failures:
- Failure to cross examine witnesses in court
- Delays in collecting and processing forensic evidence
- Lack of chain-of-custody documentation

These trials not only revealed the challenges of prosecuting wildlife crime in India, but also reflected the pressures of media scrutiny and the celebrity justice paradox.

Some publications reported how poor enforcement and weak laws make poaching an easy game (*Down to Earth*,

2012)⁷, citing the lapses in investigation, botched up evidence and hostile witnesses.

We may never know, who really killed the blackbucks and chinkaras, yet the case still, consistently makes headlines. Salman Khan has consistently denied all allegations.

What began as a series of alleged poaching incidents became a national obsession. The so-called 'Salman Khan blackbuck case' transcended the courtroom, dominating headlines, prime time television debates, and public memory. While the media and public viewed it as one consolidated 'Salman Khan blackbuck case,' the legal system saw it as three distinct trials—each with its own facts, failings, merits and implications; they remind us that justice demands more than outrage—it demands thoroughness, credibility and unwavering commitment to the rule of law.

The Other Blackbuck Case
Eight years after actor Saif Ali Khan, was named a co-accused in the high-profile blackbucks hunting case along with Salman Khan, his father also got allegedly involved poaching a blackbuck. On 5 June 2005, cricket legend Mansoor Ali Khan Pataudi, famously nicknamed 'Tiger,' found himself and seven others (Shashi Singh, Dayal Singh, Shaheed Ahmad, Daya Suddin, Mohammad Ayub Khan, Karam Singh and Balwan) not on a lush cricket field, but accused of poaching a blackbuck and rabbits in Jhajjar, Haryana. The elegance and charm that had defined his career stood in stark contrast to the serious accusations levied against him. Pataudi surrendered in court on 18 June 2005. His anticipatory bail had been rejected and with no choice left, the former captain faced the court's authority.

Booked under sections 9, 39, and 51 of the Wildlife (Protection) Act, 1972, Pataudi spent three nights in a prison cell. A .22-bore rifle registered in the name of Pataudi's daughter Soha Ali Khan, was recovered from the site. In 2009, Soha Ali's arms license was cancelled, due to violation of arms rules (*Times of India*, 2015).[8]

Pataudi's legal counsel fervently argued that the charges were baseless. Advocating for the Wildlife Trust of India (WTI), Saurabh Sharma asserted that the evidence was undeniable proof gathered with painstaking diligence, demanding justice for the slain animal. The trial's path was far from straightforward, delayed due to legal technicalities on jurisdictional debates and administrative delays that prolonged the proceedings. In 2011, Pataudi died during the trial period and his name was dropped from the accused list in the case. All the other accused were convicted by a Haryana court in 2015 (*India Today*, 2018).[9]

Another Development in the Case: The Rise of Lawrence Bishnoi

Another development that has unexpectedly brought the blackbuck case back into public memory is the rise of Lawrence Bishnoi. Bishnoi, charged in more than twenty cases ranging from attempt to murder, carjacking, and extortion to violations under the Arms Act in the Punjab–Haryana belt. He insists that he is being falsely implicated (*Financial Express*, 2018)[10.] He has issued a threat to actor Salman Khan, warning, "We do not have any enmity with anyone, but whoever helps Salman Khan, keep your accounts in order" (*Al Jazeera*, 2024).[11]

For many, this was the moment when the once-quiet name of the Bishnoi community was catapulted into the national spotlight once again, though under very different circumstances from their traditional association with ecology and non-violence.

Within the Bishnoi community itself, Lawrence Bishnoi's persona has become polarising. He is, at once, a symbol of defiance and a source of discomfort. During my travels, a young taxi driver, barely in his twenties, spoke with disarming conviction in Lawrence's defence. He saw him as a man delivering *instant justice*. His words revealed an undercurrent of generational frustration.

But not all Bishnois share that sentiment. Many elders, while empathetic to Lawrence's anger, are deeply uneasy with his methods. Some have urged Salman Khan to apologise for the alleged killing of the blackbuck; others argue that the matter belongs squarely to the courts, cautioning against taking justice into one's own hands. The community today stands divided—not over its core beliefs, but over how those beliefs should manifest in a world where law, celebrity, and emotion collide.

This division is telling. It reveals how even a shared moral compass can fragment under the pressure of modernity and media narratives. The spiritual philosophy of the Bishnois, rooted in compassion, restraint, and ecological guardianship—finds itself interpreted in starkly different ways: one invoking patience and legal process, the other claiming to act as nature's avenger.

In documenting this case, I have consciously chosen to step away from personality cults. The aim here is not to romanticise or vilify individuals, but to return to *facts, law,* and the deeper essence of Bishnoi thought. The community's legacy—born from Guru Jambheshwar's teachings within the larger frame of *Sanatan Dharma*—is not merely about protecting trees and wildlife. It is about sustaining the moral ecology of balance: between man and nature, justice and humility, passion and peace.

Poaching for Pride and Profit

While the celebrity cases drew intense media attention, poaching in India is a deeply human behaviour—wrapped in pride, tradition, and now, profit. For centuries, hunting wasn't merely about survival, but was a symbol of status and masculine prowess. Kings went on grand *shikaar* expeditions, flaunting their trophies, stuffed heads of blackbuck and deer, and tiger hides adorned palace walls. The meat from these hunts graced royal banquets and wedding feasts, a delicacy reserved for the elite.

Remnants of these beliefs persist even today. Animals like the blackbuck also have a fair degree of superstition involved. In some parts of India, displaying antlers, horns or animal hides on vehicles is believed to bring good luck—despite the fact that such possession and display can attract punishment (*Bangalore Mirror,* 2016).[12]

In 2017, a sting operation exposed how deer meat could be ordered almost on demand, in the Shekhawati belt—covering Sikar, Jhunjhunu, and Churu districts. Hotels and resorts placed direct orders with hunters, turning poaching into a doorstep delivery service for 'exotic' meals (*Rajasthan Patrika,* 2017).[13]

Incidentally a separate study revealed a concerning decline in the density of Khejri trees in the Shekhawati region. (Chaudhry, Pradeep, 2011).[14] The Khejri tree has a symbiotic relationship with wildlife. I will circle back to this in later sections.

Despite existing wildlife protection laws, enforcement remains weak, often compromised by corruption and apathy.

The demand for illegal game meat is so high that traffickers dealing in deer meat and animals parts, make up to Rs 50,000 in profits. Fuelled by false claims that the meat is 'hotter' and more potent than regular meats like chicken or mutton. This dangerous myth continues to fuel the slaughter of these animals. While hotel owners discretely serve meat to clients, poachers cash in further by selling antlers and other body parts to smugglers. What was once a symbol of wildlife protection is now hunted for profit, under a veil of misinformation and greed. (*Dainik Bhaskar,* 2024).[15]

The Impact of Legal Battles
What makes legal battles truly remarkable is their ability to put the spotlight on many aspects: hidden dimensions, unveiling deeper cultural nuances that society may have failed to see. Arguments presented in courts give us a lens to view things much beyond facts, laws, judicial precedents, and proceedings. They illuminate cultural nuances, long-overlooked traditions, and deeply held values. As the years rolled on, the Salman blackbuck case and the Pataudi case to a certain extent, did precisely this. They shone a light on the Bishnoi community, a small community from western Rajasthan—an ecological and spiritual sect largely unknown to most Indians. These cases not only brought national and international attention but also opened a window into the Bishnoi community's extraordinary worldview, while sparking broader conversations about the relationship between celebrity culture, privilege, and accountability in India's legal system.

While the government formally prosecuted these cases, it was the Bishnoi community that remained embroiled in a legal battle with unwavering determination, seeking justice, as protectors of the land and as witnesses in the legal cases. While many key witnesses turned hostile, witnesses like Chhogga Ram Bishnoi and Poona Ram Bishnoi remained firm on their testimony.

During the case proceedings, Chhogga Ram Bishnoi passed away. In the last twenty-six years Poona Ram Ji has appeared in court over 68 times (*Los Angeles Times,* 2018).[16]

Beneath the media spectacle lies a sobering truth: India's wildlife protection enforcement is fragile. On the one hand, law demands proof beyond reasonable doubt, while on the other, the cases revealed just how difficult it is to meet that requirement. When investigation falters, procedures are delayed, and witnesses withdraw. Over the span of twenty-six years, the nation grew weary keeping track of the legal proceedings, but the Bishnoi community did not relent. For most Indians, the Bishnois remained a mystery.

Who were these people taking on a megastar?
Why were they so relentless in their pursuit?
In a country where justice for humans is often elusive, why are they so bothered about a deer?

Image ©Anu Lall Bishnois and the Blackbuck

Chapter 3

Why Were the Bishnois So Relentless?

Jeev uupar jor karije, antkaal hoye si bharu.
If you exercise power over the weak, be prepared
for a painful end yourself.
—Jambho Darshan, *Sabadvaani 9*

Slowly, India woke up to the Bishnois—the fierce eco-warriors from a Hindu *Vaishnav Sampradaya* who have lived by a strict ecological code for over five centuries. To them it is their spiritual duty to protect the environment, animals and trees. Bishnoi's reverence for all life is sacrosanct, and their commitment is not merely symbolic, it's a way of life, deeply rooted in their belief that every living being is sacred and deserves protection. The Bishnoi community primarily inhabit western Rajasthan, Punjab and Haryana, with smaller populations in areas of Uttar Pradesh, Madhya Pradesh and Odisha as well.

Whether it's chasing down poachers and hunters, nursing injured animals, protecting trees, or watching over their lands, their dedication to protecting nature is woven into the very fabric of their lives. They have been living by this code for centuries. They don't just hope or pray; they act—with vigilance and determination.

They are fierce defenders, committed to the environment. The community's ethos revolves around protecting all wildlife, especially blackbucks, who are seen as delicate animals that deserve protection.

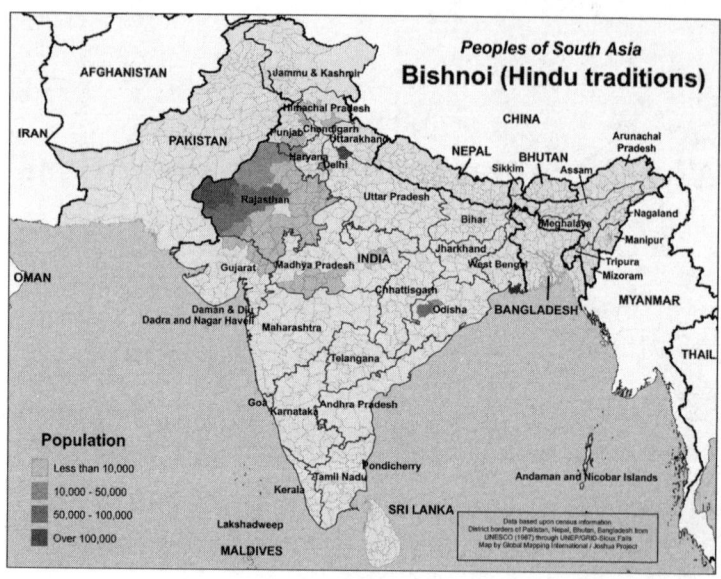

Map Source: People Group Location: Omid. Other geography/data: GMI.
Map Design: Joshua Project

At the centre of this commitment stands the blackbuck.

This graceful creature—cloaked in sleek dark brown or black fur, is one of India's most striking animals and moves with a speed and stride that is almost poetic. Male blackbucks stand out for their striking contrast of colours, white markings on the chest, belly, and chin. Their striking dark colour has earned them the name of *Krishna Jinka*. This elegant creature with its graceful spiralling horns and sophisticated stride, is amongst the fastest land animals, capable of speeds between 50 to 80 kmph—a blur of motion, nearly impossible to outrun. The only animal that can outrun a blackbuck is the cheetah.

In many spiritual and religious traditions, deer symbolise divinity, love, agility, and compassion. Japanese Shintoism considered the Nara deer as sacred, as the deity of Kasuga Taisha Shrine rode on it to Nara (*Deccan Herald*, 2025).[17] Killing a deer was once punishable by death. Once these creatures roamed freely in farms, now tourists flock to the Nara Deer Park to watch these magnificent creatures.

Blackbuck are delicate herbivores with selective feeding that allows them to thrive in open semi-arid grasslands (Choudhary, Narayan & Chisty, Nadim 2022).[18]

Blackbuck were earlier found throughout in the Indian subcontinent, but now they have disappeared largely due to habitat destruction and killing, and are found largely in protected areas like Rajasthan, Punjab, Gujarat and Haryana. (Sarita, Dave Parihar, 1999).[19] Researchers often turn to Bishnoi villages to observe and study blackbuck in the wild, for here they roam free and fearless. While blackbuck occasionally cross borders into Pakistan, but the country has no permanent residents. While blackbuck were once present in Pakistan, they are now considered extinct in local wildlife. Reintroduction efforts are being made in national parks, but their local extinction was driven by hunting and poaching from Pakistan (Ahmad, Z & Bashir, 2023).[20]

In India, the blackbuck is one of India's most safeguarded species, facing the strictest legal protections due to its endangered status. It is protected under Schedule I of the Wildlife Protection Act of 1972, which attracts the harshest punishments for poaching. With the reorganisation of Jammu & Kashmir, the protection now extends to the region, ensuring that the blackbuck's fragile existence remains shielded by law. Yet laws are barely enough to protect these magnificent creatures.

For over five hundred years, the Bishnoi's have considered wildlife protection as their sacred duty. There are accounts of kings issuing decrees barring hunting of deer in Bishnoi villages out of respect for their unflinching commitment to safeguarding trees and wildlife.

My father, Mr B R Lall, an officer of the Indian Police Service, would often recall stories from his younger days, during the 1960s, patrolling around Sirsa, Fatehabad and Hisar, districts in Haryana with a significant Bishnoi population. He would narrate stories about how the Bishnois defended blackbuck with the same fierce resolve as one would protect one's family, literally chasing down poachers and dragging them to the police station, demanding immediate legal action. The entire village would turn up, often after beating up the poachers themselves. They would routinely help forest officials, police and enforcement teams nab criminals. Bishnoi women were known to nurse abandoned fawns. Back in the day when I heard these stories as a child, they seemed like legends from a far-away land, from a different world.

Recently, I met Dr M K Ranjitsinh esteemed conservationist, as part of this book project. He shared similar memories from his photographic expeditions in Western Rajasthan. He said, the sight of his camera tripod often rang alarm bells in villages, because from a distance, it resembled a gun, sending Bishnoi women rushing towards him, shouting, and shooing him away. He added, with a laugh, that he never switched off his car engine while taking pictures in Bishnoi villages, always ready to make a quick escape if tensions escalated.

In the book, *Beyond the Tiger: Portraits of Asian Wildlife,* Ranjitsinh recounts a particularly striking incident. The headmaster of a well-known residential school in Rajasthan, a foreigner settled in India, ventured into a Bishnoi village on a hunting expedition. The outraged villagers broke his gun with their bare hands and in a show of collective anger gave him a thrashing (Ranjitsinh,1997).[21] In our conversation over a cup of tea, Dr Ranjitsinh added with wry amusement, that the Bishnoi villagers let go of the headmaster with a *'halki-phulki maar',* (a light beating), possibly because he was a foreigner. Had he been an Indian, the consequences would have been far more grave.

Bishnois have a long history of fighting tooth and nail to protect it. Today, they work together with the police and forest officials, keeping a close eye on poachers and illegal tree-felling. Cases involving celebrities capture national attention, but these are just the tip of the iceberg. Activism isn't new to this community—it is centuries old, regarded as duty backed by courage, advocacy, and historic victories.

Historical records from the Jambhani Sahitya Academy show that in 1752, Bishnois persuaded the then Maharaja Anup Singh of Bikaner to ban the cutting of green trees in Bishnoi lands. In 1878, Maharaja Man Singh of Jodhpur followed suit, issuing an official order to protect the sacred Khejri trees in Bishnoi lands. In 1900, Bishnois appealed to Maharaja Takhat Singh, the ruler of Jodhpur, who declared a complete ban on hunting within Bishnoi villages. In 1901, the Maharaja of Bikaner announced a ban on poaching in areas inhabited by Bishnois (Gehlot, and Moolaram 2017).[22]

In recent times, Bobby Luthra Sinha, social scientist, documentary maker and researcher writes about Bishnoi conservation spreading into the socio-political arena, extending beyond the realms of religion. She documents several incidents on Bishnoi activism (Bobby Luthra Sinha, Sahapedia).[23]

- Bishnois of the village Agneyu in Bikaner filed complaints against a film producer after a horse died at the film sets (January 2007).
- The Akhil Bhartiya Jeev Raksha Bishnoi Samaj demanded the ouster of Indian cricketer Mahendra Singh Dhoni for sacrificing an animal (*New India Press,* March 14, 2008).

- Bishnois surrounded the police station in Churu, Rajasthan, after over 20 Indian gazelles and three peacocks were found dead near the village of Sansatwar. The local police officers were suspended for their alleged negligence (BBC News Oct 28, 1999).
- Divisional Forest Officers at Abohar Wildlife Sanctuary regularly depend on local Bishnoi community for night patrolling against poachers (*The Times of India,* June 8, 2003).
- In Haryana, Bishnois are often the first to report poaching incidents (*The Times of India*, January 12, 2003).

The Bishnoi Tiger Force (BTF) started by a group of student activists has been very forceful. I will explore their work in later chapters.

Most recently, six hunters from Punjab were recently arrested for hunting deer around Bikaner. Once again, the Bishnoi community surrounded the police station and demanded strict action against deer hunters (*India Today,* 2025).[24]

Sometimes, poachers slip away and evidence gets destroyed. Many incidents don't make it to a legal case, yet these are impressive numbers.

A Sacred Bond Broken

The Bishnoi dedication to the many legal cases reflect the community's long-standing principle that *'all life is precious'* and must be safeguarded. Hunting is not just a violation of the law, but a desecration of the Bishnoi way of life.

In Bishnoi villages blackbucks roam free knowing they are safe—not protected by fences, but by the community's unwavering belief that all life is sacred. Men and women feed, nurture, and care for them as part of their everyday life, treating them like family. The animals develop so much trust in the community that they accept to be handfed.

If a blackbuck gets scared by an approaching vehicle, in an extremely endearing manner, it instinctively runs towards the Bishnoi *dhani,* or living quarters, to seek protection, like a scared child running towards its mother (M K Ranjitsinh, 1997 ibid).

One of the most extraordinary, touching and compassionate practices Bishnoi women practise towards the orphaned or when poaching, accidents, or natural causes leave young fawns orphaned, Bishnoi women step in to nurture them, feed them their own breast milk, caring for them like their own children, like a mother protects her child, hugging it to her bosom.

Poaching incidents strike at the heart of this bond, challenging the very values, breaking the trust the community had placed in their role as guardians of nature, for generations.

When a blackbuck, seen as part of the Bishnoi family, is killed in the very village where it was the safest, a sacred bond is broken. The killing of blackbuck is more than just the loss of an endangered species, it's the violation of a profound moral code, a disruption of the natural harmony they strive to maintain.

Animals and trees are not just resources; they are embodiments of the divine, worthy of defence at any cost.

The relentless pursuit of justice was driven by their commitment to ensuring that no one, regardless of their fame or power, could harm the animals, wildlife, flora and fauna. They sought justice not only for slain blackbuck but even more importantly, to uphold their duty, their *dharma,* to guard nature and mother Earth.

The focus of the book is on this very Bishnoi philosophy, in the larger context of *Sanatan Dharma* values which makes

Eyes of Stone, Heart of a Community

During my visit to the Bishnoi villages near Jodhpur, I witnessed a deep and lingering anger against the Bollywood superstar tied to the infamous poaching case—a case that despite years of litigation remains unresolved. The villagers' emotions were rooted in the violation of their sacred duty to protect nature, that too allegedly committed by a superstar, the world loves.

I visited the very spot where the poaching had allegedly occurred. At this site, the villagers have built a poignant memorial. I am not suggesting that the poaching was committed allegedly by the superstar. Neither is there any plaque or commemoration saying so. It is just a modest platform, in memory of the animal. It has about fifteen or twenty small steps, leading up to a life-sized statue of a blackbuck.

Though unassuming in size, standing around six feet tall, the statue's relevance in the Bishnoi community is striking. It is made of stone, in black and grey tones, with a white coloured belly, and tall twisted horns. The blackbuck's eyes are beautifully rendered, captivating, a soft, deep gaze that seems alive, as though it holds the collective sorrow and wounded spirit of the community. It is almost as if the statue is made by a community that wants to remember a place where reverence meets legal resilience. In the scorching sunlight, with not a tree to provide shade, the statue does not cast any shadow, yet in its shadow stands an entire community.

At the foot of the statue, an earthen *diya* or lamp is placed with a handmade cotton wick. I was told that the villagers replenish the oil. In these sandy deserts, where strong wind blow, the flame flickers and doesn't last long.

Through this flickering flame, the Bishnois reaffirm their commitment to their beliefs with a simple act that carries immense significance. It is a ritual of memory—a refusal to let the tragedy fade into oblivion. This memorial, humble yet profoundly moving, captures the Bishnoi legacy.

It is not just a tribute to the blackbuck, rather a representation of their compassion and duty.

humans the guardians of nature. In today's world, where wildlife faces extinction and habitats are shrinking, perhaps it's time we learn from those who see animals not as trophies or business, but as sacred life forms worth protecting, at any cost.

The Bishnoi community has a history of martyrdom for the environment. Those who lay down their lives for the environment, wildlife and trees are called *Shaheed,* or martyrs. And the community takes pride in having not one, but many *shaheeds*.

Image ©Anu Lall Bishnois and the Blackbuck

Chapter 4

Shaheed Scroll
Martyrs for 'Hirans'

प्रभवार्थाय भूतानां धर्मप्रवचनं कृतम् ।
यः स्यात् प्रभवसंयुक्तः स धर्म इति निश्चयः

Dharma has been propounded only for the welfare of living beings; therefore that which ensures welfare, is Dharma.
–Mahabharata Shanti Parva 109.10

An oft-repeated sentiment in the Bishnoi community is: when the crack of a gunshot rings out across the fields, two types of people instinctively rise to respond. One is the soldier, trained to protect human lives, who rushes out to ensure the safety of human lives. The other is a Bishnoi, usually unarmed, yet fearless, who runs toward the sound not for people, but for the animals. Both move with the same urgency, driven not by command but by *dharma*, to ensure that no innocent life has been lost. Both act in the spirit of guardianship. Both face danger. If they fall in the line of duty, both are remembered as *shaheed*, or martyrs.

Over decades, countless Bishnoi men have given their lives to protect animals, particularly *hirans*, a term in local language that includes gazelles, chinkaras, and blackbucks. Their sacrifices are neither forgotten nor treated as mere tragedies. Instead, they are honoured as martyrs and their names proudly etched into the community's collective memory. The Bishnoi community pays homage to these heroes.

In 2014, on a cold January night, Shaitan Singh Bishnoi, a 35-year-old man from Naneu, Phalodi, was jolted by the sound of gunfire. He suspected an animal must have been targeted. Without hesitation, he ran out immediately with his brother and two other farm workers. They raced after the poachers, caught up with them, and a scuffle followed. In the confrontation, the poachers shot Shaitan Singh at point blank range. His brother rushed him to the hospital but he was declared dead on arrival. He joined the ranks of Bishnoi martyrs.

The state government acknowledged the sacrifice of Shaitan Singh and announced an ex-gratia amount of five lakh rupees for his family, and sent a proposal for the Shaurya award for him (*Times of India*, 2014).[25] Two years later, he was posthumously awarded the *Rashtrapati Raksha* medal for risking his life in the line of duty, to save another life. His *samadhi* at Jambha, is a site sacred for the Bishnois.

In 1996, brave heart, Nihal Chand Bishnoi, from Sawantsar (Dungargarh), confronted hunters to save *hirans* (Gehlot, 2017).[26] His courage was recognised with the Shaurya Chakra for bravery on 22 October 1999, a posthumous honour for a life lost in service for saving another life. Several YouTube channels, dedicated to the Bishnoi faith, document his martyrdom. His family talks about his martyrdom, in the documentary film, *Willing to Sacrifice*, where Nihal Chand's father Hanuman Singh Bishnoi says,

> 'I mourn my son, but I am happy he became a shaheed (martyr), while protecting our Bishnoi faith.'

Nihal Chand's brother added,
> 'There have been many martyrs, and that's the reason the Bishnoi faith is alive today.'

Nihal Chand was buried in the heart of his own village. Martyrs are remembered and respected with prayer meetings with the frequent chant:

Vishnu, Narayan, Narayan, Narayan!
Jambho Ji Guru, Narayan, Narayan, Narayan!

Shri Ganga Ram Bishnoi, a resident of Chirai village in Jodhpur, is another remarkable example. He gave his life to protect the endangered chinkaras of Rajasthan (Government of India Announcement, 2001).[27]

In 2000, Ganga Ram Bishnoi, a farmer noticed a poacher, taking aim at a grazing chinkara, while working in his fields. He dropped everything and rushed to catch the poacher. By then, the poacher had already shot the animal and was attempting to flee with the dead *hiran* slung over his shoulder. Without hesitation, Ganga Ram confronted the armed man. A physical fight followed. Refusing to let the poacher take the animal, Ganga Ram pursued the poacher and his accomplices for over three kilometres. Another fierce fistfight ensued. Ganga Ram managed to snatch back the dead animal, and refused to let go of it. But this time, the poachers retaliated with brutal force, riddling Ganga Ram with bullets before fleeing away.

Ganga Ram's selfless act earned him national recognition. In honour of his sacrifice, he was posthumously awarded the Shaurya Chakra, one of India's most prestigious awards for acts of valour. The Ministry of Environment and Forests extended the Amrita Devi Bishnoi Award for preservation of wildlife and a cash award to his family.

A Village Pays Tribute to a Hero

I could not understand this—how could these people give up their life for an animal? To understand this, I travelled to Ganga Ram Ji's village. I had heard that the villagers had built a remembrance in his memory.

As we veered off the main village road, towards the family home, I spotted a prominent signboard—Shaheed Ganga Ram Bishnoi.

It did not take much time to realise this was not just a name on a board but a collective memory of the community.

Situated along a bustling road lined with shops, there was a memorial with the signboard which read 'Shaurya Chakra Veer, Vanya Jeevan Vishnoi Smriti'.

A huge neem tree gives shade to the area.

At the centre, stood a bust of Ganga Ram Ji—dressed in white, a hallmark of the Bishnoi community, his face proud and serene. Beside it, there was another smaller installation of a white mud tablet, with a *hiran* engraved on it, the animal he was trying to protect. Both Ganga Ram Ji and the chinkara are buried next to each other. In front of their graves are small earthen diyas—symbols of light, remembrance, and sacrifice.

The memorial was cordoned off by a wall, with an iron gate, but no lock. His family prays there every day.

As I opened the iron gate to enter the site, a shop

keeper from the neighbourhood came to greet me.

'Every morning, before opening my shop, I stop here to pay my respects and *pranam* to the *shaheed*,' he said with quiet pride.

When Ganga Ram Ji's family learnt I was writing a book on the community, they graciously invited me to attend their youngest son's wedding celebrations.

Amidst a typical Indian wedding, with colourful decorations, songs, food, customs, and traditions, I met the new bride during her welcoming rituals. I also met Ganga Ram Ji's brothers, his widowed wife, sons and daughters and extended family. The home was set up to host the entire village. Every child of the village knew of the *shaheed* and listened with rapt attention as the family elders recounted the incident. His elder brother shared with pride:

'Jab hum wahan pahunche, unke haath thande pad gaye the, aur unhone hiran ki taang abhi bhi pakdi hui thi. Unhone use chhoda nahin.'

Translated, it means, 'When we arrived at the poaching scene, we saw Ganga Ram's cold stiff body, but he was still clasping onto the leg of the dead deer. He didn't let go of the *hiran*.'

What struck me most was not the grief but the pride. The dignity with which his family honoured his legacy, proudly stating that he laid down his life for the Bishnoi tradition of protecting wildlife.

It struck me how seamlessly this act of heroism had been woven into the fabric of their daily lives.

My visit reaffirmed what I had started to believe—that for the Bishnoi community, lives lost in the

> service of nature are not tragedies, rather regarded as acts of sacrifice, triumphs of *dharma* walking the path, of their Guru's teachings. They are war heroes in the war for conservation.

The Legacy Endures

The legacy of saving *'hirans'* continues through new heroes who emerge quietly and endless reports of poaching that pour in.

In the heart of Rajasthan's Marwar region, a new hero recently emerged—Mukesh Bishnoi, a fearless 17-year-old boy who took on armed poachers to save an endangered chinkara.

It was a night like any other for Mukesh, a resident of Bhalu Rajwa village, as he set out on his usual vigil with fellow protector Pukhraj. Little did they know that this night would thrust Mukesh into the spotlight. As part of a 15-member team, Mukesh had been working tirelessly during the COVID-19 lockdown, patrolling every night to shield wildlife.

Around 8.30 pm, as they paused to drink water at a government school, the sound of a gunshot shattered the calm of the night. Without hesitation, Mukesh and Pukhraj jumped into their jeep and rushed towards the noise. In the distance, they spotted four armed men carrying the lifeless body of a chinkara. Spotting the protectors, the poachers fled. But Mukesh wasn't about to let them escape. Though their jeep got stuck in the sand, Mukesh leapt out and chased them on foot.

In an extraordinary display of courage, Mukesh confronted

one of the poachers, who pointed a gun at him. Undeterred, Mukesh charged at the armed man, engaging in a struggle to disarm him. Despite being pushed down a sand dune, Mukesh managed to wrestle the gun from the poacher's hands, forcing them to flee into the night. As the poachers disappeared, Mukesh quickly sent a message to his team through their WhatsApp group, summoning help.

Within minutes, nearly a hundred villagers arrived, following the blood trail of the chinkara to a nearby village. Though the poachers escaped before the forest department officials could arrive, Mukesh's bravery did not go unnoticed. His actions not only saved the chinkara from being forgotten, but also sent a powerful message to poachers: the Bishnois will always protect the voiceless.

With unwavering conviction he says, 'Saving chinkaras is my religion, and society is with me.'

His family, stands proud of his courage, especially after receiving countless calls of appreciation from the community.

For his bravery, Mukesh has been honoured with a certificate of appreciation by the Akhil Bharatiya Bishnoi Mahasabha, marking his place as a young hero in Rajasthan's on-going fight to protect the endangered chinkara.

These incidents of martyrdom are not isolated acts of heroism. It is a legacy deeply embedded in the Bishnoi ethos, where standing between harm and nature is not just an act of bravery but a sacred duty.

In 1947, the year India gained independence, Chimnaram Bishnoi of Barmer faced poachers along the border. Their bullets claimed his life, but not his resolve to save the chinkaras.

Gorkharam and his sons, from Barmer, were carrying water on their camels, when they spotted a herd of antelopes being chased by poachers. The brothers chased them, unarmed. The poachers opened fire killing them. The farm where they were killed, was left untilled by the farmer, as a tribute to their sacrifice. Dhookalaram Bishnoi, grabbed hold of a loaded gun of a poacher, named Mangalsar, when the latter was aiming at a chinkara. The gun fired at Dhookalaram instead, and he died on the way to the hospital. In 1995, a group of Bishnois caught an Indian Air Force Captain hunting (Jain, 2016)[28].

In recent years, Ganga Ram Jaani, from village Nehda, died on duty, fighting poachers on the border, while they were fleeing away. He also took bullets on his chest. His *samadhi* is in his village, and every year on the day of his martyrdom, the village organises a fair in his honour.

The Shaheed Scroll

Every Bishnoi village has a story, some buried in police files in various police stations at different tehsils. Others are etched into *shila-lekhs* or stone edicts at prominent sites. Some villages have created a s*mark* or prominent memorials commemorating their martyrs. Some incidents find mention in research documents and books. The names of award winners are available on the government website. Unfortunately, there is no single repository of all those who were martyred, with details of the incidents or a comprehensive list that records the names and sacrifices of all those who have laid down their lives protecting *hirans*.

The following is a partial compilation of *shaheeds* or martyrs, compiled from books, research documents and stone edicts at various places.

This is not a complete list. It is impossible to document all the martyrs, without institutional support and government assistance. However we need a starting point, which can be referenced in research and writings.

Some of the names of the list don't bear a Bishnoi surname. Many individuals use their gotra or original surnames, before adopting the Bishnoi *panth*, some also use their villages names as surnames. A couple of names do not belong to the Bishnoi community, but they also laid their lives saving '*hirans*' and are mentioned on stone edicts.

There is a need for the Bishnoi community members and government agencies to set up a documentation drive across all Bishnoi villages to update this list. I urge the Union Government and the State Government of Rajasthan to create a central public repository of all these martyrs, so that the legacy is available to all, to inspire and motivate us. This is a fight waged by ordinary people doing extraordinary things.

S. No	Year	Age	Name, Village and Details
1	1938	22	Shri Chunaram Bishnoi, son of Shri Hardanram Godara, aged 22 years, from Rohicha Kallan village, Tehsil and District–Jodhpur, was martyred on 23 May 1938, while protecting a chinkara from hunters. A case was registered in police station Luni and the hunters were sentenced to life imprisonment.
2	1947	--	Shri Dhukalram Bishnoi, son of Shri Likshmanram Mal, from Rotoo village, Tehsil–Jayal and District–Nagaur, Marwar, was martyred in 1947, while opposing the hunting of a deer by Magarasar Thakur. A case was registed in Khabariyana PS.
3	1947	2 martyrs, 29 and 35 years	Shri Chimanaram Bishnoi, son of Shri Gorakhram Manju, aged 35 years, and his brother Shri Prataparam Bishnoi, aged 29 years, from Barasan village, Tehsil–Gura Malani, District–Barmer, sacrificed their lives on April 12, 1947 while opposing the hunting of a deer. A case was registered in the Gura Malani police station.
4	1948	--	Arjun Ramji Bishnoi of Bhakatsani, received bullets in his stomach, protesting poaching around the village pond.
5	1948	--	Chunaramji Bishnoi, from district Jodhpur, was killed trying to protect a herd of blackbucks and chinkara, from illegal hunters.

6	1950	36	Shri Arjunram Bishnoi, son of Shri Prabhuram Pawar, aged 36 years, from Bhagatasani village, Tehsil and District Jodhpur, was martyred on 3 February 1950 while confronting hunters, while trying to rescue a wounded chinkara from poachers.
7	--	25	Shri Bhiyaram Bishnoi, son of Shri Lalaram Godara, aged 25 years, from Banar village, Tehsil and District – Jodhpur, sacrificed his life while resisting the hunting of a deer (Police station Luni). He was killed when he tried to intercept poachers on his camel.
8	1977	30	Shri Birbalram Bishnoi, son of Shri Biradaram Khichar, aged 30 years, from Lohawat village, Tehsil–Falodi District–Jodhpur, was martyred on December 17, 1977 while opposing hunters in Dabar area of Lohawat (Police station Lohawat)
9	1978	--	Shri Kehar Singh Jat from Bhootal Kala, Haryana, was martyred on April 8, 1978 while opposing hunters.
10	1983	--	Shri Harinarayan Vajpayee, from Mangalpur Jora, Kanpur District (Uttar Pradesh), sacrificed his life on May 1, 1983 while opposing the hunting of a nilgai.
11	1990	75	Shri Hajarilal son of Shri Bhagirath Ji Manjhu, aged 75 years, Meharana village, Tehsil–Abhor, Firojpur, Punjab, was martyred on 19 May 1990 while resisting hunters.

12	1996	35	Shri Nihalchand Bishnoi, son of Hanumanram Dharaniya, aged 35 years, from Sawantsar village, Tehsil, Dungargarh, Churu, was martyred on October 3, 1996, while opposing the hunting of deer in Rohi of Sawantsar. He was honoured by the Government of India with the Shaurya Chakra posthumously on 22 October 1999 by the President of India. The case details are in the police station at Nokha.
13	1999	--	Shri Narayanaram Jat, son of Shri Purakharam Jat, from Bheemra village, Tehsil–Bayatu, District – Barmer, was martyred on 4 July 1999, while protecting a chinkara. He was shot by hunters and succumbed to his injuries on 14 July 1999. The Rajasthan government honoured him posthumously with the prestigious Amrita Devi Bishnoi Environmental Award in recognition of his sacrifice.
14	1998	--	Shri Ali Mohammad, son of Shri Peer Mohammad, from Ummedganj village, District–Kota, was martyred on 31 July 1998 while protecting a peacock, India's national bird, from hunters. The hunters shot him and he died on the spot. The Rajasthan government posthumously awarded him the 1998 Amrita Devi Bishnoi Environmental Award in recognition of his supreme sacrifice.
15	1999	30	Shri Sukhram Jat (a disciple of the Bishnoi faith), son of Shri Surajaram Jat, from Chatara Manjara village, District-Nagaur, aged 30 years, was martyred on 30 May 1999, while protecting a chinkara from hunters at the border of Bhundel village.

16	2000	35	Shri Gangaram Bishnoi, son of Shri Pusaram Isharwal, aged 35 years, from Charai village, Tehsil–Osian, District–Jodhpur, was martyred on August 12, 2000, while resisting hunters, who were attempting to kill a chinkara. The Rajasthan government posthumously honoured him with the 2001 Amrita Devi Bishnoi Environmental Award. He was honoured by the Government of India with the Shaurya Chakra award posthumously on 29 October 2002. The Government of India posthumously awarded him the Amrita Devi Bishnoi Environmental Award for the first time in 2002 for his bravery and devotion (Police station–Osiyan).
17	2003	--	Shri Chhailoo Singh Rajput, son of Shri Chain Singh Rajput, from Dhani Miansar village, Post–Himmatsar, Tehsil–Nokha, District–Bikaner, was martyred on 29 March 2003, while protecting a chinkara from hunters. He was shot and died on the spot. The Rajasthan government honoured him posthumously with the 2003 Amrita Devi Bishnoi Environmental Award. The Rajasthan government honoured him with a Padmashri Kailash Sankhala Award in the same year. (Police Station Shri Balaji)
18	2004	30	Shri Harisingh Rajpurohit, son of Shri Radhakishan, from Jhabara village, Tehsil Pokhran, District Jaisalmer, was martyred on December 28, 2004, while protecting a blackbuck from hunters. He was shot and died on the spot.

19	2006	35	Shri Gangaram Jani, son of Shri Jiyaram from Nehara village, Tehsil–Rohat, District Pali (Rajasthan). He was martyred on duty on 26 April 2006, after being shot in the chest while performing his duty in police station Dangiyawas, district Jodhpur. He was chasing hunters on the border of Village Nandara. He was buried in his native village Nehra where a fair is held every year on 26 April.
20	2014	35	Shri Shaitan Singh Bishnoi, son of Shri Anuram Bhadoo, from Naneu, Phalodi, District Jodhpur, was martyred on January 30, 2014, while confronting hunters, who were attempting to kill a deer. He was shot and died on the spot. He was awarded the President's Defence Medal posthumously by the government of India on 15 August 2016. His *samadhi* in Jambha, is a pilgrimage site of the Bishnoi community, where a fair is organised every year.
21	2015	37	Shri Umaram Jat (police constable), son of Shri Bhuraram Bhambu from Kalari village, District Nagaur, was martyred in Police station Paanchu (Bikaner) on July 7, 2015, while opposing hunters attempting to kill a deer.

Radheshyam Pemani: The Godavan Man of India

Some are born with a mission already written out for them. While most of us wrestle with what our purpose is, Radheshyam Pemani Bishnoi seemed to have his calling early, clear, and unwavering, to protect the fragile life of the desert.

When I first spoke with him, I was struck not by his passion in the usual sense of the word, but by his stillness. '*Jo kaam diya hai Jambho Ji, kar ke jaayenge,*' he told me. (Whatever work Jambho Ji has assigned, I will do it before leaving the world). He spoke softly, almost matter-of-factly.

This young man carried a profound wisdom far beyond his years. Curiously, he referred to the inevitability of death twice in our very first conversation. However, I didn't make much of it then.

Radheshyam had grown up in Dholiya, a small village in Pokhran, in the heart of the Thar Desert where the Great Indian Bustard, the Godawan still struggles for survival. For Radheshyam, conservation is not a career but faith, flowing directly from the Bishnoi tradition that treats every living being as sacred. He often said nature was his religion. From a young age, he gained a reputation for rescuing injured animals, such as a chinkara with a broken leg or a vulture too weak to fly, and nursing them back to health.

But his childhood passion soon turned into serious commitment. In 2016, he left home for Jaipur to train as a veterinary assistant and soon began working at the Jodhpur Rescue Centre, learning to administer first aid to wild animals, gaining invaluable knowledge about animal care, habitat conservation, and the threats of poaching. It was there that he first encountered the Great Indian Bustard (GIB) up close, that was once abundantly found in India, but now barely a hundred and fifty are left in the wild. The moment he realised how critically endangered it was, protecting the Godawan became the focus of his life.

Dr Sumit Dookia, who worked closely with him, on the GIB Community Conservation Program recalls, 'He never hesitated, he was a fast learner, and soon he knew every haunt of the bird better than anyone else.' The bird lays just one egg in a year, making conservation a very difficult job. Additionally, the new solar plants in Rajasthan, had uncovered high tension wires, transmitting electricity, which made every flight of this bird fraught with danger.

Radheshyam Bishnoi's efforts to protect its habitat, while patrolling, preventing poaching, and advocating for the installation of underground power lines to prevent fatal collisions, became his defining work. His leadership of the Godawan Community Conservation project in Rajasthan, where local volunteers worked alongside authorities to protect the bird, earned him wide recognition. (Butler, Mongabay, 2025)[29]

He drove for hours, talked to villagers about poaching, dangers of wild feral dogs and overhead power lines. People listened. His presence commanded respect way beyond his years. Whenever someone spotted a Godawan in distress, the first call would go to Radheshyam.

Radheshyam was not only a protector of Godawan, but along with close friends, he rescued everything from chinkaras and camels to Himalayan Griffon vultures. He poured his earnings from organising bird watching safaris into creating water bodies across the desert. He built watering holes that turned dry sand into life-giving pools, beginning with a single litre of water in 2018 and growing until he was pouring tens of thousands of litres into the desert every summer. The results were remarkable. Vultures, once dwindling, now flocked to these oases. He filed over fifty legal cases against poachers, ensuring the arrest of more than three hundred of these poachers.

Radheshyam was well recognised for his work. In 2021, the Sanctuary Nature Foundation honoured him with the Young

Naturalist Award, calling him one of the brightest hopes for Indian conservation. (*Sanctuary Nature*, 2021).[30]

I remember telling him how rare it was for someone so young, from a small desert village, to be recognised nationally. He only laughed, as if awards were nothing to write home about.

Radheshyam was also an excellent photographer, and his work sparked conversations about conservation, inspiring visitors to see the desert not as a barren wasteland but as a vibrant sanctuary teeming with life.

I had once suggested that we should plan an exhibition for his work in Delhi. He brushed it off humbly, saying, 'Pick whichever you like, I will send high-resolution pics.' Then, almost as an afterthought, he added with a small laugh, 'Exhibition *garmiyon mein na karna… tab paani ka kaam zyada hota hai.*' Don't hold the exhibition in the summers, because that's when the desert is most thirsty, and when his hands were needed at the watering holes. Art had to await its turn, after duty.

When Operation Sindoor started in May 2025, I was scheduled to visit and document his work in the peak summer months. But his location was a prime zone of war action, so I had to cancel my trip. However the war didnt stop stop him from refilling waterholes he maintained so well.

Then one day, the news came with pictures of a twisted, blackened vehicle, and with it, the words I could not take in: Radheshyam and two others had been killed in a road accident while chasing poachers. I stared at the message, numb, feeling the world tilt. His voice, and his plans for the water holes still rang in my ears. Obituaries flew in from around the world, but the bird had taken its last flight.

'The city of Jaisalmer has been inconsolable since his death. I feel like I've lost my own brother,' said Sumer Singh, a fellow conservationist and friend of Radheshyam (*The Print*, 2025)[31].

The Bishnoi community has petitioned the government to confer the title of Godawan Man of India, and honour Radheshyam as a *Shaheed*. Titles feel too small for a life like his. He carried water into the desert not only in tanks and ponds, but in his spirit. He left behind oases, not only for birds and the antelope, but for all of us who still believe that one person, even a very young person, can hold back the tide of extinction with nothing other than courage and love.

I think often of our conversations, of the ease with which he gave, of the certainty with which he lived. Some lives stretch long but remain empty; his was brief, but full, incandescent. Radheshyam reminds me that the measure of a life is not in its years, but in the depth of its purpose and in that, he was as vast as the desert sky.

As this book went into print, it was painful to shift Radheshyam Pemani Bishnoi from a young conservationist with a future, into the past tense, a name etched in the Shaheed Scroll, a martyr in real time, in front of my own eyes. I kept putting off this change till the final edit, till the last moment, as if that was going to bring him back.

To most, these names may appear as nothing more than rows in a table, mere data points in a forgotten report. I have not met the families of all these people. I did not visit every village or capture the details of every incident. Their names are in my notes, cold, typed, itemised. And yet, each name in this *'Shaheed Scroll'* is a story of unflinching courage, silent sacrifice, and devotion that runs deeper than fear of law or fear of God.

Behind each one of these lines, is a life that stood in front of a bullet, a poacher's rage, and a hunter's greed. Some were shot in the chest; others took bullets in their stomach. Some were shot at point-blank range. Some fought with bare hands. Some died instantly; others succumbed to their injuries later. A few were awarded posthumously; many more were buried quietly in the sand, their stories swallowed by the desert wind. But their fearlessness lives on.

Heroes are made by their hearts, compassion, and courage, not by their years. Heroes don't always wear capes. Martyrs don't always wear uniforms. One doesn't need a title, badge, medal, or weapon to live by our dharma. We can fight for what is right wherever we are, armed only with conviction. The greatest acts of courage can come from the quietest corners of the earth.

Chapter 5
Khejarli Massacre
Sacrificing Heads for Trees

सर साटे रूंख रहे तो भी सस्ता जान.
*If a tree is saved even at the cost of one's head,
it's a small price to pay*
—Amrita Devi Bishnoi

Once upon a time, Khejarli, a small village in Rajasthan, was ruled by Maharaja Abhay Singh of Jodhpur. He wanted to expand his palace and paint it, which required enormous amounts of firewood. His soldiers were dispatched to the village to cut down the Khejri (*Prosopis cineraria*) trees, which were the lifeline of the village.

On 11 September 1730, Giridhar Bandhari, a representative of the king arrived with his men to fell the trees. (Sohel, Amir, 2024).[32] When the soldiers began cutting down the trees, they encountered unexpected resistance. Shri Amrita Devi Bishnoi, a mother and a staunch believer in the Bishnoi principles of environmental protection, stood in their way. With her daughters by her side, she confronted the soldiers, urging them to stop, who made it clear that resistance would cost her dearly. They didn't stop felling the trees and Amrita Devi did not stop protesting.

The soldiers asked her to step aside, warning her that they would chop off her head, along with the trees. Amrita Devi stood unwavering, hugging the Khejri, standing firm in the face of imminent danger, and her defiant last words have since become legendary:

> *Sar santey runkh rahe to bhi sasto jaan*
> *If a tree is saved even at the cost of one's head,*
> *it's a small price to pay.*

In a moment that would define the Bishnoi legacy, the soldiers brutally beheaded her. As she fell to the ground, her daughters, who witnessed their mother's ultimate sacrifice, immediately stepped forward to take her place, hugging the trees as well. They, too, were slaughtered.

What followed was nothing short of extraordinary. News of Amrita Devi's martyrdom spread throughout the village, and soon, other villages as well. These were not times where one could spread information instantly with one text message. The process lasted over a few days. One by one, the villagers embraced the trees, willingly sacrificing their lives to protect what they held sacred. By the time the news reached the Maharaja, 363 Bishnois had been killed.

The massacre shocked the Maharaja of Jodhpur, and he immediately ordered to put a stop to the tree cutting.

He visited the Bishnoi villages of Khejarli and apologised for the massacre. He accepted demands made by the Bishnoi panchayat. He issued a royal decree forbidding the cutting of trees in Bishnoi villages.

The Bishnoi community demanded this official ruling from Maharaj Abhay Singh, who issued a *Tamarapatra*, a royal decree on a copper plate, prohibiting cutting of trees and hunting animals within and around all Bishnoi villages. This decree was issued long before the Indian Forest Act 1927 came into force (Bikku, 2018).[33]

The Khejarli massacre is an enduring legacy woven into the oral history of the Bishnoi community, passed down through folk songs, sung by bards and part of folklore and stories that honour the ultimate sacrifice of their ancestors. While the exact details of the incident have faded with time, this story remains a powerful symbol of the Bishnoi community commitment to protect nature at any cost.

The community remembers the 363 Bishnoi martyrs with great reverence. During my visit to these areas, I often saw paintings of Amrita Devi Bishnoi clinging to the Khejri tree in many homes. The names of the 363 martyrs are mentioned on a stone scroll at the massacre site, along with their village and 'gotra'. The gotra in the Bishnoi community is reminiscent of the caste from where the family would have originally joined the Bishnoi community. The entire list of martyrs is reproduced as an annexure.

Mangilal Rao and Bhagirathrai Rao, from the Mehlana village of Jodhpur recorded the names. The Raos have been traditional recorders of history in Rajasthan since ancient times, and they worked to gather this information from traditional sources. From their research it is revealed that people from forty-nine villages sacrificed their lives. Of these, 294 were men and 69 were women. Among them were 36 married couples, including one newlywed couple who happened to be passing by Khejarli village when the massacre took place (Jain, 2016)[34].

The martyrs were laid to rest in the very village where they made their ultimate sacrifice, each life honoured with graves that stand as silent witnesses to their courage. Today, this hallowed ground thrives with abundant flora and fauna. Every year on *Shukla Dashmi* of the *Bhadrapad* month, the Bishnoi community gathers at this revered site. A large fair is held every year to honour the martyrs, now an annual event. They come together to remember, honour, and to renew their vows to protect the natural world, a solemn tribute to the legacy of selflessness left by their ancestors. The community's profound love for life and the environment remains as alive and vibrant as ever, echoing the timeless values they sacrificed to protect.

While research scholars and media have celebrated women environmentalists, they have rarely mentioned Amrita Devi Bishnoi (Mangilal, 2020).[35]

When we think of India's environmental movements, the *Chipko Andolan* often comes to mind. We often remember Sunderlal Bahuguna as the man often credited as the one who taught India to hug trees and save them (*BBC World News*, 2021).[36]

But the roots of *Chipko* run deeper and older, than what the headlines recall. Long before it gained national attention, the first sparks of Chipko were ignited by the courageous women of Reni village. When the forest they depended on was threatened, they didn't protest with slogans or legal petitions—they stood between the trees and the axes with nothing but their bodies. Arms outstretched, hearts unshaken, they hugged the trunks like kin, refusing to let the trees fall.

The Khejarli massacre finds several brief mentions in Vandana Shiva's writings especially her book, *Staying Alive: Women, ecology and Survival in India* (Vandana Shiva, 2010).[37] She has often said in interviews and in her writings how ecofeminism is not a borrowed idea in India. It is native to our soil. It lives in our villages. It breathes through our women. From the Himalayas to the desert, Indian women have stood as the first and fiercest line of defence for the earth, instinctively, intuitively, and fearlessly. Their bond with nature is not forged through activism but through living.

And yet, too often, their names are missing from the mainstream narrative. Their martyrdom is reduced to footnotes, their legacy handed over to men in leadership positions who arrived later.

Not many know of the details of the Khejarli incident, outside India. Wangari Maathai in *Replenishing the Earth*, shares just about a sentence on how the Chipko movement was inspired by the Khejarli movement in northwest India (Wangari Maathai, 2010).[38]

It's time we remembered the truth.

The Massacre in Popular Culture

The Khejarli massacre has been met with slightly different interpretations by other communities, especially some members of the Rajput community, who challenge and contest this massacre. There is no official mention of the massacre in the historical records of Jodhpur.

In the documentary *Bishnoi: Green Warriors of the Thar* produced by Prasar Bharati, the narrative carefully navigates these interpretations, referring to those responsible for the massacre as 'woodmen', sidestepping the question of whether they were the king's soldiers (Prasar Bharti Archives).[39]

Another portrayal, in *The Amazing Bishnois of Rajasthan*, by VegTV, an interview with a village Maharaja Bhadrajun, recounts how those soldiers from Jodhpur initially led the felling, but the horrific nature of the massacre quickly moved the ruling king to halt the destruction and later issue a royal decree safeguarding the region's trees and wildlife.

The most definitive account of the event was acknowledged by Maharaja Gaj Singh, a direct descendant of Maharaja Abhay Singh. He spoke in the award-winning documentary *Willing to Sacrifice*, that many years have passed, and the details of the incidents are not very well documented in the history of the archives of the kingdom of Jodhpur.

While historical documentation from the royal archives of Jodhpur remains sparse, Maharaja Gaj Singh attests that 'an incident did indeed occur', because there is documentation on how Maharaja Abhay Singh visited the village to intervene and order the preservation of Khejarli's sacred flora and fauna. This royal decree marked a turning point, recognising the Bishnoi lands as sacred and protecting them from exploitation, a commitment that the Bishnois uphold to this day.

This royal decree held such enduring power that it has remained in effect even after the princely state of Jodhpur merged with India at Independence, in 1947.

The documentary, *Willing to Sacrifice*[40], has been internationally recognised for capturing the Bishnois' devotion to the environment. It earned the National Award for the Best Environment and Conservation Film and two international awards at the film festival in Bratislava.

Curiously, the history of sacrifice was not a one-time incident. The tradition of sacrificing lives to protect trees and wildlife is called *Khadana* or *Saka*. In 1604, much before the Khejarli massacre, two women from Ramsari village, Karma and Gora sacrificed their lives in trying to save Khejri trees from felling by the local feudal lord, Thakur. After their protest and sacrifice, the Thakur, apologised and vowed never to fell tees in a Bishnoi village. This was the first incident of its kind. Vilho Ji, documented many sacrifices in *Sakhi*, a local language collection (Neeke Chaturvedi, 2018).[41]

A similar incident is reported in the second half of the seventeenth century, recorded as an eye witness account in *Sakhi* by Kesho Ji. In Nagar, Thakur Narasinghdas ordered some Khejri trees to be cut before Holi. When the Bishnois got to know this, they wanted to get the offenders punished. A relentless opposition was led by Bucha Ram Bishnoi, and in the struggle between the Thakur's men and the Bishnois, Busha Ram was beheaded. Later, the Thakur repented and apologised to the community. He also accepted the community's demand in the interest of the trees and animals (Neeke Chaturvedi, 2018, ibid).

Some of the important *Sakas* or sacrifices of the Bishnoi community are documented in *The Faunal Heritage of Rajasthan*.[42]

This list is primarily of the martyred for saving trees. However, two incidents overlap with those who died saving wildlife, compiled earlier in the *Shaheed Scroll* in the previous chapter.

S.No	Samvat / Year CE	Location of event	Present district	Note
1	1661–1604	Raivasadi village	Jodhpur	Two women named Karma and Gaura sacrificed their lives to save Khejri trees.
2	1604–1616	Tilvasani village	Bilada Tahsil	Khivani Devi, Neetu Devi, Nain, Motaram Khokhar sacrificed their lives to save the Khejri tree.
3	1700–1643	Polawas village	Nagour	Buchoji sacrificed his life to save trees.

4	1783–1730	Khejarli village	Jodhpur	363 men and women sacrificed their lives to save Khejri trees.
5	1940	Bahavapur Bishnoi villages	Pakistan	Army personnel in train passing from these villages killed one deer; villagers attacked them followed by court proceedings.
6	1947	Baravan village	Badmer	Chimnaram and Praapnarayan Bishnoi sacrificed their lives for protecting deer from hunters.
7	1948	Rohichangklaan village and Bhagtasani	Jodhpur	Chunnilal Bishnoi and Arjunram Bishnoi sacrificed their lives for saving wildlife.
8	1948	Rotu and Banda villages	Jodhpur	Dhonkaram Bishnoi and Lalaram Bishnoi along with two Bishnois sacrificed their lives for saving wild animals.
9	1543–1616	Bishnoi village	Jodhpur	Damodevi, Rudi Devi and other Bishnois sacrificed their lives to save goats.
10	1914–1857	Chindad village	Haryana	Bishnois protected cows and bulls from Muslims and sacrificed their lives.

Data Source: Table 3.1 Important Sakas made by Bishnois for protecting trees, deer, and wildlife in Rajasthan. Springer New York, 2013.

Again, I would like to add, data tables with line items do not serve the stories of courage they carry. If each story were brought alive, it would be an inspiration for generations.

Sako 363: A Story Waiting to be Told

In recent times, a feature film titled *Sako 363* has been under production, a cinematic tribute to Amrita Devi. The journey of this film began more than a decade ago, with the shooting commencing on 5 June 2012 on World Environment Day, in the historic city of Jodhpur.

The project was initiated after a *yagna*, and every artist of the film committed to a strictly vegetarian diet, throughout the shooting, so that every person associated with the project conveyed the feeling and spirit behind the film of sympathy for wildlife and environment (*Times of India* report, 2013).[43]

Unfortunately, the path of *Sako 363* was far from smooth.

The film's journey was riddled with controversies and delays, particularly due to a prolonged legal battle over ownership rights within the Bishnoi community members as well. At one point, the project tethered on the edge of abandonment. However, the producers reached out to the members of the community, and in an extraordinary show of solidarity, 363 members came forward with individual contributions to crowdfund the movie. This act of collective faith breathed new life into the project. Despite facing multiple financial challenges, legal hurdles, intellectual property battles, and additional delays at the hands of the censor board, the film was produced and directed by members of the community.

The producers claim the film is finally set to release in 2025 (*Dainik Bhaskar*, Rajasthan edition, 2024).[44]

The Screening and a Shared Mission

The air was thick with excitement as the chant of *Bolo Guru Jambeshwar Bhagavan ki jai* followed by *Bolo Bharat Mata ki jai* echoed loud, through Peepasar, the birthplace of Jambho Ji. I had the privilege of witnessing the unveiling of the long-awaited movie trailer of *Sako 363*. As the screen lit up, so did the faces of those gathered. The trailer saw tremendous enthusiasm and was later released across social media.

The meeting lasted over three hours. The religious leaders and the movie crew sat cross-legged on the podium covered with white cloth. In the audience, seated in large numbers, were men dressed in characteristic white *dhoti*, *kurtas* and *pagris*, sitting on one side of the tent *shamiyana*; and women in their colourful attire, heads covered, on the other side. A large white screen was put up, with numerous standees of *Sako 363*. The screening of the trailer lasted a few minutes.

As the excitement settled, the real conversations began. How do we ensure this film reaches every corner of the country?

The community came together not just as spectators but as stakeholders, discussing marketing strategies, finalising a release date, and calculating the funds needed. One by one, many members of the community stepped up to the microphone, not just to speak but to pledge their support. Some offered ideas, others promised resources, some promised support on social media, some promised to put up posters in their own towns and villages and many committed their own money to fuel the film's journey.

As the meeting ended, we all convened for lunch at the backyard of the temple, a delightful meal of *bajra roti*, *kadi*, and *halwa* overflowing with ghee. By now, during my research, I had stopped minding the calories in the meal a long time ago. After our meals, we literally picked up each speck of food on the plate, finishing every morsel and stood up to clean our *thalis* with the desert sand, without using a single drop of water. Incidentally, cleaning utensils with sand or ash is practised all over Rajasthan, and is not just a Bishnoi tradition.

Learning from Hollywood

While I have yet to watch the movie, I cannot comment on its execution, but one thing is certain: movies like this mark an important step toward reclaiming our untold stories. They bring to light events and heroes who have been overshadowed by time and neglect and waiting to be told.

Imagine if such an incident had taken place in the Western world. Imagine if people in Europe or America had given up their lives to protect deer and trees. How many films would have been made on them? How many books, documentaries, and research papers would have followed?

Their sacrifice would have been immortalised through powerful narratives, never allowing the world to forget their bravery. The massacre and the *shaheeds,* the martyrs who died protecting the trees and animals have been household names, deeply etched into the collective memory of all of humanity. Environmental studies would have been commissioned on them. The *sakas*, which are now buried deep inside data tables as local eye-witness accounts, should have been centre-stage, studied and documented.

Why, then, do we Indians hesitate to tell our own stories with the same conviction?

Cinema has, in recent years, played a crucial role in bringing environmental issues to light. Films like *Junglee* (2019), *Sherni* (2021), *Sherdil: The Pilibhit Saga* (2022), and *Bhediya* (2022) have attempted to shift public consciousness on conservation, poaching, and human-wildlife conflict (Karmakar, G Pal, 2024).[45]

Yet these movies often miss what drives the Indian conservation ethos. Storytelling is not just about preservation; it is about influence. Hollywood does not merely entertain; it shapes opinions, fosters empathy, and builds narratives that define how the world perceives history, heroism, and humanity itself. Their storytelling technique is a lesson in meticulous scriptwriting, emotionally rich arcs, immersive world-building, and, most importantly, an unparalleled ability to make local stories resonate with a global audience.

India, with its vast and diverse heritage, has all the raw material necessary to create cinema that both informs and inspires. But to truly make an impact, we must learn the art of crafting narratives that not only engage audiences but also endure beyond the screen. Investing in script development, production quality, and marketing strategies that rival international standards is no longer a choice; it is a necessity.

It is time to take control of our narratives; to present our stories with the same finesse and depth that Hollywood applies to theirs. We need to tell our stories to ensure that our martyrs, our legends, and our history are not mere footnotes in history books, not just a sentence here and a mention there, but living, breathing tales that ignite national and cultural pride. It is up to us to ensure that people see India in all its richness, courage, and glory.

Legal Implications of the Massacre

The Khejarli massacre stands as a pivotal chapter in India's environmental history, establishing a legacy that would inspire conservation laws and protect sacred lands. The decree issued by the Maharaja of Jodhpur, forbidding the cutting of trees on Bishnoi land after the Khejarli massacre foreshadows modern environmental legal frameworks and the concept of 'sacred groves' in India. While India has many sacred groves, and the term is not limited to Bishnois or Rajasthan, it is a term the Forest Department would later formalise to designate areas preserved not merely for biodiversity, but for deep-rooted cultural and religious values. I will circle back to the concept of sacred groves in later chapters.

Legacy of Amrita Devi Bishnoi

The story of Amrita Devi and the Khejarli Massacre has resonated through generations, inspiring environmental activists, who understand the intrinsic value of nature. Amrita Devi's sacrifice stands as a reminder that the protection of the environment is not just an act of curating but one of profound spiritual and moral responsibility.

In honour of Amrita Devi's unparalleled contribution to environmental conservation, the Ministry of Environment, Forest and Climate Change in India has instituted the Amrita Devi Bishnoi Smriti Puraskar. This prestigious award is awarded to individuals or organisations that have made outstanding contributions to the protection of wildlife and the environment. By recognising modern-day environmental warriors, the award ensures that Amrita Devi's sacrifice continues to inspire future generations to fight for the preservation of nature.

The day of the Khejarli massacre—11 September, has been designated as National Forest Martyrs Day by the Ministry of Environment, Forest and Climate Change, in India. Nationwide events and activities are organised to raise awareness about the importance of protecting our forests. Many schools, colleges and universities across the country organise events for preserving natural resources and reaffirm their commitment to adopt more environmentally friendly habits.

Movements Inspired by Amrita Devi Bishnoi

The courage displayed by Amrita Devi and the 363 other Bishnoi martyrs echoes in modern environmental movements like the Chipko Movement, where villagers hugged trees to protect them from being felled for logging.

In 1974, the government of present-day Uttarakhand announced the auction of 2,500 trees overlooking the Alaknanda River. When tree-fellers arrived in Raini village to begin cutting down the trees, a young local girl alerted the villagers. In response, the women of the village, in large groups, came out to confront the loggers.

Three brave women, Gaura Devi, Sudesha Devi, and Bachni Devi, physically embraced the trees, refusing to let them be felled. Through the night and the following days, these women stood their ground, their bodies becoming shields for the forest. Apparently, the Chipko movement is said to be inspired by the Khejarli massacre. 'Chipko' means to glue on to something, to hug. Sunderlal Bahuguna transformed the movement into a national cause. Eventually, the then Prime Minister, Mrs Indira Gandhi announced a 15-year ban on tree-cutting in Uttarakhand. Though the declaration was not issued on a copper plate, like the *tamrapatra* of Maharaja Abhay Singh, the intent and outcome were much the same.

Amrita Devi's ultimate sacrifice became an enduring symbol of how ordinary people can achieve extraordinary change when they unite to protect the environment. Amrita Devi Bishnoi's actions transformed what could have been a forgotten conflict into a powerful narrative of environmental activism.

Amrita Devi's sacrifice serves as a reminder that protecting nature requires not just laws and policies but a fundamental shift in how we view our relationship with the Earth. Her actions were not just about trees or a single village in Rajasthan; they were about the future of humanity and the responsibility we all share in protecting the environment for generations to come.

Courage Taller than Trees

In the words of the Bishnois, '*To harm nature is to harm oneself.*' This may sound like a slogan, but where does this community get courage that is taller than trees? I don't know of any other place on earth, or any community, where people give up their life for saving animals and birds. And that too, in such large numbers. Protecting plants, animals, and ecosystems, is not merely an act of goodwill or ecological responsibility; it is their sacred spiritual duty.

The Bishnois are fulfilling their duty, following their *dharma*. This commitment transcends the mundane, connecting them to the *Brahm*—the eternal, formless divine essence. Every tree saved and every animal protected becomes an act of spiritual realisation, a step closer to the Ultimate Truth.

How does a young man, jump in to protect an animal, unafraid to lose his life? What motivates women to give up their lives for trees? Or willingly feed their own breastmilk to animals, treating them as if they were their own children?

In a world full of selfishness, where does this sentiment come from? *Yeh haunsala kahan se aata hai?*

Where does this courage come from?

I asked this question to almost all members of the community—from religious leaders to ordinary folks, from the village *sarpanch* to women in the fields.

I received a simple one-line answer, delivered without batting an eyelid. That one-line resonates the anthem of the community—*Jeev Daya Palani, Rukh lila na ghave*—*Be compassionate to all living beings, and don't cut green trees.*

This teaching inherited from their Guru Jambheshwar, forms the spiritual backbone of the Bishnoi community—the foundation of this *desert dharma*. A faith and tradition that portrays to the world what it truly means to protect nature at any cost—even at the cost of one's life.

Khejri memorial commemorating 363 Bishnois,
Near Khejarli Village Jodhpur, Rajasthan

Bottom: Iconic photgraph of the Chipko Movement of 1970.
Image: Wikipedia commons

Chapter 6

Desert Dharma
Philosophy of Spirituality and Sustainability

Ja jan mantar Visen na japyo, nagre keer kaharoo,
kaandhe saahe dukh bhaaru
If a person does not do Vishnu japa, he lives carrying the
heavy burden sorrow of this life and the next.
—*Sabadvaani* 13

What gives ordinary humans the courage to give up their lives for what they stand for? One might argue that human behaviour is shaped by the environment and by what we are taught. A recent thought in circulation propounds that religions that emerge from the desert are more violent, and less respecting towards the environment.

Author and thinker Rajiv Malhotra suggests that the harsh landscapes of deserts foster an *'eat-or-be-eaten'* survivalist mentality. He makes a strong argument in his video titled– *Forest Religion vs Desert Religion | Wisdom Sutra EP 3 with Rajiv Malhotra*. I reproduce his argument in a short summary:

> Religions, he says are of two kinds—forest and desert. The place where a religion originates plays a huge role in the norms and adaptability of the religion. From the forest emerge dharma traditions—Hinduism, Jainism, Buddhism and Sikhism.

These traditions, mirror the biodiversity and nurturing qualities of the forest ecosystems. They are all based on harmony, peace with oneself, and with one's surroundings. Forest people instinctively see themselves as part of a larger interconnected reality.

Living in such diversity, forest dwellers accept their surroundings and respect others from different places—yet they live together in harmony. This view is reflected in the *dharma* traditions where each individual may follow their own path to God, with all *dharmic* paths ultimately leading to the same indivisible self, not separate from the divine.

In contrast, desert religions—Judaism, Christianity and Islam emerge from a geography of scarcity: barren lands, extreme temperatures, and scarcity of food. This fosters an aggressive 'eat or be eaten' mentality among desert creatures. For them nature is not a nurturing mother, but a harsh enemy that needs to be overcome.

Desert religions reflect the extremes of the desert. People following these religions look for relief from a God above who is distant, separate from the world and punishes those who don't follow his rigid rules. These religions remain rigid and view everything as black and white with little room for flexible thought. This makes them aggressive towards anyone who follows a different way of life (Rajiv Malhotra, 2022).[46]

While this argument may appear plausible and compelling, the Bishnoi community disrupts this narrative. Emerging from the arid deserts of Rajasthan, the Bishnois exemplify the nurturing principles of *dharma*, a philosophy rooted not in environmental determinism but in their alignment with righteousness. From shielding blackbucks to opposing deforestation, their actions serve as a living counterpoint to the claim that the environment alone dictates human behaviour. It depends on whether a set of people follow *dharma*, or righteousness in their conduct, and identifying their purpose of existence. The community came into existence in harsh climatic conditions, yet it didn't make them harsh, or hostile towards nature, and give in to the aggressive *eat or be eaten mentality.*'

An alignment with *dharma* has led the Bishnois to be guardians of biodiversity, even in the face of personal danger.

Panth, Sampradaya and *Dharma*

The Bishnoi *panth* is a Vaishnav *sampradaya*, and possibly one of the very few communities living the values of saving the environment in action. They have built a spiritual and practical framework for protecting nature.

Panth, sampradaya and *dharma* are integral to *Sanatan Dharma* traditions, and they serve different roles. The term *panth* literally means path, or a way that represents a specific spiritual route to reach the ultimate divine. The *panth* gives rise to a sect, community or *sampradaya*, a tradition within *Sanatan Dharma* that follows a specific spiritual leader and a way of life that encompasses shared beliefs, rituals, and practices, with the lineage of a guru.

Followers of a *panth* and *sampradaya* typically share a strong sense of community and identity, often coming together for communal worship, festivals, and other cultural activities. Each *panth* may have unique rituals, festivals, and codes of conduct that distinguish them from other groups. These practices are often rooted in the teachings of their founder.

Many times, a guru, often a realised master and charismatic

leader, also revered as a '*Bhagwan*', imparts teachings to his followers, laying the foundation of a *panth*. They contextualise broader principles in the framework for the specific *desh* and *kaal* or location and time.

Dharma, on the other hand, is an all-encompassing moral and ethical framework that guides all aspects of life. *Dharma* is considered a universal principle that applies to all individuals, regardless of their specific beliefs or affiliations. It serves as a guide for righteous living and ethical behaviour.

While *samanya dharma* or general *dharma* principles apply to all, the *vishesh dharma*, or specific *dharma* reflects the complexity and diversity of life, and may vary based on individual circumstances, age, stage of life, *varna*, and social role, providing guidelines on duties and responsibilities in various contexts, such as family life, governance, and societal roles.

The Bishnoi *Panth* of Compassion and Conservation

The Bishnoi *panth* was founded by Guru Jambeshwar Ji (1451-1536) fondly called Guru Jambhoji, who was born in Peepsar, in a Rajput family of cattle breeders. He spent the first seven years of his childhood, without talking to anyone. The villagers called him '*gahlo*' which means mute in Rajasthani, causing a lot of worry to his parents (Biswas, Rao 2022).[47]

The family tried many treatments to make him speak. At the age of seven, he spoke spontaneously, and they were words of immense wisdom. It didn't take time for everyone around to realise the divinity in the child (Bishnoi, 2018).[48]

In the coming years, as he became older, the family made some attempts to get him married, but he evaded them all. Over the next twenty-seven-year period that followed, Jambho Ji devoted himself to the yogic practices of *dhyana*, meditation, self-realisation, and cattle rearing. During this period, he performed several miracles to help people. Eventually, his parents passed away when he was about thirty-two years old. After that, he donated his parental property and started teaching his learnings as a way of life at another village close by, Samrathal Dhora, that would later become a pilgrimage spot associated with him.

Around this time, the desert land faced some of the worst famines in history. Jambho Ji was no stranger to the devastating impact of recurring droughts. Ancient Bishnoi texts and available public records, indicate that in the period between 1476 and 1486, the deserts of Rajasthan faced a series of devastating famines that ravaged the land, caused scarcity of food and water, causing deaths of countless humans and animals (Bikku, 2018).[49]

Famines are difficult times when the connection between nature and humans snaps. It is a cycle of despair and a downward spiral for humans and nature. As despair spread, the suffering caused unrest, causing people to further harm the environment, cutting down trees, killing animals, and seeking survival through unsustainable practices.

Jambho Ji witnessed the suffering, rising desperation in communities, with massive human migration. Like all realised masters, he possessed a vision beyond the ordinary. He saw what others could not. He understood it takes an immense amount of intervention to break the downward spiral. The solution to human plight was not in escaping nature's challenges, but in embracing them and creating harmony with the environment. With sustainable practices, humanity could not only survive but thrive. The Bishnoi *panth* emerged as a profound ecological awakening, amidst the harsh realities of drought, famine and suffering. Jambho Ji emerged as a reformer, offering not only solace to people around him, but a practical way to live in harmony with the natural world. He urged those suffering from drought and displacement to return to their homelands with renewed purpose, and live a life doing good *karma,* rooted in compassion and kindness toward all living beings. He gave spiritual guidance and urged people to embrace principles of compassion, and sustainability towards the environment. He guided people to dig ponds, conserve water and protect wildlife. He led initiatives to plant trees and provided food to those who assisted in these endeavours that would ensure a sustainable future for generations to come. Jambho Ji taught that the world's existence is transient, but our *karma* or our actions have lasting consequences. He taught how harming another life form, whether plant or animal, is to harm oneself, and lies at the heart of the Bishnoi *panth*, while practising compassion and sustainability.

Prahlad Panthi

Jambho Ji founded the Bishnoi sect in 1485, on the first day of the dark fortnight of the year 1542 of the Vikram Samvat calendar (Bishnoi K.R, 2002).[50]

Jambho Ji organised a grand *havan* at Samrathal Dhora. Before the *havan*, Jambho Ji bathed, held a rosary, and prepared *pahal* or holy water while chanting the name of Hari (Vishnu). As this holy water was shared, people from all walks of life embraced this new path. They took the *pahal* and became a Bishnoi, united under a common vision of compassion, simplicity, and devotion. Jambho Ji urged his followers to see protection of nature and wildlife not just as a duty, but as the highest form of spiritual practice (Chaudhary, 2022).[51]

When Jambho Ji initiated people into his fold, he sanctified them with *pahal* (consecrated water) and named them *Prahlad Panthi*—

inspired by the legendary child devotee whose unshakable faith in Vishnu defied even the might of a tyrant. Jambho Ji proclaimed:

> *Prahlada soon vacha keeve aayo baram kaajae*
> *Baara maa soon ek ghate toh, soo chelo guru laaje.*

The story of young Prahlad is one of courage, devotion, and divine justice. In ancient times, there lived a boy named Prahlad, whose heart resonated with unwavering love for Vishnu. But his father, the tyrannical King Hiranyakashipu, saw himself as supreme. He demanded that all in his kingdom worship him alone. Prahlad refused, saying he would bow only to Vishnu.

Hiranyakashipu's anger turned into fury. He tried to persuade his son, then threatened him, and when nothing worked, he unleashed unimaginable cruelty. Prahlad was thrown into snake pits, trampled by elephants, and even pushed off cliffs. But each time, he emerged unharmed, protected by his faith.

Desperate, the king sought help from his sister *Holika*, who possessed a mystical boon that made her immune to fire. She devised a plan that she would sit in a blazing fire with Prahlad in her lap. She was certain that the flames would consume him, while she remained untouched.

But divine will cannot be bent by arrogance. One cannot use a boon, divine power or privilege for harming anyone, and least of all a child devoted to *Ishvar* himself. As the fire roared, it was *Holika* who perished, reduced to ashes, while Prahlad emerged unscathed—his faith unshaken, his devotion triumphant.

Hindus remember this day through *Holika Dahan*, the ritual bonfire lit on the eve of Holi, symbolising how unwavering faith and goodness always triumph over arrogance and cruelty. The next day, Holi bursts forth in a riot of colours, celebrating joy, and the victory of righteousness.

The Bishnois, celebrate it slightly differently. They do not light the *Holika* fire. Instead, they mark it as a day of *shok* (mourning), remembering the cruelty young Prahlad endured. They prepare a simple meal of *kheechda* in quiet reflection and abstain from eating after sunset.

The following day, when Prahlad's triumph is honoured, Bishnois gather to perform *havan*, recite *Sabadvaani*, and partake in *pahal*, immersing themselves in devotion. For the Prahlad *panthis*, this day is a testament to the power of faith, a guiding light that shapes their identity and way of life.

Unlike the rest of India, they do not celebrate Holi with colours and water. However, elders often lament how younger generations, influenced by popular media, have begun adopting the more mainstream festivities.

The Ecological Manifesto

Guru Jambho Ji encapsulated his teachings in twenty-nine principles, forming the foundation of the Bishnoi way of life toward righteousness, environmental balance, and inner peace.

These twenty-nine tenets are not mere rules; they are a way of living in sync with nature, a philosophy that integrates ethics, health, society, and spirituality into a seamless whole. Some of the core beliefs and principles of this community are not just moral injunctions but sacred duties. Ecology and human existence as a symbiotic relationship, is the essence of these beliefs.

One who embraces these twenty-nine rules with a pure heart, by the grace of Jambho Ji, becomes a Bishnoi.

Unatees dharm ki aankadi, hriday dhariyo joi
Jaambho Ji kripa kari, naam Bishnoi hoi

The popular understanding is that the term Bishnoi is derived from two words *'Bish'* which means twenty and *'Noi'* that means nine. Bishnoi translates as Twenty-nine or 29 principles, that are considered sacred and have been passed down through generations as guiding lights for sustainable living.

In my discussions with the leaders of the community, they opined that the word 'Bishnoi' comes from 'Vishnu'. Jambho Ji was a Vishnu *bhakt*, and urged all his followers, to chant the Vishnu *japa*.

1	तीस दिन सूतक	Observe 30-day seclusion for a new mother and her child.
2	पांच ऋतुवन्ती न्यारो	Women should rest for 5 days during menstruation.
3	सेरो करो स्नान	Shower daily in the morning.
4	शील, संतोष, शुचि प्यारो	Practise modesty, contentment, and good virtue.
5	द्विकाल सन्ध्या करो	Meditate daily at dawn and dusk.
6	सांझ आरती गुण गावो	Do daily *aarti* to thank *Ishvar*.
7	प्रातःकाल हवन करो	Conduct *Havan Yagna* in the morning.
8	जल व दूध छानकर पियो	Filter water and milk before drinking.
9	ईंधन का बीनकर उपयोग करो	Clean fuel before using.
10	क्षमा सहनशीलता रखो	Be forgiving.
11	दया-नम्र भाव से रहो	Live with *daya bhaav* or empathy.

12	चोरी नहीं करो	Do not steal.
13	निंदा नहीं करो	Do not condemn.
14	सच बोलो	Always speak the truth.
15	व्यर्थ का वाद-विवाद नहीं करो	Do not indulge in unnecessary argument.
16	अमावस्या व्रत राखणों	Fast during *Amavasya*.
17	भजन विष्णु बतायो जोय	Pray to the Almighty Vishnu daily.
18	जीव दया पालणी	Be compassionate toward all living beings.
19	हरे वृक्ष नहीं काटो	Do not cut green trees.
20	अजर को जरो	Overcome ego, lust, rage, greed, and attachment.
21	करै रसोई हाथ सूं	Eat pure and clean food.
22	अमर रखावै थाट.	Provide shelter to animals.
23	बैल बधिया न करवौ	Do not castrate or kill bulls.
24	अम ल नहीं खाओ	Do not consume opium or other addictive products.
25	तम्बाकू नहीं खाओ	Do not consume tobacco or its products.
26	भांग नहीं पियो	Do not consume cannabis or its products.
27	मद्यपान नहीं करो	Do not drink alcohol.
28	मांस नहीं खाना	Do not eat meat.
29	नीले वस्त्र नहीं धारण करना	Avoid wearing blue clothes, made from *neel* (indigo).

Scholars have attempted to group the twenty-nine tenets into different categories. Some classifications relate ten tenets dedicated to personal hygiene and basic health; nine tenets concern social ethics and behaviour; four tenets guide spiritual practice and worship, and six tenets are focused on biodiversity conservation and animal husbandry (Mangilal 2020).[52]

Yet some scholars (Alam, Khabirul & Halder, Ujjwal, 2018)[53] argue that beyond any classifications, two core teachings embody the soul of the Bishnoi philosophy: *Jeev Daya Palani*—Be compassionate to all living beings, and *Runkh Lila Nahi Ghave*—Do not cut green trees.

Remarkably, this declaration of twenty-nine principles to save self, community and environment was nearly five hundred years prior to the Stockholm Conference at Sweden in 1972, which was the first concerted efforts at the international level, to focus on the environment as an international concern. The Stockholm Declaration gave twenty-six ethical principles to govern behaviour of societies and countries towards the environment (Shashi A Mishra, 2022).[54]

Do not Cause Wounds or Harm

Trying to understand the Jambhani philosophy, I found my way to the Jambhani Sahitya Akademi in Bikaner, an impressive, four-storeyed red building. I met Vinod 'Jambha das' Ji, the general secretary of the organisation. Later, I realised, he has adopted the name Jambha 'das', dedicating his life in service to the teachings of Jambho

Ji, True to his name, he is a living encyclopaedia about Jambhani philosophy. effortlessly recalling *Sabadvaanis* and timeless teachings of Jambho Ji, like one would expect a saint to do. I knew all my questions would be answered there. Even more, he understood the fact that knowledge needs to be presented in a modern context that resonates with today's youth.

If you ask him a question about philosophy, he will not only explain the *bhaav* behind it, the intention, but most likely, also point you to the exact publication, chapter name or even the newsletter number, where the content has been explained.

I told him what I am doing with the book, the different places that I have travelled to, and my experiences. I told him how scholars and academia are viewing the philosophy, are calling six principles, as environment-related, and the rest about personal hygiene and animals husbandry. He smiled, and said, twenty-nine *niyam achaar sanhita hai, insaan ki zindagi ke liye, saare hi* important *hai*, but *uska mool jaanan zaroori hai*.

Quickly, he contextualised the entire philosophy.

English translations often fall short of conveying the emotive power and intent of the original wisdom composed in Rajasthani. We went over many tenets. He said, if we look at *rukh lila na ghave* the English translation says, 'Don't cut green trees.' That doesn't communicate the *bhaav* behind the teaching.

The word *ghave* means to wound; it is not just about cutting trees. The teaching stretches beyond trees to include animals, rivers, birds, plants, every expression of life. To harm nature is not just to cause injury, but to commit spiritual violence against the divine that is manifest in creation. They are not ours to exploit, but companions in our spiritual journey. The spiritual DNA of Jambhoji's teachings, is a call to live consciously.

To harm another life form is not just cruelty but it is also self-violation, a wound inflicted on the universal soul that lives in us all. When a tree is cut, when a river is polluted, when an animal is killed, it is not just nature that suffers, eventually it is us. Human wellbeing is interdependent with the wellbeing of the environment. Likewise, environmental degradation is not an isolated tragedy; it mirrors a deeper moral and spiritual disconnection of humanity.

The core of Jambho *Darshan* lies in a powerful yet profoundly simple truth: Do no harm; cause no wound.

I joked how Silicon Valley companies like Google adopted, 'Do no harm' as a corporate motto, but they don't necessarily live by it.

Over the course of this book, I met Vinod Ji several times, and participated in events and discussions. I learnt about the twenty-nine tenets from Vinod Ji, which when viewed as a whole, form a complete, indivisible philosophy of living. They are not standalone rules, but interconnected strands of a conscious way of living, especially when read along with the *Sabadvaanis*.

The *Sabadvaanis*

Jambho Ji founded the Bishnoi panth at age thirty-four, and over the next fifty years he continued to teach at several places and to countless followers. Bikku (2018) analysed folk stories and songs that reveal how over the fifty years, Guru Jambho Ji travelled across Rajasthan, Punjab, Haryana, Pakistan, Kabul, and Afghanistan, spreading his message of environmental stewardship and spiritual discipline. Wherever he went, he encouraged people to plant Khejri trees, urging people to come together and conserve wildlife. At places like Rotu, he planted over 3,000 Khejri trees (Bikku, 2018, ibid).[55]

Many of these sermons were given at Samrathal Dhora, or at other places, where he travelled. Some of these teachings are answers in response to questions by his followers, written in short poetic form, in Rajasthani, also known as *marudharvaani*. His *sabads* are not merely religious hymns but guidelines for sustainable living and universal compassion, a vision that remains profoundly relevant in today's world. It is speculated that there may have been numerous preachings of Jambho Ji, which may not have been recorded in history.

Just like the Vedas are divided into *karam kaand, upasana kaand* and *gyaan kaand,* the Bishnoi *Sabadvaani* is also divided into three parts (Swami Bhagirathdas Acharya).[56]

Divinity in All

In the Bishnoi worldview, Brahm is *nirakaar*, formless, eternal, all-pervading. It transcends names and forms yet lives in every particle of existence. This is why the Bishnoi tradition does not encourage *murti-puja* (idol worship), but instead recognises divinity in nature itself (Prithwi Raj Bishnoi, 2018).[57]

This is explained beautifully in *Sabadvaani* 1, 2, and 3, which emphasises the essential unity with the *Param Brahm*, the Supreme Reality—*Ek hi roop sabai bikh dekha* or there is one divine essence in all visible forms.

While the twenty-nine rules, are often discussed, the *Sabadvaanis* are lesser known, but they stand out for their clear and bold message on the protection of forests and animals. It is impossible to include all the teachings in this book, but I have tried to include a few in the relevant sections, to maintain the authenticity of the philosophy. I have relied primarily on Prithiwi Raj Bishnoi's interpretations and translations, Swami Bhagirithdas Ji's text and my direct learnings from Bishnoi faith leaders.

Sabadvaani 6 is a stirring call to his Hindu followers. Jambho Ji questions them directly: You call yourself a Hindu, then why don't you chant the divine name? Why do you let your mind wander in ten directions? And why, oh why, do you cut down living, green trees without a second thought? It's a plea to stop the mindless destruction of nature, destruction of your own mind, its focus and of your sacred responsibility.

Sabadvaani 7, 8 and 9: Jambho Ji turns toward his Muslim followers with the same fearless clarity. He implores them: The goat, the sheep, the cow—who created them? The same Lord who gave you life gave them life, too. Then what gives you the right to butcher them? In one searing line, he says it all: One's bull is dearer than one's own brother, why kill him? Every living being has a right to life, and the knife of violence cuts through our own humanity.

Jambho Ji delivers a thunderous warning proclaiming, '*Jeev uupar jor karije, antkaal hoye si bharu*'. If you exercise power over the weak with cruelty, then be prepared for a painful end yourself; no act of violence goes unaccounted, your karma will come back to you.

In *Sabadvaani* 11: Jambho Ji appeals to our conscience. *Re binhi gunhe jeev kyon maaro?* Why kill innocent creatures that have done no harm? These verses echo with the virtue of *ahimsa*, of living gently in a world that sustains us all.

Among the twenty-nine sacred principles, the seventeenth principle urges followers to chant *Om Vishnu* as a form of *japa* (meditative repetition).

While doing circumambulations at temples, devotees repeatedly chant *Om Vishnu japa*. In *Sabadvaani 119*, he says, *Vishnu Vishnu tu bhad re prani, painkhe lakh upaju.*

Sabadvaani 13: is a powerful wake-up call for spiritual discipline. *Ja jan mantar Visen na japya, nagre keer kaharoo, kaandhe saahe dukh bhaaru*. If you don't chant the name of Vishnu, if you forget the path to liberation (*mukti*), you'll live like '*keers and kahaars*', people who carry physical loads like donkeys, beasts of burden, carrying heavy sorrow of this life and the next.

He doesn't sugar-coat it. Without spiritual focus, we're nothing more than labourers of our own suffering, eating excessively, steeped in toxicity, and doomed to cycles of painful rebirth, condemned to be born as animals in future lives.

No Soft Sermons. Bold Call to Save Environment

The *Sabadvaanis* don't just inspire. They demand a life full of courage and responsibility toward all living beings. What makes the philosophy so striking is its fierce honesty. His words don't whisper, they thunder with urgency, cutting through excuses and apathy. There's no diplomacy in these teachings. He doesn't flatter the human ego. Rather he exposes it. He forces us to confront our own cruelty, our careless relationship with nature, and our complicity in a world where compassion has become optional.

Reading these *Sabadvaanis* is like holding up a mirror to our worst habits and being asked to do better. Jambho Ji doesn't give you a soft sermon. He gives you truth, raw and real.

This intensity in Jambho Ji's teachings comes from the fact that this philosophy was not born in comfort; it was forged in catastrophe. He was teaching during a time of famine and disaster, when human suffering was widespread, and hope was scarce. His message was not of despair, but of live-and let-live, not because it sounds good, but because there is no other option for humanity.

It is almost as if he looks humanity in the eye and says: You think you're the highest form of creation, but you destroy what sustains you. You bear loads of sorrow because you've broken your covenant with nature.

What makes Jambho *darshan* or philosophy even more relevant, is that the world we live in today mirrors those conditions. Disasters, ecological collapse, and rising violence while humanity stands again at the edge. Jambho Ji's urgency taught over five hundred years ago, feels eerily present. His call to rebuild our relationship with the Earth and environment is not just poetic, but is a warning flare. The time to act is now.

Incidentally, it is this same unflinching spirit that I've encountered in the Bishnoi community. They carry forward his message with boldness. They don't dilute the truth. They don't dance around the issue. They speak with a clarity that's rare—because they bear the weight of a message that's rooted in compassion, and they've inherited the courage to defend it.

Dharmic Environmental Philanthropy

Jambho Ji also recommended what may be an early form of environmental taxation, to nurture the environment, protect wildlife, and treat all beings with reverence. Every Bishnoi was urged to leave one-tenth of their harvest for birds and wild animals. Bishnoi families keep away harvest for *chuga* or grains to feed the birds. Every temple has a *chuga-ghar* or a granary dedicated to store grains. During *melas* and festivals, families carry harvested grains to store in the temple granary that can store up to quintals of *chuga*. In some large temples, up to one or two quintals of *chuga* is fed each day; that's between 100 or 200 kilograms of grain.

Travelling through Bishnoi areas, a village sarpanch, shared with me a *bahi* or general ledger, that maintained accounts of *chuga* contribution from his family, for the last 200 years. It shocked me to the core, as it was a powerful enough testimony to make my jaw drop. The ledger was in tatters, but carried an amazing account of philanthropy that isn't even mentioned in any studies.

This was an account from just one family, in a small village, out of the hundreds of Bishnoi families that support numerous temples. There has never been a formal study of how much does this contribution, amount to as a percentage of a farmer's produce. A farmer giving away 10 per cent of his produce, amounts to a very large number.

International organisations often say Indians are not generous enough, implying that we are less inclined to charitable activities. India is ranked eighty-two of 128 nations on the World Giving Index, published by World Charities Organisation (World Giving Index, 2024).[58]

Western models of philanthropy assume that the entire world should follow their system, disregarding our native practices.

Ancient Indian wisdom applauds 'Giving' as a source of joy. *Skanda Puran* recommends 10 per cent of one's justly earned income should be given away for greater good, spent on good deeds and works of public service. This recommendation is still followed by many Hindus.

> *Nyayopaarjita vittasya daśhamaanshena dhimataḥ*
> *Kartavyo viniyogashcha ishvaraprityarthameva cha*
> *(Skand Puran V 7)*

The assertion that Indians are less charitable, is simply bogus. In *Sanatan Dharma,* people contribute generously to temples and communities in funds, cash and in kind and the resources are used to help not just their own community, but people across religions through government participation.

The Tirupati Tirumala Tirupati Devasthanam (TTD) board had a budget of ₹ 5,141.74 crore for 2024-2025, all from devotee donations. It has Fixed Deposits in banks of ₹ 13,287 crore, under the various trusts operated by the temple body (*Economic Times*, 2024).[59] The trust has 11,329 kg of gold worth ₹ 8,496 crore deposited with various nationalised banks (*Times of India*, 2023).[60]

Since its establishment, the Shri Ram Janmabhoomi Teerth Kshetra Trust has collected ₹3,500 crore in donations (*Hindu Business Line*, 2024).[61]

The trend is not new. In 2012, Venkateswara Temple in Andhra Pradesh had an annual income of $340m from donations (*BBC Online* 2012).[62]

The *Sanatan Dharma* spirit of giving and community participation was so strong, that our British colonisers enacted a law, The Religious Endowments Act (1863) allowing governments to withdraw temple funds, from places of worship of Hindus, Buddhists, Jains and Sikhs.

While other religious institutions receive money from the government, for the last 150 years, temples have been contributing to government projects. In many states, temple *hundi* collections are used by the secular government as administration fee, and 'Common Good Fund'. Laws to this effect exist in almost every Indian state, especially in Tamil Nadu, Karnataka, Andhra Pradesh and Telangana. Bills have been passed recently to take more control of temple contributions.

In addition to the above contributions, Tirupati Devasthanam remits ₹ 50 crores as contributions to the state government. The Ram Mandir trust's financial records are regularly audited by officials from the Comptroller and Auditor General (CAG) and the trust has paid over ₹ 400 crores as tax to the government (*Economic Times*, 2025).[63]

Perhaps, the *Sanatan Dharma* system of charity, helps build a close-knit community, where not just humans, but the entire ecosystem survives. Perhaps, the world needs to learn from this *dharmic* way of philanthropy instead.

Nasha: The Opium Dilemma in Rajasthan

The Bishnoi way of not harming life, nor 'wounding' trees and animals is consistent with not harming oneself as well. Jambho Ji taught addiction is not just a personal failing or a social ill, but a form of self-directed violence that disrupts harmony. Addiction, by its very nature, erodes balance of life. It fogs the mind, numbs the spirit, and weakens the body, rendering a person less capable of living in harmony with others and with nature, itself. Just as harming a tree or killing a deer is seen as a grave sin in the Bishnoi worldview, so too is the directive of not harming the sacred body-temple entrusted to each of us.

Out of the twenty-nine *niyams*, four *niyams* stand as

unwavering sentinels against substance abuse. These four rules explicitly prohibit the consumption of opium, tobacco, cannabis, and alcohol, not just as arbitrary moral edicts, but as an understanding that the preservation of nature must walk hand-in-hand with the preservation of the self, body, mind, and soul.

Interestingly, Jambhani scholars point out that the four substances are listed in the precise order of their degrading impact on the human body and mind—starting from opium and ending with alcohol. This is no coincidence; it reflects a nuanced understanding of human physiology and psychology long before the advent of modern neuroscience. In today's context it means choosing not to pollute one's own body with toxic substances. It means refusing to harm one's mind with stimulants or depressants that cloud judgement and upset emotional balance.

In the truest spirit of Guru Jambho Ji's philosophy, many Bishnoi families embrace this discipline with unwavering dedication. Some are so devoted that even *chai*, India's unofficial national drink, and the lifeline of most social conversations, is quietly absent from many Bishnoi kitchens.

If the body is a temple, why cloud its sanctity with even a mild stimulant?

So, when you step into a Bishnoi home, welcomed with warmth and unmatched hospitality, don't be surprised if your expected cup of tea never arrives. It is not out of oversight, but out of conviction and restraint as the highest form of respect, both for the guest and the self.

However, there is another reality on the ground that tells a more complex tale. Rajasthan is a hub for drug trafficking. The annual report of the Narcotics Control Bureau (2020) maps western Rajasthan as one of the key corridors in India's opium trade, and a major hub for drug trafficking.

Map showing Rajasthan as one among the states on opium trafficking areas.
(Source: NCB Annual report, 2020)

Drinks made from opium, along with poppy husk, or *doda*, has been a long-standing custom as a part of ceremonies in western Rajasthan, especially Jodhpur, Barmer, Jalore, Jaisalmer and the neighbouring districts. It is said warriors in the army would take a dose before going to battle to overcome their fear. In social functions, it is offered to guests as a token of respect, and is a significant part of celebrations, in marriages, birth of a male child, festivals, post-death rituals and even mourning ceremonies. Traditionally, opium or *afeem* is perceived as a comparatively lesser harmful substance. According to estimates 60 per cent to 70 per cent of drug addicts consume opium or its derivatives, including *doda* (poppy husk), a cheaper and more addictive cousin (Jethu Bharti, 2023).[64]

Bishnois are not untouched by this. Tradition is taken as refuge to justify *afeem* consumption. In response to the growing tide of addiction, activists, spiritual leaders, and educators have begun reclaiming the lost narrative. Organisations like the Jambhani Sahitya Akademi, local NGOs, and individual leaders have taken up the mantle to restore the purity of Jambho Ji's teachings.

Sanskaar Shivirs, or value-based camps for children and teens are organised to teach the dangers of substance abuse and to cultivate inner strength. Many influencers within the community are speaking out against the misuse of tradition. These are not just drug awareness programmes, but are movements to restore *dharma*, and to reconnect young minds with purpose, restraint, and spiritual clarity.

The Blue Ban: Tradition Meets Ecology

The Bishnoi community avoids wearing blue garments. Among the twenty-nine sacred principles laid down by Guru Jambho Ji, the twenty-ninth is a prohibition against wearing the colour—blue. At first glance, it may sound odd. How can a colour be against *dharma*? But when you understand the environmental wisdom behind it, the reason unfolds beautifully.

While traditional attire for Bishnoi men consists of pristine white *dhotis, kurtas*, and turbans; women adorn vibrant *ghagras* and *cholis*. Blue, however, remains conspicuously absent. Even today, during community gatherings and rituals, one rarely sees women or girls wearing blue, though younger men, influenced by modern fashion, can be seen wearing blue denim jeans; perhaps the comfort of a good pair of denims is hard to resist. In Bishnoi religious meetings even today, the saints remind listeners, not to wear the colour blue to bathe, meditate, while doing *japa, havan* or studying the Vedas, else benefits do not accrue to the person.

This principle is rooted in ecological awareness and has a fair bit of mythological relevance as well. Some devout followers take this observance a step further—some sadhus and spiritual teachers refuse to use pens with blue ink, recognising the symbolic weight of the prohibition.

The colour blue is considered 'impure' and has several references to it in *Sanatan Dharma* literature. There is an interesting episode of King Trishanku's ascent to heaven in the *Bala Kanda* of the Valmiki Ramayana, and a description of how a curse caused his body and clothes to go blue. The famous poet and mystic Kabir, spoke of *neel rang* as an insult. *Apastamba Smriti*, an ancient text, with insights into rituals and social laws mentions in the sixth chapter, how the cultivation of blue indigo makes the land impure for twelve years (Maheshwari, 2011).[65]

The Environmental Cost of Blue

Jambho Ji's stance against blue was not merely symbolic, or purely mythological. It was a direct response to the ecological damage caused by the cultivation and processing of the indigo plant (*indigofera tinctoria*). While synthetic dyes now dominate the textile industry, the historical association of blue with the indigo plant serves as a reminder of the environmental destruction and is worth understanding.

The plant was cultivated as early as the Indus Valley Civilisation, and for centuries, it remained a valuable dye for textiles. Jambho Ji recognised how its large-scale cultivation could damage the already fragile ecosystem of the desert. Traditionally, blue dye was extracted from the leaves of the indigo plant harvested while it was still green. The short shrubs undergo multiple stages of soaking, fermenting, and oxidation, a labour-intensive process which consumes vast quantities of water. This extraction process not only depletes water sources but also renders the soil barren, making it unfit for growing food crops. Over time, indigo farming devastated large tracts of land, leaving behind infertile fields and struggling communities.

Dark History of Indigo Cultivation

Indigo's history in India during the colonial rule took a darker turn and was steeped in exploitation. The British, recognising the profitability of indigo, aggressively expanded its cultivation in India. Under the oppressive system enforced particularly in Bengal and Bihar, Indian farmers were coerced into growing indigo instead of food crops.

By the early nineteenth century, India was supplying nearly 95 per cent of the indigo used in Britain's textile industry. A system of predatory lending and loans trapped farmers in a cycle of debt. The financial burden was compounded by the destruction of soil fertility. Once a field was used for indigo, it became unsuitable for other crops, exacerbating famine and poverty. The exploitation was to such a large extent that it led to the Indigo Rebellion (1859-1860) also known in Bangla as the *Neel Bidroha*—one of the first organised peasant uprisings against British rule. Farmers in Bengal, pushed to the brink of survival, refused to cultivate indigo, attacked plantations, and demanded fair treatment (National Council of Science Museums, 2017).[66]

When the rebellion was investigated, the Indigo Commission, 1860, was formed. The magistrate of Faridpur, EWL Tower, famously said that 'not a chest of indigo reached England without being stained with human blood' (Bhattacharya, S. 1977).[67]

The Indigo Rebellion was a defining moment in India's resistance against colonial oppression and later influenced Mahatma Gandhi's *Champaran Satyagraha*, where he fought for the rights of indigo farmers in Bihar.

The history of indigo serves as a reminder of the environmental and human costs of unchecked industrial practices, mindless capitalism and colonialism. The Bishnoi principle against wearing blue is not merely a cultural dictate; it is a powerful ecological stance that underscores the need for mindful consumption and sustainable practices.

Modern-day Impact and the Bishnoi Stance

Sometimes I wonder what Jambho Ji would have said if he were to witness the waste, pollution and environmental degradation caused by modern-day fast fashion, driven by consumerism and fleeting trends. It generates enormous textile waste, pollutes rivers with toxic dyes, producing cheap, disposable clothing that consumes vast amounts of water and energy.

Fast fashion, synthetic fabric and polyester clothing, contribute 35 per cent of all microplastics, contributing to 20 per cent of the world's wastewater, fast filling landfills (Climate Change Initiative, Princeton, 2020).[68] Ironically, today natural indigo dyeing is beginning to be considered less harmful than synthetic dyes. Some villages in India are seeing a resurgence of indigo cultivation (*Al Jazeera*, 2020).[69]

If the world can truly follow Jambho Ji's wisdom, we must extend our resistance to all forms of environmentally harmful clothing practices and move away from natural clothing to synthetic wear. True sustainability lies in deeply rooted values that prioritise the well-being of the planet and its people, above mindless consumerism. In an age where trends change with every season, the Bishnoi refusal to wear blue can be seen as a timeless reminder that the planet comes before personal adornment.

550-year-old Blueprint for a Sustainable Future

Long before the world began to speak the language of sustainability, carbon footprints and ethics, Guru Jambho Ji had laid down a way of life that echoed these principles, 550 years ago. Sustainability is not an invention, but an ancient wisdom we've forgotten. What we need now is a global ecological manifesto, rooted not just in policy, but in philosophy. Guru Jambho Ji's teachings can be adapted as beacons for the future.

Image ©Anu Lall Bishnois and the Blackbuck

Chapter 7
Festivals, Traditions and Rituals

द्रव्ययज्ञास्तपोयज्ञा योगयज्ञास्तथापरे
स्वाध्यायज्ञानयज्ञाश्च यतयः संशितव्रताः

Some offer wealth, austerity as sacrifice, some practice the eight-fold path of yogic practices, some study and cultivate knowledge as sacrifice, while observing strict vows.
—Bhagavad Gita 4.28

India loves celebrations. Festivals here are not mere dates on a calendar; they are vibrant expressions of culture, faith, and community. The tradition of *melas*—bustling fairs filled with colour and joy—is woven into the very fabric of rural life. Among them, the Bishnoi *melas* stand out, offering a unique glimpse into the spirit of this deeply rooted community.

I hesitated before writing this chapter. Would readers truly care about the festivals and customs of a small, close-knit community?

But I soon realised that to understand any community without its celebrations is to read a story without its soul. Festivals and rituals are not adornments; they are living embodiments of belief and identity. When scholars ignore living traditions in their study, they risk serious errors and misinterpretations—something the next chapter will make clear. I would be doing a grave disservice to this book, if I don't take you, dear reader through a journey of Jambho Ji's sacred trail.

In recent years, India has witnessed a growing interest in *dharmic tourism*—pilgrimages and spiritual journeys to sacred sites. Perhaps, this chapter will inspire you to follow the trail of the Bishnoi faith. Yet, as much as I encourage these journeys, I must also offer a word of caution. The fragile desert ecosystem that cradles these pilgrim spots is no place for plastic waste or discarded wrappers. If you do choose to visit, tread carefully. Carry reusable bottles, respect the land, and do not leave empty packets of chips behind. This reminder holds true for all pilgrimages.

So, with mindful steps and an open heart, let's embark on this journey together to the fairs, the festivals, the sacred sites, and rituals that tell the story of the Bishnoi spirit.

Jambho Ji's journey is etched into the sands of Rajasthan, leaving behind sacred footprints at several places. Among these are *the ashtdham,* eight revered vibrant pilgrimage centres, where he lived, preached and ultimately left his mortal form. Alongside the *ashtdham* exist the *saathris,* places where he stayed for significant periods, and where relics of his life are

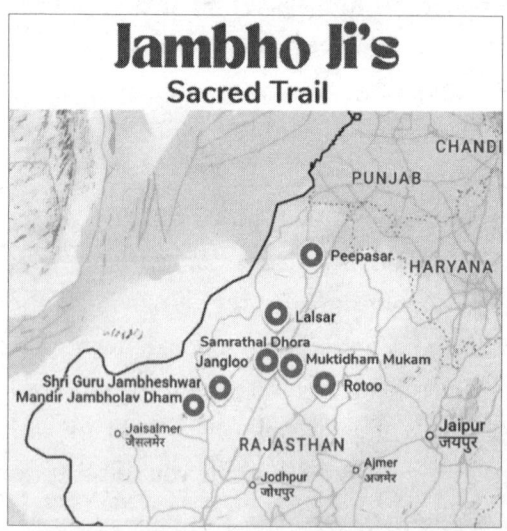

preserved. During melas and events, the pilgrim spots see lakhs of devotes in attendance.

Peepasar: The *Avatar Sthal*
Nestled in the heart of Nagaur, Peepasar is where it all began, the birthplace of Guru Jambho Ji. Not only is it an *avatar sthal*, marking his divine arrival, but also a *saathri*, where objects associated with his life still exist.

***Samrathal Dhora*: The Guru's Seat of Wisdom**
A vast sand dune, known as *Samrathal Dhora*, has deep spiritual significance. *Dhora* means sand dune. *Guru aasan Samrathale* means the Guru's presence is eternally bound to *Samarathal*. At its peak, stands a magnificent marble temple close to a sacred pond. Devotees collect the sand from the pond and carry it to the top of the dune, almost 200 metres away, a ritual symbolising devotion and continuity.

Laalsar: The *Nirvana Sthal*
Laalsar, close to Bikaner, is where Jambho Ji took his final breath under the shade of an ancient *kenkadi* tree. The pilgrim site is also known as *Nirvana Sthal*. Devotees slowly walk in circles, around the *kenkadi* tree, where a large temple stands nearby.

***Muktidham* Mukam: The Ultimate Pilgrimage**
About seventy kilometres from Bikaner lies the most important pilgrimage site for the Bishnois. Jambho Ji's body was brought here from Laalsar. When they dug the earth to bury his body, a *trishul* was found during the excavation, which is now placed on top of the grand marble mandir that enshrines his sacred remains, covered by an orche *chhadar*. Mukam is surrounded by

towering sand dunes and clusters of khejri trees, around which deer, peacocks, and antelope roam freely, untouched by fear.

Jambha Dham: An Oasis of Faith

Jambho Ji's teachings took deep root here. A vast marble temple stands in his honour, alongside a miracle of nature—a perennial water pool, called *Jambh Sarovar*. In a land where water is a rare blessing, this sacred pond has defied time and terrain. On every *Amavasya* men, women and children undertake the holy task of de-silting it, ensuring that life-giving water remains abundant.

Rotu Dham: The Forest of Miracles

Rotu Dham in Nagaur tells a story whispered by the wind of a miracle where Jambho Ji is said to have made thousands of khejri trees appear from the barren earth. Today, these trees stand tall, a green sanctuary amidst the desert. It holds the greatest significance for pilgrims and researchers.

Jaanglu: The Guru's Chola

About 15 km from Bikaner are preserved Jambhoji's *chola*, or robes and his *chippi*, a wooden spoon with a handle. Close to the temple, is a water body constructed on the orders of Guru Ji which is still maintained by the community.

Lodhipur: The Easternmost Pilgrimage

Far from the sands of Rajasthan in Muradabad (Uttar Pradesh), lies the final stop in the sacred circuit of *ashtadham* (not shown in the map).

Each of these sites, are not merely locations, but a map of faith, living chapters of a legacy, a pilgrimage for the Bishnoi community that continues to guide their life. Each sacred site has its own schedule of *amavasya* melas, according to the *Hindu Samvat* calendar. Bishnoi poets have extensively written about the significance of *melas* adding a literary dimension to the spiritual fervour of these gatherings.

At Mukam, the Jambheswar mela is held twice annually, in the months of *asoj* and *phalgun*. In recent times, about half a lakh or more people gather at Mukkam, on every *amavasya*, even when a mela is not organised formally. The *phalgun* mela was first organised in 1537 CE. The *asoj* mela, was started in 1544 CE by Sant Vilho Ji, the first *panth-pramukh* after Jambho Ji. Devotees offer *dhok* or obeisance at the temple. Some offer *bhagwa chhadars*, and still others offer *chhatirs* made of gold and silver.

Night-long *jaagrans* are held, with devotional songs and poetry recitations. One of the unique features of Bishnoi temples is the absence of traditional *prasad*. *Pahal* or sanctified water is given to devotees, which most Hindus might know as *charnamrit*.

Melas: Vibrant Marketplaces

Melas or fairs are not just religious gatherings but also vibrant marketplaces, where goods are sold and agricultural equipment traded. Families and friends meet, children run around, with plenty of food stalls, and with joy reverberating in the atmosphere. Historically, leather goods were also sold during these gatherings, a practice that conflicted with the Bishnoi ethos of non-violence and environmental conservation.

Many raised voices against it. It is said that poet Raju Ram Bishnoi, famously protested this practice in the court of Maharaja Ganga Singh of Bikaner, by reciting powerful verses imploring the king to ban the sale of leather at the fairs. The poem had such an impact on the king that he issued a decree that leather goods will not be traded at Bishnoi fairs. It is a tradition that continues to this day.

Raju Ram Bishnoi's poems are said to be very powerful and poignant. Unfortunately, most of the poems are lost. Whatever remains are also undocumented. Only a few *katha-vaachaks* or religious story tellers use these poems to open their meetings.

The Khejarli mela is also an annual mela remembering Amrita Devi Bishnoi. Each year, lakhs of people congregate there, and organisers give away thousands of tree saplings that the devotees take away and plant in their respective cities.

Fasting on *Amavasya*

Many Bishnois observe fasts on *amavasya* recognising its spiritual and health benefits. Since melas are organised on the day of *amavasya,* most people attend the mela, while fasting. Families that rear cows refrain from selling milk on *amavasya* days, reinforcing the idea of ethical consumption.

One of nature's most fundamental patterns is the two phases of the waxing and waning moon. The first fifteen days, as the moon waxes, are known as *shuklapaksh* or the white fortnight, culminating in *poornima*, the full moon. The next fifteen days mark the waning phase, called *krishnapaksh*, which ends in *amavasya*, the dark moon. In Hindu *sampradaya,* fasting systems align with these natural rhythms, as fasting on specific lunar days is believed to aid in detoxification and balance bodily functions.

Scientifically, it is well established that the gravitational pull of the moon influences oceanic waters. Given that the human body is composed of nearly 70 per cent water, these lunar phases are believed to have a profound effect on human physiology and energy levels. The world over, there are plenty of scientific studies being done on the benefits of fasting.

The daily *Havan*

Jambho Ji laid plenty of emphasis on performing *havan*. The seventh *niyam*, prescribes a daily *havan* at home and at temples. He famously said:

जादिन तेरे होम न जाप न तप न किरिया।
जाण कै भागी कपिला गाई॥
(Sabadvaani 7)

When you don't perform a *homa* with austerity, the *kapila* cow, symbol of wisdom leaves you. There are two mythological cows in Hindu religious literature, the *kamadhenu* and the *kapila*. The *kamadhenu* cow is a symbol of plenty and the *kapila* cow is a symbol of wisdom, and its leaving symbolises destruction of general wisdom in the family (Prithwi Raj Bishnoi, 2018).[70]

Bishnois take pride in the fact that in the last 550 years of faith, they have been amply blessed with food, prosperity, *roop* and *gunas*, pleasant qualities, both external and internal, because of following these principles. The Bishnoi *havan vidhi*, or process is very similar to the *Vedic vidhi*, with *kande* (cow dung cakes) ceremonial coconuts and ghee received from devotees. The *Havan samagri* includes *dhoop, guggul, karpur*, sesame seeds, spices, condiments and herbs. (Swami Bhagirathdas).[71]

Men, women and children participate in *havans*, makings offerings of ghee to the fire, while chanting selected mantras from the *Sabadvaani*. The ritual is led by the temple priest, and in homes, by members of the family, with continuous chanting of mantras and tending to fire, continuously seeing it burns properly, and if elements are vapourised properly. At *melas*, a large format *havan* is organised for community participation, and the fire is left to burn on its own.

There are several references to Vedic philosophy in Bishnoi

literature. It is often said *devo bhutva devam yatej* which means that to pray to a deity, one must become like the deity; signifying that one has to rise above one's smaller self and expand one's consciousness and imbibe qualities like the deity itself. During *havans,* offerings are made to *agni* and *Prajapati*. The starting mantras are:

ओम् अग्नये स्वाहा । ओम् सोमाय स्वाहा ।
ओम् प्रजापतये स्वाहा । ओम् इन्द्राय स्वाहा ।
ओम् विष्णवे स्वाहा । ओम् श्री जम्भेश्वर भगवते स्वाहा ।
ओम् अग्नये स्वाहा इदम् न मम

Idam-na-mama literally means, not mine, detaching oneself from the offering and reward.

The terms *yagya, havan, homa* and *agnihotra* are used interchangeably in daily life across India. *Yagya* means sacrifice. The Bhagavad Gita mentions several types of *yagya*, including *tapaḥ-yagya*, which implies austerities as a means of controlling the mind. Similarly, *gyan-yagya*, or offering of knowledge and *dravya yagya,* where material offerings are given up or sacrificed.

Agnihotra means offerings made to *agni* or fire. It is commonly called *havan*, where the sacred fire is lit in a prescribed copper, metal or mud *havan kund*. Sacrificial offerings of ghee, cow dung cakes, herbs, bark or wood, are made while chanting mantras.

The sacred fire is tended in such a manner that the elements heat appropriately, evaporate and vaporise. The vapour rising from this ritual is regarded as a medicated infusion and is believed to cleanse the environment and the individual. It is believed that natural ingredients used in *havan* have anti-polluting properties, purifying the air and contributing to environmental wellness.

Rituals like *havan* and *yagya,* are not just acts of devotion, but are profound acknowledgments of nature's central role in sustaining life. The fire in the *yagya* symbolises not only purification but also the transformative power of nature, reminding us of the cyclical processes of creation, sustenance, and destruction. In ancient texts, fire rituals were regarded as acts to maintain the balance of the cosmos, purify the environment, and replenish nature. As offerings are consumed by the sacred fire, it is believed they go back to the *panch-mahabhoota*, symbolising human responsibility to maintain harmony with the elements, welfare of animals, and sustenance of all life.

Several essential Hindu rites of passage such as initiations, weddings, and cremations involve fire sacrifices and rituals called *yajna, yaga, havan,* or *homa* and often involve Vedic chants and recitations (Beck, 2012).[72]

Not many scientific studies have been done on *havan*. In one of the few documented works, researchers set up special chambers to study air quality—before, during, and up to 72 hours—after the *havan*, analysing the compounds released in the smoke using advanced tools like GC-MS (Gas Chromatography-Mass Spectrometry). They found that after the *havan*, harmful bacteria in the air dropped by 88–90 per cent, and only good bacteria like *Bacillus* were left behind. Initially, there was a short spike in gases like CO_2 and Nox, but all within safe limits. Remarkably, these levels dropped below the starting point within 24 hours in natural settings. During the *havan*, the herbal smoke contained a wide range of bioactive substances, known for their antimicrobial, antioxidant, and air-purifying properties (Rastogi, Krishnanand, Panwar et al 2022).[73]

During the COVID 19 pandemic, as the world grappled with uncertainty, there was a renewed interest and even modifications in *havan* rituals across the country. Symbolic coronavirus balls were offered to the fire. Corona-*mukti yagya* and *panchagavya havan* involving the five substances obtained from the cow to eradicate COVID were performed (Kapoor V, Belk R, 2022).[74]

Some researchers have explored the role of *agnihotra* in maternal and child health, where cow dung cakes, ghee, and rice grains used in these rituals can be antimicrobial (Sanu, Usharani Shyamasundar et al 2023).[75] *Havan* with special herbs have several volatile oils that are specifically useful for epilepsy, a neuropsychiatric disorder. Due to the high temperature of the fire, the vapours of these oils enter the central nervous system through the nasal route (Bansal et al 2015).[76] Few case studies indicate that *yagya* may reduce stress levels, measured by galvanic skin responses, change of electrical properties of skin, before and after the *yagya* (Nilachal N, Trivedi, 2019).[77] A clinical study reported benefits of *agnihotra* as adjunct therapy in alcoholism, leading to abstinence after two weeks of continuous practice (Golechha G and Deshpande 1987).[78] More research on *havans* and its impact is needed, given its importance in all *Sanatan* traditions. Environmental degradation is a symptom of humanity's moral and spiritual detachment from nature. We must revive religious values and create a society where the conservation becomes a moral imperative. *Dharmic* beliefs offer a way to reconnect with the divine through reverence for nature (O P Dwivedi, 2003).[79]

Fire, Faith and Problems of Modernity
As we approached Mukam for the *phalgun* mela, the first thing I noticed was the thick, black smoke curling into the bright spring blue sky, a sight impossible to miss. I asked

my companions, locals from the community, about it. 'It's coming from the *havan*,' they said.

On entering the *mela* premises one could see the teeming crowds, brimming with faith, making offerings at a massive *havan kund* from which the thick black smoke was rising. I am no stranger to *havans* and by now I have participated in countless *havans* at Bishnoi temples and homes. But I had never seen anything like this. And this wasn't just any place—Mukam is the largest gathering of a community known for its commitment to environmental preservation.

Smoke, especially thick, black smoke, rises if there is incomplete combustion. It means the fire lacks sufficient oxygen, or proper ventilation, leaving behind unburned carbon particles.

I sought out senior faith leaders for answers. They acknowledged the issue is a recent one and they were actively exploring better ways to manage large-scale *havans* at *melas* while ensuring mass public participation.

Melas are held on a grand scale and lakhs of devotees participate in the *havan*, and make offerings continuously, throughout the day. The temple management had constructed a *havan kund,* nearly 15 feet by 15 feet in width, about 5 feet deep, with about 4 feet rising above the ground—large enough to receive everyone's offerings. People toss in small coconuts smeared with ghee, but since no one is actively tending to the fire, it burns erratically and unevenly, producing smoke.

Image ©Anu Lall Bishnois and the Blackbuck

Chapter 8
Are Bishnois Hindus or Muslims?

प्रवृत्तिं च निवृत्तिं च जना न विदुरासुरा: |
न शौचं नापि चाचारो न सत्यं तेषु विद्यते ||

Those who possess a demonic nature do not comprehend which actions are proper and improper. They possess neither purity, nor good conduct, or even truthfulness.
Bhagavad Gita 16.7

Are Bishnoi's a mix of Hinduism or Islam? Do they have Muslim origins?

This peculiar idea often appears in popular media and many mainstream writings. It has trickled down from misinformed academia and research community. But it is an absolute distortion and an uninformed dismissal of the lived history of the community and their sacred beliefs.

The curious question came up so frequently in writings that I felt compelled to address it conclusively.

'The Bishnois are a mixture of Hinduism and Islam', claims *Sunday Observer*. The article opens with the paragraph:

The Bishnois, a community native to the Thar Desert in the North Indian state of Rajasthan are unique. Though they are generically classified as 'Hindu', their folk religion is very distinct. Besides being a mixture of Hinduism and Islam, it is all about environmental

protection. Bishnoi's are today recognised as Hindus. They were unorthodox and were recorded as Muslims until the 1891 Census in Marwar. They practised both Hindu and Muslim rites.
November 3, 2024, by P K Balachandran

When one reads the history of fthe *Bishnoi* community, it becomes clear the seeds of this confusion—*whether Bishnois are a mixture of Hindus and Muslims*—were sown during the 1891 Census of Marwar, conducted by the British that record so-called 'syncretic practices.' The census classified Bishnois as a minor agricultural community, with a population of 40,023 people, in the area of Marwar. They were originally Jats, who became Bishnois under Jambho Ji (Chapter II, on pages 41–42 of Marwar Census, reproduced as Annexure No 2).

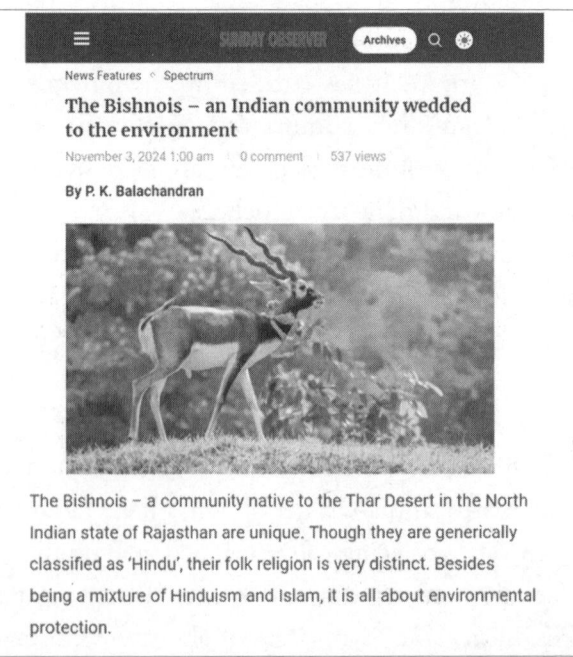

The British hinted that Bishnois straddled between Hindu and Muslims practices, simply because the Bishnois buried their dead, unlike most conventional Hindus. Whether this confusion was deliberately introduced by the British, by mischief or by error, is an impossible assessment.

In later publications, *Tribes and Castes of the Central Provinces of India*, an ethnological study of the caste system, Robert Vane Russell, offers a long list of sub-castes and detailed accounts of social, marriage and death rituals in British India. Bishnois are classified as cultivators, placing them in the higher agricultural castes along with Rajputs. In some kind of obsession with death, Russell Vane documented death rituals for many other Hindu tribes and sub-castes, marking out many communities that buried their dead. There are many more Hindu communities in all parts of India, who bury their dead, but I have limited the list to areas around Rajasthan alone:

Hindus cremate their dead as a rule; but infants who die before they are weaned, Sanyasis, Gosains, Bishnois, and Naths are buried. Again, some of the low castes bury when they cannot afford to burn. The first victim of an outbreak of smallpox is buried, and if, within a certain time, no one else in the village dies of the disease, the body is disinterred and burnt (Russel Vane, pp 34). [80]

Satnamis always bury the dead, laying the body with the face downwards, and spread clothes in the grave above and below it, so that it may be warm and comfortable (ibid pp 313).

Are is a cultivating caste of the Chanda District. Some of them wear the sacred thread…they also cremate their dead, but bury those who die unmarried, placing their feet towards the north like the forest tribes.

The *Dohor*, a small caste of *Berar*, burn dead bodies, but also practise burial.

The *Kamads* wear yellow ochre clothes and bury their dead in a sitting posture, placing crushed bread and water beside the corpse.

When the British undertook the documentation of castes and conducted a census in India, it was perhaps the first time such an exercise had been carried out on such a scale. However, it was done through the lens of foreign rulers who neither understood nor respected the fluidity of our culture. Instead of reflecting the organic nature of caste dynamics, the census made them even more rigid, laying the groundwork for a deeply divided India. The British, driven by their colonial agenda, were already set on fragmenting Indian society and dismantling its *dharmic* traditions using every tool at their disposal, every tactic in the playbook. As a result, the confusion in the Marwar census cast a long shadow over Bishnoi history—one that still lingers to this day.

I was quite surprised to read, that even Dr Pankaj Jain, mentions in his book, that the British classified Bishnois as Muslims. He writes:

> Today Bishnois are considered a caste group within the Hindu community but in the 1891 Census of Marwar, they were classified as Muslims. Some scholars have situated them as a 'liminal' community with common features from Hinduism and Islam. (Jain, 2016)[81]

The 1891 Census of Marwar, certainly created a lot of confusion, however, it did not officially classify Bishnois as

Muslims. The census also did not refer to any Islamic faith traditions. But the myth of the Census of Marwar, simply refuses to die, especially in academic circles and in scholarly debates.

This theory that the Bishnois have Muslim origins, was popularised by Dr Dominique-Sila Khan in her book *Conversions and Shifting Identities* 1997.[82] She describes the Bishnois as an 'obscure cult' with not just strong Islamic influences, but even Muslim roots and origins. She based her arguments on the premise that Bishnois do not practice idol worship and cremate their dead, indicating an Islamic pedigree.

Indian history is replete with such confusions. The Bishnois are not the first victims of such errors, mistakes, omissions, commissions or even deliberate confusions.

In his book *Eminent Distorians*, Utpal Kumar gives multiple examples how Indian history has been distorted, misrepresented, mostly deliberately, sometimes accidentally. History was written by invaders and colonisers who created new heroes, new causes, and new villains, often disregarding the obvious evidence that was right in front of them (Kumar, 2025).[83]

Academic research has a strange way of keeping bad ideas alive. Once a seed of confusion is planted, it keeps sprouting new shoots, passed around in endless loops of references and cross-references. Each citation breathes fresh life into the nonsense, and before you know it, a flimsy theory becomes an 'established fact.'

Unless conscious steps are taken to uproot these bogus claims with solid rebuttals and demands their removal from academic literature, they just keep flourishing, watered by every scholar who comes along next. Now with Artificial Intelligence models like GPT (Generative Pre-trained Transformer) and MLM (Masked Language Modelling) churning out content based on whatever they're fed, these distortions are spreading faster than ever. Western academia, of course, has a soft spot for such confusion—it thrives on keeping questionable narratives alive, letting them creep into every discussion like an unkillable weed, a vicious vein in perpetual academic memory.

Debunking the Myth of Bishnoi Muslim Origins

According to Dominique-Sila Khan, the Bishnoi community underwent a phase of Ismaili conversion in the 13th and 14th centuries before a process of 're-Hinduisation' took place. Today Bishnoi followers, spare no effort to prove their Hindu identity. But many gurus in this geographic area like Ramdev, Mahanati and Jambho Ji were perceived and are still perceived, as having dual Hindu-Muslim personality, and even their devotional hymns, *bhajans* and *vanis*, have Islamic terms and concepts. (Khan, 1997)[84]

Dominique-Sila Khan, a French scholar, settled in Jaipur, was married to a Rajasthani Muslim. Her personal history of transcending religious boundaries reflected in her writings on 'syncretic' or 'liminal' religious traditions (*Islamic Voice*, 2016).[85]

Her erroneous thesis laid the foundation for numerous researchers, such as Meera Anna Oommen (2021)[86], who also labelled the Bishnois as a syncretic or liminal community—one that straddles multiple religious identities.

This idea suggests that the Bishnois occupy a fluid, in-between space between Hinduism and Islam. Further, Khan claims that many revered Bishnoi spiritual figures, including Jambho Ji himself, were buried following Islamic rites, even though their tombs are now referred to as *samadhis*. Yet, crucially, she fails to provide any evidence for this claim.

While some marriage rituals and burial practices may overlap with Muslims, but to claim that these indicate Muslim roots is far-fetched. Jambho Ji even had Muslim followers, and some of his discourses were addressed to them, but this does not translate to the Bishnoi community or Jambho Ji having Muslim origins. The claims of 're-Hinduisation' is not substantiated in any historical document. In many *Sabadvaanis*, Jambho Ji urges his Muslim followers to renounce animal slaughter and meat consumption. Jambho Ji's repeated use of Hindu symbols, myths, and spiritual references, combined with his direct criticism of animal slaughter, does not support Khan's claim of Islamic influence.

Dr Jain, in his critique of Khan's arguments, refutes these speculations. Based on his own fieldwork, he says his informants strongly rejected any notion of Muslim origins. Jain further points out a fundamental flaw in Khan's research: most of her informants were from the Meghwal and Muslim communities, groups historically marginalised and in social tension with the Bishnois. Given these longstanding divisions, it is not surprising that alternative narratives exist about Jambho Ji's origins. However, such perspectives cannot be taken as conclusive evidence (Jain, 2016)[87]

Furthermore, Khan's work is riddled with factual errors and misleading interpretations. She claims that Jambheshwar Ji is regarded as a form of Krishna, when in fact he is seen as an incarnation of Vishnu. She equates *shakti*—a fundamental force in Hinduism—with charisma and *barkat* in Islam, a term associated with divine blessings. But *shakti* is not charisma, nor does it have the same connotations as *barkat*—they are entirely different spiritual concepts. (Khan, 1997)[88]

Perhaps most questionable is Khan's personal account of visiting Mukam, the Bishnoi pilgrimage site with Jambho Ji's *samadhi*, where she claims to have seen a dark green *chhadar* (a colour associated with Islamic shrines) beneath the traditional ochre cloth that covered Jambho Ji's *samadhi*, and concludes that Mukam was being 'Hinduised.'

Now, this was quite the claim, and I was determined to verify it for myself.

Missing Green Chhadar: Case of Imaginary History
Fieldwork has its moments; some insightful, some frustrating, and some downright hilarious. My visit to Mukam, the Bishnoi pilgrimage site, turned out to be a mix of all three.

Mukam on a regular day, is a temple against the stillness of the desert, with a slow trickle of visitors, and a quiet reverence that is almost meditative. As I walked up the marble steps, I couldn't help but notice the strong resemblance to a Sikh gurudwara. Inside the main temple stood the *samadhi*, with a bright orange *chhadar* covering the sacred space.

But thanks to Khan's claim, I found myself thinking: *What if there really is a green one underneath?*

Such is the power of a well-planted seed of confusion; it makes you second-guess even the most obvious truths.

After the prayer, I sat outside on the steps, observing visitors. Unmindfully, I started mentally categorising them by age, telling myself anyone in their mid-40s today, might have been an adult when Khan made this alleged discovery in 1997.

In the warmth of the winter sun, I spent countless hours at the shrine, chatting with several people about the possibility of a green *chhadar*. Not a single person had ever seen one.

One elderly gentleman, in his sixties explained that Jambho Ji's *samadhi* had always been protected, first by watchful *sadhus*, and now by a glass enclosure. Even when devotees offer new *chhadars*, they do so through the priests. No one could ever simply lift the sacred cloth at will.

Then, I took my inquiry to the head of the *math*, and the temple caretakers. Their reaction ranged from bemusement to exasperation.

'A green *chhadar*, hidden beneath? Impossible!' they said.

Another elderly gentleman pointed out a simple but often overlooked truth: the colour of a *chhadar* (offering cloth) at a shrine doesn't necessarily indicate the religious identity of the saint, site, or community itself. It also reflects the devotion of the person making the offering.

At Muslim *dargahs,* Hindu devotees sometimes place orange *chhadars*. This doesn't mean the saint buried there was Hindu or that the shrine is being 'Hinduised.' It just means that a Hindu devotee, following their own reverence chose to offer an orange cloth as a mark of respect.

Similarly, the presence of a green *chhadar* (if there

ever was one) wouldn't mean the shrine had Islamic origins. It would simply signify that at some point, someone, possibly a Muslim devotee, made an offering in a colour they found sacred.

And, back in the day, Jambho Ji had many Muslim devotees. In fact, many *Sabadvaanis* are addressed to his Muslim followers.

What a wise way of highlighting the foolishness of researchers and academicians, creating unnecessary controversies based on superficial observations, I thought.

My biggest takeaway, from the orange vs green debate was that it was much ado about nothing! A community's identity was being questioned based on the colour of a cloth, one that no one had seen, and was being passed off as history, when it was creative fiction at best.

As we drove back from Mukam, I was convinced that the truth is often far more ordinary than the academic theories spun around it.

However, this was not the end of the peculiar theories offered how Bishnois have Muslim origins. Dominique-Sila Khan presents yet another peculiar theory, one she herself describes as amusing and absurd, yet grants space in her book.

According to this theory, the Bishnois were once orthodox Muslims who began their prayers with *Bismillah*. Later, to dissociate themselves from Islam, they supposedly developed a habit of stopping after the first vowel sound, turning Bismillah into *Bisen Bisen*. Over time, this mispronunciation allegedly led to them being called Bishnois. Furthermore, Bisen was supposedly mistaken for the Hindu chant—*Om Vishnu! Om Vishnu!* (Khan,1997)[89]

Khan completely misses the basic philosophy of Jambho Ji. All his hymns begin with *Om*, a deeply significant and unequivocally Hindu invocation. The seventeenth tenet out of twenty-nine, urges followers to pray to Vishnu Ji every day, chanting Om *Vishnu, Om Vishnu!* a mantra to be repeated during circumambulation in all temples. The entire philosophy is about reaching *vaikunth*, laced with references to *brahm*, everywhere. How can we ignore all this?

In her eagerness to apply the 're-Hinduisation' theory, Khan possibly made a forced attempt to fit the Bishnois into a narrative that disregards their deeply rooted *dharmic* traditions. Scholars like Khan, in their overzealous pursuit, fall into what is known as the *law of the instrument*, often referred to as Maslow's hammer. This cognitive bias can be summed up as: *'If the only tool you have is a hammer, you tend to see everything as a nail.'*

The absence of idol worship also does not indicate Muslim origins. Many Hindu sects, such as Arya Samaj and Satya Mahima Dharma, also reject idol worship. *Sanatan Dharma* traditions are open to any form of worship that connect us to the divine, including rivers, trees, plants, animals, as all these are regarded as manifestations of the divine. It also has a long-standing *Nirguna* tradition, which venerates the divine as formless. The Vedas contain numerous passages describing the *param-brahm* beyond any physical form. Nowhere in the Vedic tradition is there a rigid prescription to worship deities in a particular form. Nor is there a prohibition against doing so.

> न तस्य प्रतिमा अस्ति यस्य नाम महद्यशः ।
> हिरण्यगर्भ इत्येष मा हिंसीदित्येष यस्मान्न जात इत्येषः ॥
>
> *na tasya pratima asti yasya nama mahadyashah*
> *hiranyagarbha ityeaha ma ma himsidityesha*
> *yasmanna jata ityeshah ॥*
>
> Yajur Veda 32:3

The formless Supreme Spirit that is all pervasive has no material representation or image. The Sanskrit word *pratima* may be taken to mean an image or idol or also mean that there is no one 'like' the formless supreme spirit.

Further, coming to the practice of burial, it may surprise many, but Hindus do not exclusively cremate their dead; they also practise burial, as discussed in earlier sections. In some cases, a *jal samadhi* (water burial) is also performed.

In the context of the Bishnoi tradition, burying the dead reflects a profound commitment to nature, where spiritual practices have been adapted to suit the harsh conditions of the arid desert.

Firewood is a scarce and precious resource. Their reverence for nature does not allow them to cut trees for a funeral pyre. Interestingly, unlike other communities, the Bishnois do not claim designated lands for cemeteries or have separate burial grounds. Bishnois bury their dead on their own land, ensuring no additional space is taken from the earth. Only in rare cases, such as for *shaheeds* (martyrs), does the community build memorials to honour their sacrifice.

This is an example of the inherent adaptability of *Sanātana Dharma* and one of its greatest strengths. This understanding is fundamentally rooted in the understanding, of that one eternal truth and many paths that take us towards it. This flexibility allows diverse practices to emerge in response to geography, climate, community needs, and evolving times, without losing sight of the underlying spiritual unity. This enables *Sanātana Dharma* to remain living and relevant, accommodating variation while preserving coherence within a shared philosophical framework.

It is imperative that the Bishnoi community, along with historians, cultural anthropologists, writers, and policymakers, work towards correcting these glaring misrepresentations in historical narratives.

Bishnois need to tell their own story, and researchers should seek clarity from primary sources, explore evidence from the ground, rather than engage in endless debates, and a circular referencing wrong studies.

Bishnois are *not* a community torn between two religions. They are and always have been an unshakable *dharmic* tradition, with festivals and rituals, that have a deep *dharmic* connection.

Image ©Anu Lall Bishnois and the Blackbuck

Chapter 9
The Bishnoi Effect

धारणाद् धर्ममित्याहुर्धर्मेण विधृताः प्रजाः ।
यः स्याद् धारणसंयुक्तः स धर्म इति निश्चयः ॥

Dharma comes from the ability to bear or sustain. Through Dharma are people sustained. Hence whatever has the ability to sustain, that for sure is Dharma
— *Mahabharata Shanti Parva 109.11*

In a world where conservation is a buzzword, sustainability is debated at conferences, funded by grants, and championed by influencers, the *Bishnoi Effect*, rarely gets too much coverage. Does such a phenomenon even exist, and does the community even make a difference.

> *Does Bishnoi philosophy live up to its promise of ecological conservation?*
> *Are Bishnoi villages greener? Do they have more wildlife?*
> *Are they more prosperous?*

The Proof is in the Pudding

Researchers have documented it. Travellers have marvelled at it. And locals take pride in it. Many studies with very thorough research leave no doubt. Bishnoi villages are greener, with more Khejri trees standing tall, blackbuck roaming freely, *unafraid*. Drive through Rajasthan; the answer is obvious.

You can see it with your own eyes.

Bishnoi villages have a greater number of wild animals compared to non-Bishnoi villages (Hall and Chhangani, 2015).[90]

Bishnoi Effect is a term first used in a two-year long study, conducted across nineteen villages, eight villages with Bishnoi populations and eleven without Bishnoi. It was found that villages with Bishnois had significantly more Khejri trees (Jonathan Hall 2011).[91] Hall traced five 500-metre paths through agricultural lands in these villages and found that the number of Khejri trees on Bishnoi land was significantly higher than in non-Bishnoi areas. This difference wasn't merely a matter of tradition but had practical implications. For communities with Bishnoi populations, the higher density of these trees correlated directly with greater agricultural productivity and stability.

Blackbuck population was much higher in villages with Bishnoi population and abundance of trees was associated with income as well (Hall Hamilton, 2014).[92]

Neekee Chaturvedi writes a personal account of how the Bishnois treat water conservation as if it's a sacred duty. She documents her experiences of surveying water conservation efforts of the desert villagers, where she came across many community-maintained water reservoirs. Unfortunately, the ponds lacked maintenance, and hardly had any water stored in them. As she went through several villages photographing these traditional water harvesting structures, she walked across the village periphery in Phlaudi, expecting another ill-kempt, semi-arid pond. But once she and her team reached the other side of the sandy hill, they found a large water reservoir brimming with clean and sparkling water. The shady trees, the peacock sounds and the beauty of a camel guzzling water to quench his thirst added to its spectacular beauty. This man-made oasis was startling as well as soothing in an otherwise dreary landscape. She found out that this water body was maintained by the Bishnoi community, who unfailingly labour on every new moon night for its upkeep. Every man, woman and most children contributed fortnightly to the cause as if it were a sacred duty. It was a touching spectacle (Chaturvedi, 2018).[93]

I have witnessed the *Bishnoi Effect*, first-hand, too. Driving through the vast, unforgiving landscape of Rajasthan, the land stretched barren and dry, mile after mile, with the sun shimmering on the road. As we came closer to the temple at Jambha, one of the most sacred sites of the Bishnois, the transformation was almost surreal. Birds circled overhead, their calls breaking the silence. Trees rose high against the green desert sky. Where there should have been no water, a permanent water body reflected the sun, preserved by the efforts of local people who manage it, and de-silt it as a sacrosanct sacred duty.

I spent plenty of time at the Kaushal gaushala at Jambha. The Swamiji told me that the 4,000 cows there were cared for with devotion. He told me of the conservation efforts taken by the community. We were in an oasis of greenery with peacocks and birds, and I didn't want to leave. Jambha wasn't an anomaly. I had the same experience when driving to other Bishnoi places, like the Jajiwal Dhora temple. The landscape is different in Bishnoi villages.

Many other researchers have shared similar experiences. Alexis Reichert talks about the sharp contrast in patches of land owned by Bishnois and non-Bishnois. Reichert narrates the story how one afternoon, he, along with his hosts, took a trip to climb the Rotu dune and circumambulate the temple. The area is almost entirely populated by Bishnoi who don't allow a single branch to be cut. As a result, large, lush, green trees and wild animals are scattered around the dune for miles. As they climbed the dune, he noticed some barren trees amidst the dense green, a perfect rectangle of land where the trees had been stripped of their branches. On inquiry, he learnt that a non-Bishnoi person had moved there. He further adds, that it in the course of his research it was quite evident that Bishnoi villages were far more green than other villages. But this was the first time, it was laid out so clearly, in a little box in front of him. Bishnoi dharma and a green landscape are inextricably linked (Reichert, A. 2015).[94]

Dr Jain shares a strikingly similar account in his travels. He recounts that while driving along the state highway, he was struck by the sudden appearance of a huge number of deer freely grazing on both sides of the highway. The area was protected by fences and notices posted by the department of forests. He later discovered that this was one of the famous sanctuaries for blackbuck, protected by the Bishnois. The biodiversity of the desert state of Rajasthan is managed not by human isolation but by active human participation, Bishnoi's being one of the prime examples of it (Jain, 2016).[95]

M K Ranjitsinh offers a beautiful account from the 1970s. He notes when driving through the Rajasthan desert if one suddenly notices clusters of blackbuck, it is safe to assume that there is a Bishnoi settlement nearby. Blackbuck and chinkara survived not because of any governmental action, rather despite poaching by government officials, both civilian and military. They survived because of the religious zeal of the Bishnoi community. In fact, even Vala Rajputs and Kathis of Saurashtra held the blackbuck sacred. Over 9,000 of the approximately 11,000 black bucks of Rajasthan are in Bishnoi areas. The only viable blackbuck population in the state of Punjab, reported to be about 5,500, is also in the Bishnoi area of Abohar. One of the largest concentrations of chinkara now surviving the Indian subcontinent, estimated at over 2,000 in 1974 is around Jambha, the main shrine of the Bishnois. Another is around Lohawat in Jodhpur district, where in a shrine venerating the footprint of Jambho Ji, animals and birds are offered grain twice a day. No community deserves to be recognised for its services to conservation more than the Bishnoi (M K Ranjitsinh 1997).[96]

Are Blackbucks Sacred?
Most people believe that blackbuck are sacred to the Bishnoi community. Mainstream media has reported on several occasions that the Bishnois regard blackbuck as sacred embodiments of their Guru (*India Today*, 2024).[97]

They believe blackbuck to be a reincarnation of Jambho Ji (*Indian Express*, 2018).[98] Bishnois worship blackbuck like Jambha Ji (*Times of India*, 2006).[99]

No evidence exists in Jambhani literature that bears testimony to these claims. No Bishnoi religious leaders claim that Jambho Ji was reincarnated as a deer. But the media finds it an easy way to explain the devotion of the community towards nature.

Incidentally, I came across a study by Jonathan Clarence Hall, that substantiated the vulture story narrated by Swami Ji at the temple.

***

Every Species Follows its Own *Dharma*

During one of my visits to the Bishnoi temple at Jajiwal Dhora, on a cold windy winter morning, I sat in the morning sun, speaking to the Swami Ji at the temple.

The *havan* had just concluded. The energy of collective chanting and the beautiful scent of the fire was still in the air. Devotees were preparing to leave the temple premises, after paying their respects. Some children quickly ran out to the rescue centre at the back of the temple, to see the animals.

I asked Swami Ji:

But why just the blackbuck? Why not all animals?

Do Bishnois believe Jambho Ji reincarnated as a blackbuck?

Swami Ji smiled, as if he had been asked this before. Knowing that this would be a long conversation, he paused there and asked me if I would like to have some milk. I readily nodded my head.

Milk from the temple *gau-shala* is *amrit*, never to be refused. Desert winters, like the summers can also be very harsh, with sudden temperature changes, and winds that almost blow away your mind. Swami Ji went inside his kitchen himself to prepare some warm milk.

He eats only what he cooked, said someone sitting beside me. Soon, Swami Ji returned with a *batti* of warm milk, laced with crushed *elaichi* and *gur*, warming my cold hands.

As we drank the goodness, he explained.

'It is not just the blackbuck. It is every creature that faces persecution.'

He recounted an incident, from a few years ago, when a group of villagers discovered several vultures, large, majestic birds, on the verge of death. Perhaps poisoned or simply starving, they had collapsed, wings limp, their sharp eyes dulled with exhaustion. The community did what it always does in the face of suffering—they rescued them.

Bishnoi temples are often used to provide shelters for animals. Most temples have a rescue centre and a sanctuary attached where animals are taken care of with the same devotion as if towards a divine deity.

But there was a problem. Unlike the deer, which could graze peacefully in the Bishnoi fields and could be handfed grains, these flesh-eating birds refused to eat seeds or grains. The temple could not provide for them.

'*Eating flesh is the dharma of the vulture,*' Swami Ji explained. '*Ishvar has created it that way. It is bound by instinct, and does not have a choice to eat anything else.*'

The community was forced to arrange for the forest department to transfer the vultures to a government conservation facility where they could be properly cared for until they were fit enough to fly.

It was a powerful story, with the moral being—help any living creature in danger that needs your help.

> If the blackbuck is the Bishnois' icon of protection, then the vulture, often reviled, yet ecologically essential, was another silent beneficiary of the same devotion. It also made me wonder: Was this just a one-time act of kindness, just an anecdote or folklore?
>
> But one thing was clear, wherever the Bishnois exist, life finds a way.

In 2011, Hall analysed the population of vultures in Bishnoi and non-Bishnoi villages. Vulture species across the globe face numerous threats to their survival, due to human persecution, climate change, or unintentional poisoning. There were reports that the vultures had been poisoned, because local poultries medicated their farm birds with a drug called diclofenac, which was well tolerated by the poultry birds. But the vultures died, after feeding on the carcasses of these medicated farm birds.

Between 1996 and 2005, the El Niño Southern Oscillation (ENSO) triggered environmental disruptions that also critically endangered Indian vultures across western Rajasthan.

This study monitored vulture populations in and around eleven villages within 175 km of Jodhpur, for many years. Year after year, they counted the dwindling numbers and found that in villages with a significant Bishnoi presence, something unusual was happening (Jonathan Hall 2011).[100]

The vultures were surviving.

Unlike other areas where vulture populations plummeted,

Bishnoi villages acted as sanctuaries for these scavengers of the sky. The researchers speculated that religion-based conservation, woven into the fabric of Bishnoi life, was shielding and buffering these birds (Hall, 2010).[101]

Khejri, Blackbuck and Desert Ecology

Amrita Devi Bishnoi's willingness to give her life for a tree epitomises the deep reverence the Bishnois have for nature that transcends material needs and personal safety. It is about sustaining future generations. When the landscape is a daily negotiation with nature for water and survival, one tree stands tall, unyielding, generous, and vital. This tree is Khejri, botanically known as *Prosopis cineraria*. We have seen how desert communities have for centuries revered it.

Prosopis cineraria is officially recognised as the state tree of Rajasthan, and for good reason. In Rajasthan, Khejri reigns supreme, not only ecologically, but also culturally and spiritually. Known for its resilience and unmatched usefulness, the Khejri tree is deeply woven into the rural life of Rajasthan. Villagers rely on it for almost everything: food, fodder, fuel wood, medicines, and even soil enhancement. Its pods called *sangri*, are harvested and sun-dried, and used all year around as a vegetable, often combined with *ker*, to create the classic Rajasthani dish, *ker-sangri*.

Every farmer I met told me how every part of the Khejri tree serves a purpose. The roots bind the soil, leaves are for cattle and for nourishing the soil, its fruits and pods feed humans, and the tree provides shade to crops and wildlife, protecting them from the harsh sun. It grows slowly and stays strong even without rain.

Kuch maangti hi nahin Khejri, deti hi hai—was the common sentiment.

Science backs this claim amply. Monika Sharma writes: *Prosopis* the '*Kalpvriksha* of desert', does not wait for rain to bloom; whether the skies bless the land with water or not, it bears fruit, earning it the title of an 'unfailing crop'. With a root system that dives deep into the earth, far beyond the reach of most plants, this tree draws water from invisible aquifers, allowing it to flower and fruit reliably, even when surrounding crops wither under drought.

> The tree does not merely survive; it heals the earth. Its ability to fix atmospheric nitrogen rejuvenates the soil, making it more fertile and giving farmers hope when conventional agriculture struggles.
>
> Its leaves are rich in protein, calcium, and phosphorus, making them excellent cattle fodder. The leaves are crushed into a paste, and applied to blisters, boils, and mouth ulcers. Traditional healers use them in remedies that modern studies now support with evidence of antifungal, antibacterial, and antioxidant properties. Khejri flowers are often mixed with sugar and used as a natural blood purifier and a supplement.
>
> In an amazing symbiotic relationship, animals like chinkaras and blackbuck, survive the harsh sun beneath the Khejri trees. They feed on the fruit pods that drop from the tree and help in propagating the tree wherever they go as they carry the Khejri seed in their faeces. Khejri is generous even in decay. When its leaves fall, they enrich the soil. Farmers often mix dried leaves into farms to boost fertility. Blackbuck and chinkaras are known to rely on its shade and pods during extreme summers, surviving where other food sources vanish. And so, calling Khejri the *Kalpavriksha* of

the desert is no poetic exaggeration, it is simply the truth (Monika Sharma, 2022).[102]

It is quite clear that centuries ago, when the Bishnois laid down their lives to protect the Khejri tree, they weren't just hugging wood and leaves. They were standing guard over life itself. They did not die for a tree; they died for the future.

Official programmes of afforestation are based on heavy funding and centralised decision making, and act against the local knowledge systems regarding indigenous knowledge as worthless and unscientific. Local trees that are venerated often play a crucial role in local ecosystems. Sacred forestry is a life support system. This aspect is often overlooked by modern environmentalists who seek to replace 'sacred' forestry, by 'social' forestry seeing natural forests and trees as 'weeds'. Development and afforestation programmes conceived at the international level by experts, adopt a reductionist philosophy of tree planting. It is about producing wood for the market, not for maintaining ecological cycles or satisfying local needs for food, fodder and fertiliser (Vandana Shiva, 2012).[103]

***

138 | Bishnois and the Blackbuck: Can Dharma Save the Environment?

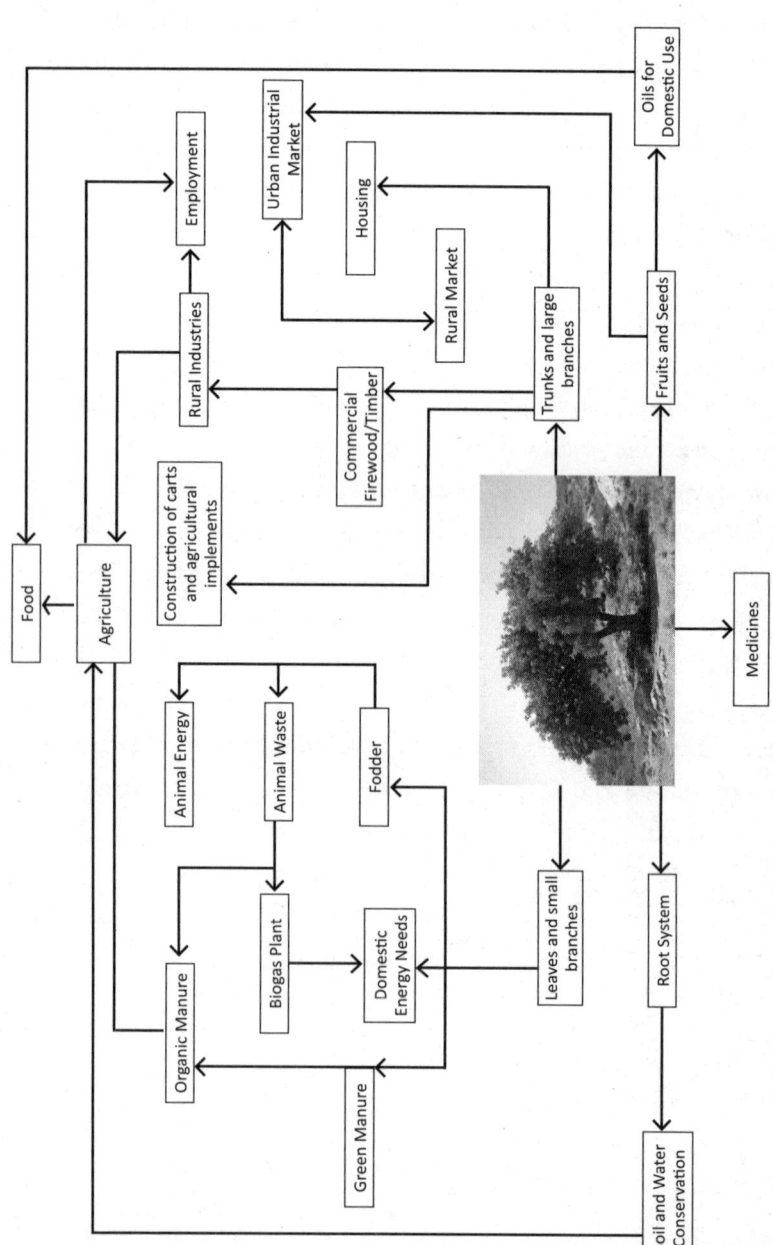

Image Source: Dr Shiva's model on local trees, often venerated play a crucial role in local ecosystems, Monocultures of the Mind, 2012

The *Bishnoi Effect* is not a theory or mere philosophy, sheer good luck or just a policy on paper. It's proof, visible to all that wherever Bishnois are, nature flourishes. Where they aren't, the land struggles. Seeing it with my own eyes, I didn't need any study to tell me the truth. The *Bishnoi Effect* is real, and it's undeniable. It's proof that when people treat nature as sacred, she responds back in kind.

What if protecting nature like this was a part of everyone's daily life, woven so seamlessly into daily rituals that conservation happened effortlessly? At some point of time in ancient India, such daily life rituals were sacred duty or *dharma*. Across India, many communities guarded nature as if it was their sacred duty. Ritual offerings weren't just symbols; they are survival strategies, passed down from generations. *Dharma* was supposed to guard holy rivers and environment, but most of Bharat forgot *dharma*.

For a few communities even now, faith doesn't just inspire conservation, it *demands* it. Trees, water bodies, and animals become sacred trusts, shielded from harm through customs that outlive policies and laws. These sacred spaces become more than places of worship; they are the heart of communal life, where festivals, gatherings, and agrarian rituals reinforce a deeper, almost instinctive commitment to the land. And in these traditions lies a lesson for the modern world: when belief and faith survive, *faith* becomes *forest*. Both thrive.

Chapter 10
When Faith Becomes Forest

विश्वस्वं मातरमोषधीनां ध्रुवां भूमिं पृथिवीं धर्मणा धृताम्
शिवां स्योनामनु चरेम विश्वहा

The plants are like mothers that sustain the world grow on the earth (bhoomi) which is held by dharma, in which auspiciousness gently pervades throughout the world.
—Bhumi Suktam, Atharva Veda, 12.1.17

We began this journey in the mystical forest of *Kantara,* where *prakriti* was safeguarded through faith, customs, rituals, and reverence for the divine. That sacred grove, where nature and spirit merge, finds its reflection in many places in India. Deep in the heart of Rajasthan's parched landscape, where the golden sands stretch endlessly under an unforgiving sun, exist islands of life: *Orans,* the sacred groves of the desert. These clusters of trees stand like living temples, where conservation is not just a practice, but a way of life.

An *Oran* is not just land—it is a sacred trust, guarded for generations by many different communities that survive along with nature. Like Kantara's enchanted forests, *Orans* embody an ancient pact between man and nature, where protection is devotion, and destruction is sacrilege.

The Orans provide a much-needed lifeline and safeguard communities dependent on them, functioning as an infrastructure for resilience in the face of extreme hardships.

The Orans are where communities conserve the environment for their socio-material sustenance and as part of their religious beliefs. They become important gathering points for communal congregations, festivals and other social events, the performance of which is linked to agrarian rhythms and the continued commitment of the communities towards environmental conservation (Aditi Veena et al, *Adawal ki Devbani*).[104]

Sacred 'Orans' of Rajasthan

The Rajasthan Forest Department documents a remarkable number of sacred groves. Many communities preserve these Orans and their daily life depends on them. In Mewar, Rajasthan, these groves are called *Vani* and *Kenkri* in Ajmer. The people of Jodhpur, Bikaner, and Jaisalmer, including the Bishnoi community, call their groves, *Orans*. In Alwar, they are called *Devbani*. Though their names vary, their purpose is deeply unified; they're dedicated to divine guardians, who protect and sanctify the land. The common saying across many communities, whether Bishnoi or not is: *Jungle mein hariyali hogi, ghar ghar mein khush-hali hogi* (Where forests are green, only then, every household can prosper).

At the heart of these Orans, stands the Khejri tree (*Prosopis cineraria*), a symbol of resilience, revered as the life giver of the desert. This unassuming tree, with its deep roots and ability to thrive in harsh conditions, has sustained both humans and wildlife for generations.

Till recently, several *Orans* had not been clearly defined, or declared as forest lands, which makes it difficult to apply protective legislation. These lands were being protected by the indigenous Bishnois alone.

The world-famous Oran of Pipasar and Khejarli are found in areas where the Bishnoi are in the majority. The birth place of Jambho Ji, Pipasar has five sacred groves, Jambheswar Ji ki oran (31 acres), Pipajikioran (10 acres), Maharaja Kioran (42 acres), Hanuman Jikioran (5 acres), and Oodjijkioran (2 acres). This covers a total area of 90 acres, which is heaven for desert wildlife. Other major orans are: Samrathal, Mukam, Lalasar, Lalwas, Bajju, Nokha, Pithasar, (Bikaner), Kishanpura (Ajmer), Dariba, Samelia (Bhilwara), GudaMalani, Dhorimanna, Sonri (Barmer), Khetolai and Dholia (Jaisalmer), Sawantsar (Churu), Rawatsar, Lakhasar, Ber (Hanumangarh), Jambha, Guda Bishnoian, Jajiwal Dhora, Artiya Khurd, Lohawat, Ramdawas, Jurd, Osian, Akelkhori, Kosana, Lamba, Tilwasani (Jodhpur), Karawari, Malwara, Charnau (Jalore), areas where the Bishnois settled. Due to their conservation efforts, a Bishnoi-dominated area of Jodhpur district has been declared a Conservation Reserve (Guda Bishnoian Conservation Reserve) by the Rajasthan State Government for recognition of their wildlife value (Gehlot, Hemsingh, 2017).[105]

The Bishnoi conservation ethic, passed down across generations, intertwined in religion and faith, highlights how community-driven conservation practices can support economic needs, agricultural stability and strengthen the very fabric of rural livelihoods. Trees in these groves are protected by centuries-old traditions that place spiritual value on the land, adding a profound layer of cultural significance to environmental conservation efforts. (Gehlot Hemsingh, ibid)

Dr Pankaj Jain notes that the biodiversity in the state of Rajasthan is managed not by human isolation but by active human participation. The Bishnois are a prime example of that. Many animals are found in and around Bishnoi villages, in addition to blackbucks, Great Indian Bustard, Indian gazelles, peacocks, bulbul, bayas, sparrows, crows, vultures, chinkaras, neelgais, wild pig, wolves, jackals, and desert foxes. The trees that are commonly found in and around Bishnoi villages are Khejri, Jal, Peepal, Khais, Rohira, Babool and Neem. The Bishnois have consistently preserved this biodiversity for generations. In 1981, village Janvi in Jalore district of Rajasthan was surveyed after twenty years and it was found that a similar number of flora and fauna was counted, as in the India Census of 1961 (Jain, 2016 ibid).[106]

Sacred Groves of India
India's landscape is dotted with unique patches of greenery that are, quite literally, *sacred*. These ancient sanctuaries, known as *sacred groves* are not merely preserved by chance but are protected by deep-rooted spiritual beliefs that span millennia.

In the heart of these groves, the hum of life is palpable. Birds fly through the trees, medicinal plants grow freely, and animals roam with a rare sense of security. These sanctuaries of biodiversity exist in a world of their own, and their stories tell of a bond between people and nature that is as old as civilisation itself.

The reverence for sacred groves is woven into the cultural and religious fabric of India. These groves often house shrines and deities, along with trees, flora and fauna embodying divinity and natural wisdom.

Two prominent Indian ecologists, Professor Madhav Gadgil and Vartak explored how 'sacred groves' became a fundamental part of forest conservation. Before the advent of agriculture, when people relied on foraging and hunting, small forest sections were consecrated to local deities and ancestors. Forests were not just a resource but a realm of sanctity. These sacred spots, often untouched by humans were vibrant with life and became centres of cultural and religious significance, where local beliefs encouraged complete protection of nature (Dhanapati Shougrakpam, 2024).[107]

Guarding these groves often became the responsibility of the local or tribal communities, who deeply believed that any harm, like cutting trees or even gathering fallen leaves, could bring divine wrath. Their traditions tell of natural calamities like floods or droughts, believed to have arisen when the grove's sanctity was violated, affecting surrounding fields and lives. Even today, this tradition of preserving sacred groves endures in various parts of India, where the community's connection to these untouched spaces remains intertwined with spirituality and respect for nature's own balance. (Dhanapati Shougrakpam, ibid)

This legacy can have a lasting impact on modern-day ideas about conservation and show modern society the power of respecting natural spaces as sacred entities.

Murugesan (2016)[108] compiled one of the best compendiums of sacred groves, with state-wise descriptions, trivia about groves, sacred practices and their importance and roles in communities, acting as spiritual sanctuaries and guardians of biodiversity.

He describes the management and significance of groves that vary across regions and social structures:

> *Local Village Groves* are community-managed and often involve participation from the entire village. Typically, even villages with multiple tribal and ethnic groups unite to protect and maintain these sacred spaces.

Regional Groves are managed by temple trusts. These groves attract people from various areas for worship. For example, Sabarimala is a regional sacred grove in Kanjikkuzhi, Kottayam in Kerala, which draws visitors due to its religious significance.

Pan-Indian Sacred Groves, are larger in size and serve as national pilgrimage destinations, fostering a pan-Indian spiritual unity. Finally, *Sacred Groves* are dedicated to ancestral spirits, often acting as burial grounds.... These groves serve both as sacred sites for worshipping deities and as places to honour ancestral spirits, linking generations of the community to the land and each other (Murugesan, 2016, ibid)

The estimates regarding the number of sacred forests have been quite varied. It was estimated that there are around 13,270 groves all over the country (Malhotra, 1998).[109]

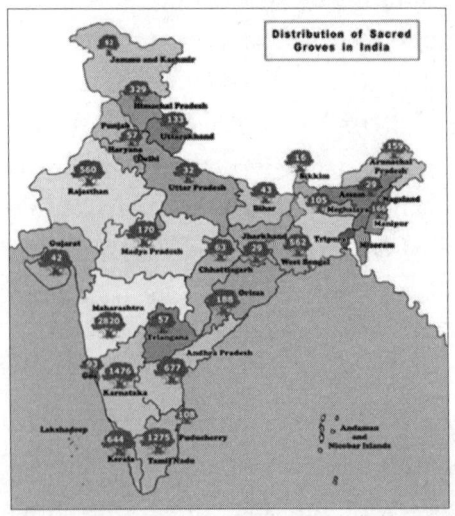

Source: Sacred groves of India, Home: ENVIS Centre on Conservation of Ecological Heritage and Sacred Sites of India

The Government's website mentions almost 10,000 sacred forests all over India. Maharashtra has the highest number—2,820 sacred groves (Deshmukh, 1999).[110]

Each sacred forest serves as a testament to India's rich cultural diversity and profound respect for nature and ancestral traditions. Indian environmental policies have acknowledged the importance of these sacred groves, protected by cultural and religious practices rather than formal legal systems, demonstrating a powerful, community-driven approach to conservation. This incorporation of traditional ecological knowledge into formal frameworks reflects the timeless relevance of India's environmental heritage.

The religious belief serves as an instrument of protection of rare forest species. Traditional knowledge-based sacred groves conservation has a significant contribution in the process of biodiversity conservation. Most of the plants and trees have medicinal importance. Sacred groves are indicative of positive consequential combination of religion and ecology (Jamir and Pandey 2003).[111]

Tribal people of the Bhotiya community (Uttarakhand) have an ancient practice of conserving the medicinal plants of the region for centuries, mainly attributed to their religious belief. They believe that if someone from outside the village uproots medicinal plants, it is an evil act which may bring misery to the village folk. Almost all Hindu Gods are associated with animals, birds and creatures as their vehicles or *vahanas* promoting harmony in nature to maintain the ecosystem (Kandari, LS, Bisht, VK, Bhardwaj, M et al., 2014).[112]

Murugesan also compiles many interesting stories and folklore associated with various sacred groves across India:

In Assam, the ancient Vaishnav temples known as *Shankara Deva Mathas* are centres of devotion and intrinsically linked to sacred groves. Each village has its identity associated with the plant or tree available in that area, and its importance to the villagers. For the villagers, every species has a story, a purpose, and a spirit to honour and protect. Hunting is prohibited in the mating season. During the nesting season, the community enforces strict protection, prohibiting hunting and ensuring that all wildlife, especially birds, can thrive undisturbed.

In Himachal Pradesh, stories of ancient gods and myths play a vital role in keeping sacred groves intact and untouched, in the *dev-vans* or revered forests dedicated to *devi* and *devtas*. The community imposes strict rules. Not even a dry leaf may be taken beyond the grove's boundaries, protecting it from any form of exploitation. Across the state's 10,000 temples, each deity is supported by a dedicated community *biradari* panchayat, that ensures the grove's preservation.

In Tamil Nadu, nearly every village is blessed with its sacred grove, some spanning from 1 to 500 acres, protected with a unique set of customs. These groves are kept spotless; urination or defecation is strictly forbidden. At festival time, villagers prepare *pongal*, using only the fallen dry twigs for the ritual, leaving the branches of the trees untouched. (Murugesan, 2016).[113]

The Living Root Bridges of Meghalaya (a UNESCO World Heritage Site) are maintained by the community. Sacred forests managed by *Khasi Lyngdoh* or the priest had greater species richness, across trees, shrubs, and herbs, including a number of endemic and threatened plant species, than in the unprotected community forests. However, a decrease in sacred groves and their degradation caused by erosion of religious beliefs are matters of concern (Barik, Gogoi, Rashmi, 2008).[114]

This practice echoes the beliefs of the Bishnoi women of Rajasthan's *orans*, who believe that cutting the green branches of the Khejri tree would hurt the tree itself.

As the hold of religion and community declines, the preservation and conservation of groves also goes down. In Andhra Pradesh, many sacred groves are now under threat as religious practices evolve and modern developments encroach on their traditional lands. The modernisation of temples has led to the clearing of the very vegetation that was once preserved as a mark of reverence—similarly in Mizoram, where large tracts of sacred groves have been cleared to make space for churches. It must be added, however, that the local community has continued to preserve these spaces, despite conversion of religion (Murugesan, 2016).[115]

There is a need for more projects and studies on these sacred groves. It remains to be seen how these groves will be preserved in the future once the hold of religion decreases further, and conversions occur on an even larger scale.

Sacred Groves in Ancient Times

India's sacred groves did not spring overnight. They also did not arise as the result of some activist movement. These sanctuaries have religious significance woven through millennia, carefully curated to be part of *Dharma* consciousness making them more than protected lands. They are revered extensions of the divine in *Bharatvarsha*. From the *itihaas* of Ramayana and Mahabharata to the philosophical insights of the Upanishads and the poetry of Kalidasa, India's ancient texts are filled with references to forests, rivers, mountains, plants, and animals.

Together, they paint a picture of a civilisation where humans are inseparable from and protective of their natural surroundings.

Valmiki Ji's *Ramcharitmanas* has the *Aranya kaanda*, or the 'forest episode'. The Mahabharata, also has the *Vana Parva* or *Aranya Parva*, or the 'book of the forest', which is the third and the longest of eighteen books, documenting the twelve-year long journey of the Pandavas in the forest. In both compositions, the forests play critical roles beyond being mere backdrops for events in history.

Both texts present forests as places of transformation, the backdrop for profound experiences and learnings, and where characters undergo trials, meditate, and connect with the divine. The experiences in these forests highlight the importance of the natural world in human learning and human resilience. In these texts, the forest isn't simply a place to pass through; it is a living, breathing entity worthy of respect and reverence, embodying the divine spirit in all its forms.

As Ram, Lakshman and Sita traverse vast regions, they journey from present-day Uttar Pradesh's lush Chitrakuta to the dense forests of Dandakaranya, followed by Panchavati, Kishkindha, and the distant evergreen forests of Lanka. The verses of the Ramayana, beautifully describe the vegetation, plants, flora and fauna that are found in these areas even today.

This geographical sweep provides not just a backdrop but a window into ancient ecosystems.

Murugesan (2019)[116] writes about the Dandakaranya forest, that stretches approximately 92,200 square kilometres across modern-day Chhattisgarh, Odisha, Telangana, and

Andhra Pradesh. It derives its names from the Sanskrit *dandaka* (punishment) and *aranya* (forest), symbolising its association to remote wilderness, exiles, and banishment. He adds that Rama, Lakshmana and Sita were cautioned to be careful when entering the Dandakaranya that was known to be full of lions and tigers. However, in current times, lions no longer inhabit the area. Curiously, prehistoric paintings found at the Bhimbetka rock shelters, show a lion and a tiger, which validates Valmiki Ji's reference in the Ramayana. Bhimbetka is often called a Buddhist site by historians, even though Bhimbetka means 'Bhima's resting place'.

Bhimbetka rock shelters is now a UNESCO World Heritage site with its 750 rock shelters, with some of the oldest paintings that date back to Palaeolithic and Mesolithic periods (Rock Shelters of Bhimbetka, by ASI India).[117]

Chitrakuta and Panchavati are *vanas,* or cultivated forests, in contrast to Dandakaranya, a fierce forest. The forests in Ramayana pulse with life and emotion, each one embodying a unique quality and atmosphere of *shanta* (calm), *madhura* (sweet), *raudra* (angry), and *vibhatsa* (fearful); the four moods of the forest (Lutgendorf, 2001).[118]

Ram and Sita spent many years in *panchvati,* a grove or *vatika* with five tree types—Peepal, Ashoka, Bael, Banyan and Amla. The Ashoka tree becomes a significant symbol when Sita Ji is held captive in Ashoka Vatika, where she finds solace and strength amidst a grove of Ashoka trees.

There are 182 plant species in Valmiki's Ramayana, classified as trees, small trees, shrubs and creepers (Murugesan, 2019).[119] Trees like Ashoka burst into flower as spring begins, filling the landscape with colour and vibrancy, while, Flame of the Forest, another remarkable tree, flares up with bright red flowers toward the end of winter. The Ramayana further brings the environment alive through its seasonal references, which are closely tied to India's natural cycles.

This environmental philosophy for humans and nature is found in the Vedas and *Puranas*, that have an ecological code of conduct built on reverence for nature (Sudhir Rawat, Anjana Vashishtha). [120]

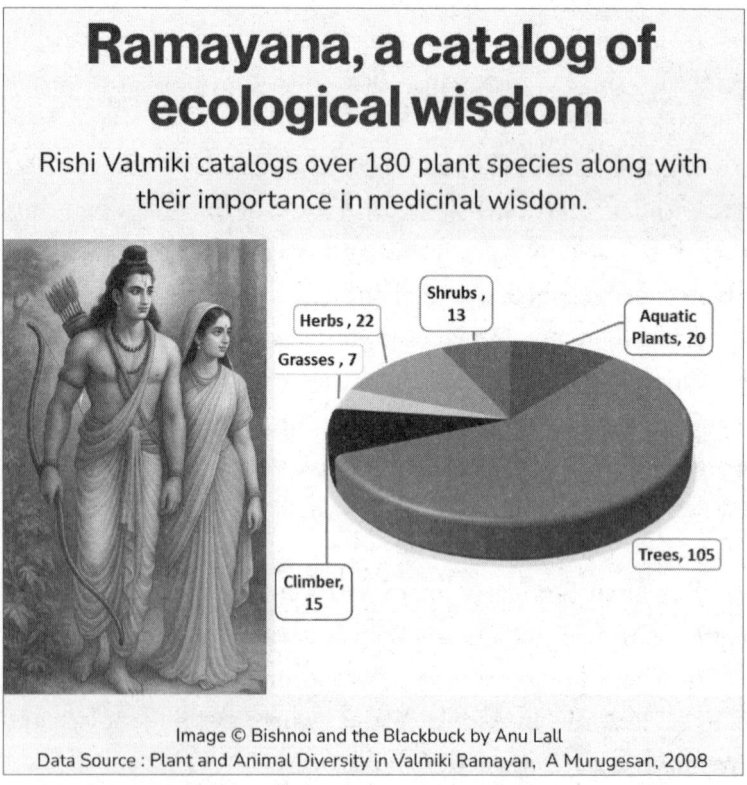

Image © Bishnoi and the Blackbuck by Anu Lall
Data Source : Plant and Animal Diversity in Valmiki Ramayan, A Murugesan, 2008

Do not cut trees because they remove pollution.
Rig Veda 6:48:17
Do not disturb the sky and do not pollute the atmosphere
Yajur Veda 5:43

Top: Blackbucks in open landscapes.
Bottom: Freedom finds a home, roaming freely in Bishnoi villages, without fear. Photo ©Vinod Karwasara

Top: Nilgai lock horns in Badopal.
Bottom: Demoiselle Cranes, the graceful 'little ladies' in Jambha, lovingly fed by generations of Bishnoi and non-Bishnoi farmers.
Photo ©Vinod Karwasara

During winters, desert ecosystems transform into global meeting spots, offering refuge to migratory birds escaping harsh climate in Siberia, Europe and Mongolia.
Top: Birds at Dhanger village. Photo ©Vinod Karwasara
Bottom: Pink flamingos. Photo ©Nirmal Verma

A blur in motion—with incredible leaps and lightning speed, between 50 to 80 kmph, the only animal that can outrun a blackbuck is the cheetah.
Photo ©Vinod Karwasara

Nature gave Blackbucks speed to survive. Humans created traps for them that allows even wild feral dogs to hunt them. Photo ©Vinod Karwasara. Bottom Left: Nursing an injured animal. Photo ©Late Radheshyam Bishnoi

Several animals hunted in a single night. After securing each kill, the poachers continue their search for more animals, turning trees into hiding places, protecting the hunt from other animals.
Photo ©Om Prakash Bishnoi (Ledha)

Top: Filling watering holes for birds and animals to survive the harsh summers. Photo ©Late Radheshyam Bishnoi
Bottom: After just a few monsoon showers, the barren, dry desert transforms into a lifeline for wildlife and humans.
Photo ©Nirmal Verma

Devotees gather to offer respects to Ma Amrita Devi Bishnoi at Khejarli Mela (Fair). The Khejarli Trust provides tree saplings to all, free of charge.
Photo ©Vinod Karwasara

The Great Indian Bustard (GIB) one of the heaviest flying birds. GIB is critically endangered and vulnerable to power line collisions due to lack of frontal vision. Photo ©Late Radheshyam Bishnoi

Western Rajasthan's solar future unfolds. The Bishnois call for a balance between development and the desert's delicate ecology.
Photo © Nirmal Verma

Shaheed Shri Ganga Ram Bishnoi Memorial. The proud family relives the sacrifice and narrates the incident. Joining wedding festivities with the family. Photo ©Anu Lall

Not every martyr's story has been told. There is a pressing need for collective effort to recover names from village stone edicts, police records and place in the public domain.
Top: Shaheed Shri Birbal Bishnoi, Lohawat.
Bottom: Stone edict honoring martyrs for wildlife. Photo ©Anu Lall

Clockwise from Top: Learning to feed baby animals at the conservation at Jambha. Learning age-old wisdom and listening to stories from another era.
Photo ©Anu Lall

Jambhani Sahitya Exam at Gudamalani Barmer. Girls and boys across 600 exam centres took a pledge to work for the nation and environment. Water dispensed from reusable jugs and copper cups.
Photo ©Anu Lall

Top : Awareness and Protest at Badopal in 2013.
Photos ©Vinod Karwasara.
Bottom: Environment Awareness Meet.
Photo ©Khamu Ram Bishnoi.

Muktidhaam Mukkam, the final resting place and samadhi of Jambho Ji.
Photo ©Vinod Karwasara

Don't destroy forests with tigers and don't make forests devoid of tigers. Forests can't be saved without tigers and tigers can't live without forests because forests protect tigers and tigers protect forests. (*Virat Parrva* 5:45-46).

Siddhartha Gautam received realisation under the Bodhi tree to become Gautam Buddha, the realised one. The Bodhi tree as a tree of knowledge finds it way in pop culture as well.

In Jainism, all 24 Jain *Trithankars* attained Pure Knowledge or *Kevali* (*kaivalya*) under the shade of a Kevali tree. (Jain & Kapoor, 2007).[121]

Name of Tirthankara	Tree
Adinath	Banyan (*Ficusbenghalensis*)
Ajitnath	Saptaparni (*Alstoniascholaris*)
Sambhawnath	Sal (*Shorearobusta*)
Abhinandannath	Chir (*Pinusroxburghii*)
Sumatnath	Priyangu (*Calicarpamacrophyya*)
Padamnath	Priyangu (*Calicarpamacrophyya*)
Suparshvnath	Siris (*Albizialebbek*)
Chandranath	Nagkesar (*Mesuaferrea*)
Pushpadantnath	Bahera (*Terminaliabellirica*)
Sheetalnath	Bel (*Aeglemarmelos*)
Shriyansnath	Tendu (*Diospyrosperegrina*)
Vasupujnath	Kadam (*Neolamarckiacadamba*)
Vimalnath	Jamun (*Syzgiumcumini*)

Anantnath	Pipal (*Ficusreligiosa*)
Dhramnath	Kaitha (*Limoniaacidissima*)
Shantinath	Tuna (*Cedrellatoona*)
Kunthnath	Tilak (*Wendlandiaexserta*)
Arahnath	Mango (*Mangiferaindica*)
Mallinath	Ashok (*Saracaasoca*)
Munisubratnath	Champa (*Micheliachampaca*)
Naminath	Maulshiri (*Mimuscopselengi*)
Neminath	Bamboos (*Bamboo species*)
Parshwanath	Deodar (*Cedrusdeodara*)
Mahaveernath	Sal (*Shorearobusta*)

Data Source: Plants associated with salvation of 24 Jain Tirthankars Jain & Kapoor, 2007.

In the *Guru Granth Sahib,* trees are said to be Gods and the universe itself are described as their branches. Trees growing near the places where langar is served are known as *Guru ke Bagh*. Gurus delivered spiritual talks and sang devotional songs under trees. At the Anandpur Sahib Gurudwara, plants are distributed as *prasad* to the devotees. The success rate of these plants is 100 per cent according to the devotees (Jain & Kapoor, 2007, ibid).

In the *Mahabharata,* forest hermitages are described as places of study, meditation, and ascetic practice, symbolising peace and the unbroken harmony between nature and human life. Mahabharata and Ramayana suggest an advanced and nuanced understanding of ecological wisdom, emphasising that forests and the creatures within them are not merely resources to be exploited but entities that deserve respect and preservation.

They maintain the symbolism where nature often mirrors human emotions and transitions.

In the forest of Kamyaka, Yudhisthira prays to Surya, who grants him the boon and supplies food for thirteen years. In another section, Arjuna meditates in the forest to gain knowledge. The *Vana Parva* also has a summary of the story of Shri Ram in exile, to comfort the Pandavas when they are suffering for twelve years in the forest.

Interestingly, the Mahabharata contains a lone, singular episode of large-scale destruction, the burning of the Khandava forest. The story goes, that Agni, the fire god is weak and emaciated, and approaches Krishna and Arjuna, who are relaxing by the river for help. He seeks to consume the forest since it harbours demons, but is too weak to do it alone. With their assistance, the forest is set ablaze, and all animals, demons, and countless other beings, are destroyed. The fire rages so intensely that even Indra, king of the gods, cannot douse it. While some modern historians interpret this episode as symbolic of habitat destruction to build Indraprastha, the Pandavas' capital, the timeline doesn't support that theory. Indraprastha was already established by the time this incident of Khandava forest comes in the Mahabharata.

Overall, in the Mahabharata, the *Vana Parva* has many incidents that emphasise the importance of the forest, where they learn life lessons and build character (Debroy, 2011).[122]

The Upanishads, and Puranas echo this reverence for nature. In literature, and in Kalidasa's poetry, the natural world serves as a backdrop for human emotion and divine activity.

The *Chandogya Upanishad,* emphasises the interconnectedness of all life, portraying rivers, mountains, and plants as part of a larger cosmic order. This interconnectedness is celebrated, urging humanity to recognise the divinity in all forms of life, a sentiment foundational to the concept of sacred groves.

The *Advaita Vedanta* philosophy, which emphasises the interconnectedness of all existence, plays a significant role in shaping how Indians perceived the natural world. This worldview proposes that all life is one and interconnected, an idea encapsulated in the principle of *Brahman*, the universal soul or cosmic consciousness.

According to Advaita, there is no separation between humans, animals, plants, and even inanimate objects. All are manifestations of the same divine essence, urging individuals to respect and cherish every aspect of the universe.

In the Bhagavad Gita, Shri Krishna emphasises on non-duality, saying:

> *I am the ritual, I am the sacrifice, I am the offering, I am the herb, I am the sacred verse, and I am the ghee*
> (Chapter 9, Verse 16).

In addition to the sacred texts, classical Indian literature is replete with ecological wisdom. Kalidasa vividly describes the natural world in works like *Meghadootam*, literally translated as the Cloud Messenger, where he portrays the cloud as a messenger that carries love across vast landscapes, describing each natural scene with profound respect and admiration. Kalidasa's poetic landscapes are alive with rivers, mountains, and forests that serve as living entities, bearing witness to human emotions and spiritual growth. Through Kalidasa's writings, readers experience a deep sense of environmental beauty and subtle calls to protect it.

In his celebrated work, *Abhijnana Shakuntalam*, nature flourishes around the protagonist, Shakuntala, as she cares for plants and animals with a nurturing hand, her relationship with nature mirroring her inner purity and connection to the divine. Through Kalidasa's verses, forests and natural habitats gain spiritual importance, revealing nature as an ally, a teacher, and a companion.

This alliteration with nature, can be seen across the Indian subcontinent. In Sangam literature, the landscape was divided into five *thinais* or geographies.

These landscapes are *kurinji* (mountains), presided over by Lord Murugan or Kartikeya; *mullai* (forests), whose reigning deity was Lord Krishna; *marutham* (agricultural lands), ruled by Lord Indra; *neithal* (coastal regions), the world of Lord Varuna; and *paalai* (wasteland/desert), which was the region of Goddess Kotravai (Durga). Each *tinai* has its own characteristic flowers, trees, animals, birds, climate and other geographical features. (Nanditha, Krishna, 2005).[123]

These geographies play an important role in Tamil poems and ballads as well. Blackbuck are called *Iralai Maan* in Tamil. They are revered and feature in the *Kurunthokai,* a collection of classic love poems in Sangam literature (*Down to Earth*, 2024).[124]

Bharat's ancient texts view nature as an extension of the divine, reinforcing that humanity's connection to the earth is not just a matter of survival but of spirituality. The narrative of nature woven throughout these texts offers guidance that remains relevant, inspiring reverence for the environment as both a cultural and spiritual obligation.

Sacred *Orans* or Deemed Forests

India's sacred groves and history offer a refreshing reminder of an ancient conservation model—one that requires no fences, government directives, fines or complicated carbon credit systems. They are acts of faith sustained through *dharma,* and reverence towards nature. The surest way to preserve ecology is possibly by living the eternal dharma.

However, today, sacred groves stand at the crossroads. With erosion of faith, the *dharmic* outlook towards sacred groves is reducing. Will future generations maintain sacred groves, with as much devotion? With new developments, and changing city landscapes, there is little knowledge about sacred groves. Despite their deep cultural and ecological significance, these sacred groves face relentless encroachment, deforestation, and exploitation in the name of 'development.'

In response, a new wave of legislative measures aim to protect these last bastions of biodiversity. Should the government step in to take care of these groves, declaring them as forests?

In 2024, in a landmark judgement in 2024, (T N Godavarman Thirumulpad vs Union of India case),[125] the Supreme Court reignited a long-standing dilemma of whether Rajasthan's sacred groves, or *orans* be declared deemed forests under the law? The Supreme Court acknowledged the role of community traditions in protecting these lands. However, by declaring *orans* as deemed forests, perhaps the state will be able to protect them from encroachment and exploitation.

The Court's nuanced stance tries to balance legal protection along with community devotion. It directed the states to prepare local lists of *orans* supported by satellite mapping to identify and classify sacred groves as forests, regardless of their size. A five-member committee of forestry and administrative experts, would oversee the process. This attempts to respect both the legal framework and the cultural and religious aspects.

Most environmentalists and communities were excited about this development, where previously unregistered land, would get protected as deemed forests. But others expressed caution at whether a government, often swayed by corporate interests and policy changes, could be trusted more than the local communities who have preserved these groves for centuries without any legal labels.

While the court sees legal protection as a shield, some critics see it as a trap. Once notified under forest wildlife laws, these lands come under bureaucratic control, and can be reclassified via a change in land use. This could later allow mining, highways, or tourism projects to eat away these once sacred spaces.

Villagers, often following oral traditions and strict taboos, have protected *orans* without fencing or paperwork. The moment the state steps in, communities may lose ownership—not just of land, but of their identity and agency.

The verdict is progressive on paper. But whether it protects *orans* or endangers them will depend on implementation and community participation, not just legal classification.

Can modern conservation efforts match the unwavering commitment of the traditions who have treated nature as sacred for over 500 years?

Chapter 11
Portraits of Devotion

यज्ञार्थात्कर्मणोऽन्यत्र लोकोऽयं कर्मबन्धन: |
तदर्थं कर्म कौन्तेय मुक्तसङ्ग: समाचर ||

Work must be done as a yajna; else work causes bondage in this material world. Hence O son of Kunti, perform your duty without being attached to the results.
—Bhagavad Gita 3.9

The Bishnoi *spanda* or pulsation, refuses to stand by as nature suffers. For over five centuries, the community has lived by a simple principle: to protect the environment in the belief that by doing so, is protecting life, itself. By the time this book reached completion, I had met so many achievers and listened to so many tales of quiet heroism of ordinary men and women. I had encountered many silent warriors, standing up against poaching, environmental degradation, defending a way of life, ensuring that the principles of their ancestors endure. I felt compelled to bring together a few such stories, giving a glimpse into their perspectives.

These are portraits of devotion, stories of fierce love for the Earth that demands action—farmers shielding blackbuck from hunters, homemakers nursing injured fawns, rallies against deforestation, and activists taking on policies that threaten their sacred bond with nature.

Choosing a handful of stories was perhaps the hardest part.

Countless more are waiting to be told, each as powerful and inspiring as the other. If I were to do justice to them all, I would have to write an entirely new book. But for now, these few voices stand as proof that you don't need a title to be a warrior, only the courage to stand up for what is right.

Very early in my exploration of the Bishnoi world, I stumbled upon the remarkable work of French photojournalist and documentary filmmaker, Franck Vogel, known for his environmental and water-focused work. He immersed himself in the community to capture their unique relationship with nature. Vogel created a deeply moving, beautiful and inspiring visual narrative of the Bishnoi people. His photographs and documentary captured the community's sacred connection with nature—a commitment that's both cultural and spiritual.

His imagery reveals symbolic reverence, for instance how Khejri trees are honoured as wise elders; Demoiselle cranes are regarded as *sisters* by the women; blackbuck are viewed as cherished *sons*, and oxen are seen as integral family members.

The Bishnoi community acknowledged Vogel's dedication by bestowing upon him an award at the Mukam festival, solidifying the lasting connection he built with them.

When I spoke to Vogel, it was clear that his experiences with the Bishnois had been both inspiring and transformative. He told me that his exhibition in Paris featuring the Bishnois attracted over 15 million unique visitors, allowing viewers worldwide to glimpse the Bishnoi ethos. He had stayed in the Bishnoi villages for over six months, visiting often, and covering many events and festivals. I was struck by the stories he shared and later met some people he had photographed, and many of them offered further insights into their work. One person whom

Vogel formed a great bond with was Khamu Ram Bishnoi. Incidentally, Khamu Ram Ji was also one the first people I met during my journey, that started at the Jodhpur High Court. He was one of the most enthusiastic and 'young at heart' heroes from the community. Let's begin with this hero.

Khamu Ram Bishnoi: Battling Plastic on Sand Dunes
At Samrathal Dhora, Bishnoi pilgrims perform a sacred act—carrying handfuls of sand from a pond below, creating little sand dunes as symbols of prayer. They then climb 200 metres to deposit it atop a man-made dune. This symbolic gesture dates back to the time of Jambho Ji and reinforces the importance of dunes as barriers against winds.

In earlier times, pilgrims used the folds of their traditional clothing to carry the sand, blending reverence with sustainability. The same garments, once used for prayer would be used for daily life.

But times changed. Plastic crept into the rituals. Colourful but destructive plastic bags replaced cloth folds, leaving a trail of waste strewn across the sacred dunes. The pristine slopes of Samrathal Dhora became littered with waste plastic marring the landscape. Documentaries like *Willing to Sacrifice (1999)* captured the growing concern.

The community could no longer ignore the problem.

The sight of plastic bags scattered across the sacred dunes pained Khamu Ram Bishnoi, and he decided to act. Working as an Assistant Registrar at the Jodhpur High Court, Khamu Ram Ji used his modest savings, to buy a loudspeaker and a thousand cotton bags. With passion in his voice and determination in his step, he plunged into the pilgrimage crowd, shouting:

> *'Plastic dushman hai! Yeh plastic theli uthao yahan se, aur yeh lo, mere sooti thaili. Free hai! Sab ko do.'*
> *(Plastic is the enemy! Pick up that plastic bag from here and take this cloth bag instead. It's free! Distribute them to all.)*

At first, some people laughed, while others ignored him. But Khamu Ram Ji remained resolute. When no one listened, he took matters into his own hands, literally. He began collecting plastic bags left behind on the dunes, his only companions being two young teenagers who believed in his cause. Over time, others joined. His persistence grew into a movement. He even installed mobile dustbins at festivals and at pilgrim sites, and the community slowly embraced his message (*Sharad Krishi* magazine, 2017).[126]

But Khamu Ram Ji didn't stop at pilgrimages. His passion extended to weddings, community gatherings, and schools. You cannot miss his team at most Bishnoi events, wearing placards, reminding people not to waste food and encouraging the use of reusable copper water tumblers instead of plastic bottles. Ever resourceful, they wear recycled posters around their necks, displaying messages against plastic pollution and food wastage. It was activism at its most grassroots level, simple, effective, and heartfelt.

Khamu Ram Ji often jokes that had Jambho Ji been alive today, he would have added a thirtieth *Niyam* (rule) banning single-use plastic.

And perhaps, he's right.

His commitment did not go unnoticed. He also gained recognition on the global stage, thanks in part to his friendship with Franck Vogel, who not only photographed Khamu Ram Ji's remarkable efforts, but also invited him to speak at international eco-citizenship conferences in Paris and Switzerland. His experience in Paris is beautifully blogged by several bloggers and media, especially in: *A Bishnoi in Paris* (2012).[127]

In 2013, he was honoured with the Extraordinary Man of India award, one of the more than fifty national and international accolades he has since received. He received the Sidharth Social Award in 2016 for his unconditional services for preservation of the environment.

I have travelled with Khamu Ram Ji, attended several events, weddings and conferences. His team goes to weddings wearing placards urging people not to waste food. In a typical, Indian style welcome coupled with Rajasthani hospitality, we urge guests to eat more and load their plates with food. At such events, Khamu Ram Ji requests people to take only as much food as they can eat.

At international environment conferences, dressed in pristine white clothes, he calls out environmental hypocrisy from the stage, delivering his speech with typical Bishnoi-style *chutzpah*. At a conference in posh South Delhi, he scolded the high-profile attendees, saying, that if at an environment conference, they couldn't carry their own reusable plates and spoons, then what environment were we trying to save.

Watching him in action, it is hard to believe he is approaching retirement from his official role. Khamu Ram Ji laughs at the irony, saying most people look forward to resting after retirement, but for him, it will be a time to double his efforts. He exudes a youthful energy and everyone is inspired by his insurmountable courage and indomitable spirit.

Anil Bishnoi: Lifelong Commitment to Wildlife

Anil Bishnoi, another award-winning conservationist, has garnered recognition for his dedication to preserving wildlife and natural habitats of Rajasthan. This humble farmer and ardent wildlife activist has become a beacon of hope for India's endangered species, especially the majestic blackbuck and the graceful chinkara.

Over the years, he has saved thousands of blackbuck and chinkaras. He and his team have rescued injured animals, nursing them back to health, and returning them to the wild. Along with a dedicated group of Bishnoi volunteers, Anil patrols vast stretches of the desert, acting as a wildlife guardian. His team of volunteers, often working without any formal support from government bodies, monitor wildlife areas and keep a watch over animals.

These patrols are no small task. The terrain is rugged, the distances long, and the resources scarce. Often, volunteers are armed with little more than their knowledge of the land and their unwavering resolve. Yet, this has not deterred Anil from his mission. Over the years, he has tirelessly pursued poachers, reported illegal hunting activities to authorities, and worked with other conservationists to establish networks that one can quickly mobilise in times of crisis.

Anil's quick action has foiled many poaching attempts.

Parineeti Bishnoi: Little Yogini with a Big Heart

Parineeti Bishnoi is an eleven-year-old dynamo who radiates energy, joy, and an unshakable love for nature. A yoga champion and a social media sensation, she has taken the internet and media by storm, inspiring thousands to embrace a healthier, more natural way of life.

She has been a media sensation (*Dainik Bhaskar*, 2022),[128] and even been called a guru (*ABP Live*, 15 June 2024).[129] Her infectious spirit even caught the eye of industrialist Anand

Mahindra, who retweeted one of her videos turning her into an even bigger star. Parineeti is a familiar face now, sharing the stage with Baba Ramdev Ji and captivating audiences with her poise and confidence.

Her parents manage her social media accounts that has over 800,000 followers. But every post reflects her genuine voice. Scrolling through her videos, you'll see her heartfelt stories about the environment, Bishnoi traditions and the divine devotion of Prahlad Vishnu.

In addition to her yoga *asana* championships, she is often seen feeding blackbuck, affectionately tying protective Jambho Ji amulets on the deer and speaking passionately about the Bishnoi way of living.

She uses her social media status very effectively reminding everyone of the twenty-nine principles, out of which four principles urge people to stay away from *nasha* or drugs, opium, tobacco and alcohol, and all products that are harmful for our mind and body.

When I met Parineeti, she was fasting for *Amavasya*. But fasting did nothing to dull her enthusiasm. She gleefully invited me to the grassy patch at her house, challenging me to a yoga session:

'Will you be able to do *Surya Namaskar*?' she said, her eyes gleaming with playful curiosity.

She guided me, counting the steps as her father filmed a reel, with her family cow lazing around in the background, and her mischievous kid brother popping into the frame, an absolutely adorable photobomber.

Endearingly, she begins her sentences with, 'I've been doing yoga since I was a child…' only to be gently reminded that she is still very much a child, with a contagious smile and inspiring spirit. On stage, she transforms into a captivating orator, confidently reciting the *Hanuman Chalisa* to large audiences with a presence far beyond her years.

She boldly calls out the harmful effects of processed food, chemicals, sodas and colas, urging her followers to choose natural alternatives. With her emotional, physical and spiritual health in place, she will be an even bigger force to watch out for in the coming years.

Lesson in Zero-Waste, *Dharma* and Patriotism
I had the opportunity to witness an initiative by the Jambhani Sahitya Akademi. The organisation conducts conferences, workshops, and academic interventions that bridge the ancient and the contemporary. They also conduct drives to reduce drug abuse and addiction in young adults.

One of the academy's most impactful initiatives is its annual exam series on the Jambhani philosophy. Spanning across ten states, forty-two districts, and nearly 600 centres, last year this massive endeavour saw over 50,000 girls and boys register, with approximately 37,000 students participating, backed by countless volunteers. On a bright Sunday morning, we drove to the small village of Gudamalani, in Barmer, to witness one such exam. Despite being in Western Rajasthan, Gudamalani seemed slightly greener than the rest of the Thar desert. About 2,000 children from neighbouring villages gathered at the centre, their eagerness palpable for an important exam that was being conducted. Without the comfort of desks and chairs, they sat cross-legged on the floor, while some directly sat on the sand.

The exam, divided into three levels, was conducted using OMR (Optical Mark Recognition) sheets, a method that not only evaluates their knowledge but also familiarises rural students with the process of competitive exams.

School teachers volunteered as invigilators, ensuring the examination ran smoothly. As the exam sheets were collected and were being tabulated, the air came alive with the soulful echoes of Jambhani songs and *bhajans*. Cultural performances unfolded blending devotion with festivity. Then came the moment that always stood out—the resounding *jaykaara* or chants that punctuated every speech till the results were announced:

Guru Jambeshwar Bhagwaan ki Jai!
Om! Vishnu Bhagwaan ki Jai!
Bharata Mata ki Jai!

The voices of so many children united in fervour, their chants ringing through the air. The heartfelt tribute to their Guru came through, along with a reverence for the nation woven into their minds from a young age.

I don't know, if city kids ever chant *Bharat Mata ki Jai* like this. It was a delight to see the award ceremony. Students from each category were awarded books and mementoes.

Despite the large crowd, the event had zero plastic waste. Drinking water was brought in tankers, stored in reusable large dispensers, and served in copper tumblers—a practice steeped in tradition. Volunteers managed the water service. The children carefully held their tumblers away from their mouth, pouring the water by using their hand. Some of them also tried to teach others how to pour water into the hand and drink simultaneously.

As the programme ended, simple meals were served on eco-friendly *pattal* (plates made of leaves), with steaming *chholey* and ghee-laden *halwa* adding a sweet note to the day. The children stashed away their bio-degradable plates in one corner of the event grounds and went back home, jumping and joyfully piling into their buses.

Ironically, as I came back to my hotel late that night, I couldn't help noticing the plastic bottles of water placed neatly by the housekeeping staff. In the name of hygiene, most hotels have stopped putting jugs of water that can be refilled.

They provide individual plastic bottles, instead. Everything else in the room—from water to bathroom accessories—is placed in disposable bottles. At some level, the privileged are destroying the earth far more than anyone else, but we don't want to see it, face it or even talk about it.

Dr Shiv Pratap Bishnoi: Crusader Against Addiction

One man stands out in this fight against addiction, Dr Shiv Pratap Bishnoi. For over three decades, Dr Bishnoi has waged a relentless war against substance abuse, blending his medical expertise with the spiritual wisdom of Jambho Ji. His efforts go beyond mere medical intervention. He has organised hundreds of residential de-addiction camps, offering free food, medication, counselling, and motivational talks.

These camps, accommodating anywhere from 100 to 300 people, not only provide rehabilitation but also serve as platforms to engage government officials, environmental bodies, and policymakers in discussions about tackling the addiction crisis more effectively. Through awareness drives and large camps, he has touched the lives of close to one lakh families by helping people reclaim their lives from addiction.

Honestly, I would have believed the huge numbers, but it was so humbling when he showed me a pile of notebooks and registers with patient details going back years, with each line entry saying a story.

Remarkably, much of this work is self-funded. Dr Bishnoi pours his own resources into these initiatives, occasionally securing sponsorships for food and medicine. Many of his camps operate out of schools or government buildings, repurposed as temporary rehabilitation centres.

In a region where addiction is deeply entrenched, Dr Shiv Pratap Bishnoi is not just a doctor, he is a movement. Through his unwavering dedication, he is restoring lives, one de-addiction camp at a time, one counselling and one consultation, at a time.

Peera Ram Bishnoi: Nurturer of Injured Animals

Peera Ram Ji has won several awards for his work and is famous as the roadside mechanic who has rescued over 1,180 injured animals (*Better India*, 2018).[130] He runs a humble little tyre repair shop on the highway. Often, he would hear from drivers how animals were injured or killed by speeding vehicles. Peera was an animal lover right from childhood, and such stories would pain him. There were no guards or institutional support, to take care of these injured animals.

Once he found a chinkara that had been hit by a vehicle and he took him to the veterinary doctor immediately, later taking him home. Slowly, he started nursing more animals and soon his home became a rescue shelter for peacocks, chinkaras, blackbuck and demoiselle cranes. People started taking notice. Anytime an animal was found injured, they would ferry the animal to Peera's shelter. He received government help with a small patch of land in his village to create a small rescue centre.

In 2012, Peera Ram and a few of his associates started the Shri Jambheshwar Paryavaran Jeev Raksha Pardes Sanstha, dedicated to protecting wildlife. What started as a home shelter is now spread over six acres, taking care of over 400 animals at a time, with a much higher survival rate, than in the hospital.

In 2018, the Vice President of India, Venkaiah Naidu felicitated Peera Ram Bishnoi as an 'Earth Hero' and awarded him the 'Save the Species' award (*Business News This Week*, 2018),[131] for protecting endangered species and contributing to education, awareness programmes, capacity building and resolving man-animal conflict.

Ranaram Bishnoi: Tree Man
Ranaram Bishnoi, affectionately known as the Tree Man, has devoted over five decades to greening the desert. Born in a village near Jodhpur, Ranaram's journey began as a teenager, after attending the Mukam mela, where impassioned discussions ignited a lifelong mission within him to work for the environment. Determined to combat desertification, he returned home with several saplings and a vision to transform

his arid surroundings.

Over the years, Ranaram Ji has planted several indigenous trees, including Neem, Rohida, Fig, Khejri, Kankeri, Babool, and Bougainvillea, totalling more than 50,000 thereby significantly altering the landscape and fostering biodiversity in the region.

Ranaram Ji is now eighty-eight years old, but his spirit is undeterred. His approach to afforestation is both labour-intensive and innovative. Every other day, he embarks on a three-kilometre journey to a towering sand dune, carrying a large earthen pitcher. He first ascends the dune, then descends to a friend's tube well to fetch water, and climbs back up to nourish his cherished saplings.

Back in the day, to conserve water, he ingeniously created a water collection system using a large polythene sheet, ensuring his plants received adequate hydration despite the harsh climate. Understanding the power of collective effort, Ranaram established a nursery at his home to cultivate seeds and saplings, which he disperses across the dunes during the rainy season. He actively involves his family and villagers in his mission. He would offer a modest sum of two rupees to women and girls who assisted him in watering the plants. This initiative not only accelerated the greening process, but also instilled a sense of environmental responsibility within the community.

Despite his monumental contributions, Ranaram remains humble, often declining financial assistance. His selfless work for environmental conservation has garnered recognition from the local administration and the forest department, who have honoured him with awards for his efforts. His work has not only halted the encroachment of the desert onto arable land but has also created a habitat for various species.

Vishek Bishnoi: Fight for Recognition

I first reached out to Vishek Bishnoi with the aim of speaking to his father, Ranaram Ji. What I did not anticipate was the fire of devotion and determination that he had inherited from his father. He wasn't just a passive admirer of his father's work; he had been right there since his childhood watching and helping his father. He had planted trees, mobilised villagers, and ensured that the legacy of environmental protection thrived. But Vishek had ambitions of his own, and audacious ones at that!

His mission is to secure long-overdue recognition for the Khejarli Massacre, an international acknowledgement of the momentous sacrifice of 363 Bishnoi men and women who laid down their lives for trees.

Vishek has been relentless in this pursuit, working with government agencies, lobbying politicians, and organising conferences to keep the memory of Khejarli alive. He has drafted a five-point agenda that he tirelessly pushes forward:

1. Initiating discussions in the Rajasthan Assembly to officially recognise the significance of the Khejarli Massacre.
2. Get Khejarli listed as a tourist site in Rajasthan.
3. Ensure basic development of the site and surrounding areas.
4. Discuss the event on the floor of the Indian Parliament.
5. Campaign to include Khejarli in UNESCO's Intangible Cultural Heritage list.

Forty-four-year-old Vishek speaks with a broad, infectious smile and the unshakable confidence of a man who refuses to take 'no' for an answer. He says that the first three have been done over time.

When we spoke, I casually suggested, 'Why not push for the massacre's anniversary, September 11, to be declared as World Environment Day?'

He broke into a big smile, 'Why not! Let's add it to the list.'

But beneath the humour, lies sheer grit. Vishek has spent nights camping outside ministers' offices and homes, campaigning at Jantar Mantar in Delhi, and refusing to leave until they acknowledged his demands. The family doesn't make that much money, and they don't take donations for their work.

Using his own meagre funds, he has made countless trips to the Capital, lobbying for the massacre's inclusion in UNESCO's heritage records.

He has taken the story of Khejarli to conferences in Kenya, Tanzania, and Ethiopia.

He shakes his head, laughing again. 'And just when I was about to present at a conference in Sri Lanka, the country went bankrupt!'

He adds with a chuckle, 'I once met the Green Belt lady, Wangari Maathai. She had no idea about Khejarli. Imagine, she has worked on tree plantation, won the Nobel Prize written books on environment, yet, she didn't know anything substantial about the 363 people who had sacrificed their lives for trees! Can you believe it?'

I wasn't sure where he had met her, or which of her books he had read. But to my amazement, he was not wrong. Maathai's books and writings barely mention the Bishnoi sacrifice, except for a single sentence, and that too, is referenced from Wikipedia. There is indeed a lot of merit in educating the world about the Bishnoi community.

There's something surreal about the juxtaposition of Vishek's earthy, unpolished manner and the magnitude of his global ambitions.

'We have to be a little aggressive in today's world,' he says with unwavering determination. 'People don't realise what India has given to the world. We struggle to tell our own story.'

I couldn't agree more. It felt as if I was looking into a mirror, hearing my own thoughts echoed back to me. India has a wealth of stories, but too often, we fail to share them with the world. By the end of our conversation, I had made him a promise—to stand beside him in his mission to bring Khejarli to the global stage.

During my research, I would write these personal experiences at the back of my notebook, and slowly, they started adding up. Sometimes, when I sat alone at cafes, pondering over my research, flipping over these personal stories, gave me goosebumps.

Why do these people choose the harder path, the lonelier road? Why do changemakers exist, not just in the Bishnoi community, but in any community?

Wouldn't life be simpler if everyone just quietly went with the flow?

Why does **Khamu Ram Ji** bend down to pick up garbage that isn't even his?

Why does an eleven-year-old **Parineeti** feel compelled to warn strangers about the dangers of junk food?

No one pays **Shiv Pratap Ji** to spend his days battling the inner demons of drug addicts. No one rewards **Anil** or **Peera Ram Ji** for protecting animals.

What were the *shaheeds* thinking when they laid down their lives for deer?

What was that moment of courage that led Amrita Devi to give up her life, with her own children looking on?

Our 'practical' society would mock them, calling them 'fools' and *junooni*. But it is these so-called fools with fire in their bellies and passion in their hearts, who awaken our sleeping conscience. They are the spark in a dark room, the quiet whisper of hope in a world drowning in noise. They dream when the world tells them to be practical. They act when others turn away. They sacrifice comfort for conviction. And through them, humanity remembers what it means to care. These people don't have wealth or power. They aren't celebrated at red carpet events.

What they do have is a deep, quiet conviction that they did not let the world pass them by, untouched. That they chose to make a difference, no matter how small, no matter at what personal cost. In the end, it is not the rich or the powerful who shape the soul of society. It is the believers. The ones who hurt deeply and love fiercely. The ones who care for the world they were born in. The world needs more stories about devotion. About these rebels of hope. They are the heartbeat of our collective future.

While penning these stories, I was reminded of that haunting song from *La La Land*, that repeatedly ran in my head:

> *Here's to the ones who dream,*
> *Foolish as they may seem,*
> *Here's to the hearts that ache,*
> *Here's to the mess we make.*
> *A bit of madness is key*
> *To give us new colours to see,*
> *Who knows where it will lead us*
> *And that's why they need us.*
> *So, bring on the rebels, The ripples from pebbles,*
> *The painters and poets and plays.*
> *Here's to the fools who dream.*

(*La La Land*, 2016)

Image ©Anurag Bishnoi and the Blackbuck

Chapter 12

From Protest to Policy
The Art of Environmental Advocacy

निर्वनो वध्यते व्याघ्रो निर्व्याघ्रं छिद्यते वनम् ।
तस्माद् व्याघ्रो वनं रक्षेद् वनं व्याघ्रं च पालयेत् ॥

A tiger is killed without a forest, and a forest without a tiger is cut down. Therefore the tiger should protect the forest and the forest should maintain the tiger
—Mahabharata, Udyoga Parva: 5.29.55

The world needs more stories about devotion and rebels of hope. In modern times, saving the environment is not just about passion and perseverance—a never-ending battle—but is both a war and a mission. As cities sprawl and forests vanish, the delicate balance of the ecosystem is under constant threat. This battle demands strategic action, political engagement, and policy influence. Individuals need to be more and more engaged in the domain of public policy and legal advocacy.

In the past, the Bishnois took their grievances to kings and rulers, who gave decrees on *tamprapatra*, whether it was about a ban on hunting, not cutting trees, or stopping leather trade in Bishnoi *melas*. Now we need the same spirit of advocacy in the constitutional and legal framework governing our forest areas.

The Indian Constitution provides for safeguarding the environment. Article 48A of the Indian Constitution, a Directive Principle of State Policy, directs the state to protect the environment, safeguard forests, and wildlife. On the other side, Article 51A (g) makes it a fundamental duty of every citizen to protect the natural environment, forests, and wildlife.

Whether you are a Bishnoi or not, the secular law beseeches you to defend forests, lakes, rivers, and wildlife. This brings the power of compassion towards the environment into the domain of policy and activism.

Every decision made in the name of development, from highways that slice through forests to factories that pollute rivers, has lasting consequences. To stand against this tide, the advocates of nature, the warriors of the earth, must enter the corridors of power, ensuring that environmental preservation is not an afterthought in policy making, but is centrestage.

Bishnoi leaders have been increasingly engaging in legislative processes, championing stronger environmental protections and holding policymakers accountable. Their cultural legacy, rooted in a profound respect for nature, lends weight to their advocacy and strengthens their call for ecological stewardship.

Bishnoi Tiger Force

This is an organisation that is moving contemporary efforts into the domain of legal activism, policy advocacy, and community mobilisation. Recognising the need to operate within formal institutions, the Bishnoi Tiger Force (BTF) was started by a group of young student activists in 1999, in response to the Salman Khan case. It was later registered as an organisation in 2007, with the aim of bringing poachers and environmental criminals to justice. BTF aims to take the Bishnoi values about the environment and wildlife, to the modern legal arena, bridging the gap between villagers and environmental law.

BTF works to preserve the Thar Desert, much like the rest

of their community, by carrying forward the customs and values that have been a part of their lives for centuries, combining old traditions with modern activism. They actively engage with government officials, political and legal systems to ensure that the desert is protected. They take a stand against environmental crimes, poaching, illegal logging, and other threats to the desert's delicate ecosystem. To do this, they collaborate with wildlife officials and use India's environmental laws to bring wrongdoers to justice.

Their efforts go beyond the call of religious duty; they enter the world of conservation politics, engaging directly with the state to fight for the land they hold sacred (Luthra, 2014; 2016).[132] Ram Niwas Budhnagar, formerly part of BTF and later part of the Executive Committee of the All-India Bishnoi Mahasabha, in an interview (*Sahapedia*, 2018),[133] spoke about how they work:

'Whenever an incident of poaching, injured wildlife, or illegal tree cutting happens, we immediately reach the spot and initiate legal proceedings. First, we file an FIR and then pursue legal action in court. We help people file reports, follows up on legal action, hire lawyers, and fight in court. No other community does this.'

On being asked why they are sometimes called troublemakers by the authorities, he responded, 'We only raise our voices when the forest department, police, district administration, or state government fail in their duties.'

'They wonder: Who are these people and why are they doing this? To silence us, they accuse us…the ones doing the right thing are then labeled as troublemakers. They question us, asking who are we to tell them what to do. We are protecting the environment, and until wildlife protection laws are fully effective, our movement will continue.'

He goes on to say that he studied law, primarily to work better and save himself from the false cases being filed by the forest department, police and poachers. He narrates how once, they were peacefully protesting, and he had personally taken permission for using a loudspeaker, when the police blocked the road from both sides, and charged them under the Noise Pollution Act and also for blocking the road. He said, he was acquitted in the noise pollution case—the court found he wasn't guilty. But the trial lasted six years.

The relationship between the Bishnoi community members, organisations like BTF and government officials is not always marked by animosity. On numerous occasions, wildlife officers have sought the assistance of local Bishnois to apprehend poachers. The government has also acknowledged and appreciated their active role in conservation efforts.

Wildlife census figures are not easily available, but senior government officials acknowledge that the Bishnois have been far more effective against poachers than many official conservation efforts. In many areas, divisional forest officers, regularly depend on the Bishnois for night patrolling against poachers (Luthra-Sinha, Bobby 2020).[134]

Additionally, the Akhil Bhartiya Jeeva Raksha Bishnoi Sabha has meticulously documented reports and cases of poaching across Rajasthan and Haryana. Countless individuals in various districts and tehsils have filed independent reports, complaints and FIRs (First Information Report) against poaching. Communities all over India, can learn how to organise themselves for political relevance, take inspiration and show that by coming together, standing up for what's right, and working with the right partners, we can all contribute to saving our environment for future generations.

Khejri aur Hiran vote nahin karte. Jungle mein election nahin hote

I arrived at the home of Rampal Bhavad of the Bishnoi Tiger Force (BTF) in the outskirts of Jodhpur on Nagaur Road, a little earlier than scheduled. While waiting, Rampal Ji's mother, a grand old lady, stuttering around in bright red traditional clothes welcomed me warmly. She showed me some beautifully preserved traditional clothes, and we had a delightful conversation, full of laughs. It was a light and joyful start.

When Rampal Ji arrived, the gears quickly shifted to more serious topics. Bhavad is a lawyer, and started as a student activist. He carries both his words and convictions with clarity and makes no effort to hide his political affiliations.

Before getting into the details, I asked him, 'Why the name 'Bishnoi Tiger Force'? Why 'Tiger'? There are no tigers in the region.'

He laughed and said he's often asked this, *'Sahi hai.'* That's true, he said. The name is symbolic. In the jungle, the tiger is the top predator, as it maintains the balance. Without the tiger, wild feral dogs rule the forest, who breed and proliferate indiscriminately, destroying the entire ecosystem.

'That's what we're trying to prevent. We want to be the tiger, that keeps the balance intact, and in turn the forest protects the tiger,' he said.

He took me through the work BTF has done on

the ground. With the help of Bishnoi villagers, BTF has helped file over 425 legal cases against poachers, all in coordination with the Forest Department of Rajasthan. 'In many more cases, we guide locals on how to take legal action,' he added.

'Many challenges arise. Most villagers give their testimonies in Marwari, which are often misinterpreted or lost in translation in the legal process. That weakens the poaching case,' he explained.

I had read in previous interviews about the misuse of laws by poachers.

He replied, '*Bahut baar* poachers protected tribe *se aate hain. Jab hum unhe rokte hain, woh law ko humare against kar dete hain, aur* SC/ST Act *mein case darz kar dete hain.*'

(Many poachers come from protected tribes, Scheduled Caste and Scheduled Tribes. They turn the law against us using the SC/ST Act, filing false cases and accusing us of caste-based assault.)

'We act in defence of an animal, or even in self-defence when they attack us. Only if the police find the poached animal's body during the initial investigation do some of these false charges get dropped. Otherwise, these false cases drag on for years.'

He said they were now training villagers—not just in conservation, but in legal literacy. 'We need to save wildlife and also know how to defend ourselves legally,' he says.

Rampal Ji is right. The misuse of the SC/ST Act is a larger issue in India. Even the Supreme Court has acknowledged that conviction rates are very low, and they can destroy lives and delay justice (*The Hindu*, 2018).[135]

He calls for tough laws, and even tougher implementation. He says, right now, it's too easy for poachers. They get bail immediately, which is a small amount, and does not act as a deterrent.

'Sarkaar ko sanshodhan laana chahiye, 10 se 14 saal ki saza ho, tabhi toh rok lagegi."

(We need legal changes. Only a 10 to 14-year sentence can act as a true deterrent.)

He added, there's another side to this—tourism. 'Hotels and restaurants serve deer meat behind the scenes. These are organised networks. Nobody goes after the real buyers, only the ones holding the weapon. But the deer must be sold somewhere, right? Why isn't the government tapping the entire network,' he asks.

I asked him, 'How do how do these poachers hunt, what kind of guns are usually used?'

Rampal Ji shared how poachers have become smarter. They don't use weapons now, but use some poaching tribes to chase the deer, herd it toward a fence, and then trap it before killing it with a single fist blow, at the back of the neck—clean, silent, with no trace. 'It happens fast, and often we don't even get to know in time,' he explained.

I asked him for photos or documents from recent poaching incidents. Within minutes, my inbox was flooded with newspaper clippings, FIRs, post-mortem reports of animals killed and rescued. He says the rescue rate is only about 25 per cent. These animals are very delicate, and usually don't survive after an assault, despite their efforts. Seeing pictures of those lifeless, graceful beings, mercilessly killed, was enough to send jitters down the spine.

We spoke about many issues. Bishnois are opposing indiscriminate destruction of trees for solar plant projects, too. As we wrapped up, there came the final remark with the trademark Bishnoi bluntness:

'Dekho madam, na Khejri vote karti hai, na Hiran. Jungle mein chunav nahin hote, inki awaaz kaun sunega?

Jeev daya palani, rukh leelna na ghaave, insaan ka dharam hai.'

(Plants and animals don't vote. There is no election in the jungle, so who will listen to their voice? It is the duty of human beings to protect them.)

And the penny dropped. In that one sentence, he had summed up everything. That's why animal welfare rarely figures in policymaking. But humans forget that our own welfare depends on their survival.

The Bishnois and the Solar Plants

A fierce disagreement is brewing in western Rajasthan over solar panels. The rapid expansion of solar power plants has ignited a dispute over energy infrastructure; it's a clash for environment, trees, livelihoods, and farming.

As solar panel plants were beginning to be set up in many areas and trees were cut, the Bishnois were one of the first to stand up, as a community against destruction of trees.

Today, people from thirty-three *khom* (communities) are

standing together for this cause. While many environmental groups unite around secular causes, for the Bishnois protecting nature isn't just a choice—it's a sacred duty, woven into the fabric of their existence. Their resistance is powered by centuries-old devotion to all living beings.

I will not break down technical nuances of the solar panel debate, and step into the domain of energy and environmental experts. I will provide a brief overview of the solar panel landscape, to understand the perspective of the environmentalists, the Bishnois, and the government's.

My focus in this discussion remains on the role of faith-driven communities in modern decision-making.

> *How can a belief system that has stood the test of time, be a force for environmental protection in today's world?*

Solar energy is a high priority area for India and a stated goal of public policy. Under the Green Energy Corridor Scheme, India attracts $6.1 billion FDI in the renewable sector (*Economic Times*, 2023).[136] With abundant sunshine, Rajasthan is set to play a pivotal role and is seen as a land of great opportunity, ranking first in the country in solar energy production.

It emerged as a prime destination for solar energy investment, not just for India, but also for global giants, with an impressive installed capacity of 22,860 megawatt. As India pushes toward its ambitious goal of achieving 500 giga watt of non-fossil fuel energy capacity by 2030, the state's potential solar generation capacity is estimated at 142 giga watt, almost one-fourth of India's total solar capacity (*Financial Express*, 2024).[137]

The state government has signed ambitious agreements to build solar power plants in desert areas. More than 100 solar plants are in operation or being planned. While this seems like a win for clean energy, there are serious concerns about the environmental and social costs of these projects.

Green Energy, Grey Areas

Solar farms, the emblems of India's renewable energy ambitions, are rapidly transforming the landscape. To accommodate these installations, extensive tracts of land are cleared, trees and shrubs uprooted, and concrete pillars embedded in the land. These pillars support gleaming photovoltaic panels that resemble glass panes, harness solar energy, which is then transmitted via open lines across the desert to the grid.

This green energy revolution casts a long ecological shadow. The removal of trees not only disrupts the ecological balance, but also renders the land infertile and unsuitable for agriculture or grazing, as the concrete foundations of solar installations make the soil impermeable. There are claims that large-scale photovoltaic installations can alter local biodiversity and increase desertification processes. However, no longitudinal study has yet been done to validate these claims.

However, widespread destruction of native vegetation, shrubs, cutting of trees, particularly the Khejri tree has ignited deep-seated unrest among local communities, especially the Bishnois, whose emotions are fuelled by the civilisational memories of Amrita Devi, countless *sakas* and *shaheeds,* including the Khejarli massacre. The Bishnoi community has been at the forefront, now for almost two years or perhaps more, and have been leading sustained protests against solar plants in Bikaner, Jodhpur, Phalodi, Sanchore and other proposed development sites and districts.

What began as a peaceful *dharna* or sit-in and symbolic shutdowns or *bands* has grown into a broader, grassroots movement, resonating strongest in areas where the Bishnoi ethos runs deep. These protests are no longer just about one community; they are a larger outcry against ecological disregard caused by huge solar plants.

The representatives of the people repeatedly state that they are not anti-development. They say they also want development, but it should not come at the cost of destruction of the ecosystems that provide sustenance to them.

The Scale of Destruction

The proposed installation of eight solar power plants in Phalodi (Jodhpur district) has led to a major confrontation with Bishnoi activists, who have strongly protested the felling of Khejri trees. Here, solar energy companies have acquired 25,000-*bigha* land on lease in the region, and have already cut down many Khejri trees, the state tree of Rajasthan (*Hindu*, 2022).[138]

In Jodhpur, it was reported that a solar firm illegally axed 250 Khejri trees, and buried the tree trunks inside the same land. The pictures of these revered trees buried in sand, hurt the sentiments of the villagers. The National Green Tribunal stepped in, ordering the company to plant 10 times the number of trees destroyed (*Economic Times*, 2022).[139]

Meanwhile, in Baran, a proposal allowing the felling of over 119,000 trees for a hydro power project was approved. Locals are protesting the government decision (*ETV Bharat*, 2024).[140]

The High Court has asked the government to take a decision on the matter (*Times of India*, 2025).[141]

Dr Sumit Dookia (in a personal interview),[142] who works on restoration ecology in the Thar Desert pointed out that while clean energy is important, it's crucial to carefully weigh the benefits and environmental costs of such projects.

Unlike traditional development projects, solar farms often don't undergo environmental impact assessments. This can lead to major damage to the local environment. Large stretches of farmland and grazing lands are being cleared of Indigenous trees like Khejri, Kumtiya, and Rohida to make place for solar panels. Rajasthan has many pastoral communities and marginal farmers who rely on these lands for grazing their livestock.

The provisions of Environmental Impact Assessment (EIA), which mandate environmental clearance for various projects, do not apply to solar photovoltaic power projects, solar power projects and solar parks. However, they have to ensure that the project area does not involve any agricultural land, wetlands and bio-diversity rich areas with a large habitation and ecologically sensitive areas (*The Mint*, 2017).[143]

Several environmentalists opine that India does not have a policy for wastelands and grazing lands. This probably comes from a colonial mindset, where any land, that could not generate revenue by way of tax, or timber, was classified as wasteland. Hence what the land records classify as wasteland, is often not waste.

Dr Ranjitsinh says the Thar desert in India, is a semi-arid desert, and one of the most highly populated deserts in the world, unlike the Sahara and Atacama that house virtually no population. People have survived here for centuries grazing cattle and growing hardy crops and it is important for biodiversity.

Vast solar plants, take away the livelihood of these people who subsist on land. Besides, solar panels gather dust and heat up and require water for cleaning and cooling down the panels, a resource already scarce in the desert. As solar plants consume more water, nearby communities are left struggling to meet their basic needs (International Conference at SCDR, Delhi).[144] He suggests, solutions like deploying solar panels over canals and rooftops of homes to reduce the need for large solar farms. By making smarter choices now, Rajasthan can truly lead the way in green energy—without sacrificing its natural heritage.

While many individuals flagged the solar panels and destruction of biodiversity, the Bishnois were one of the earliest communities, to stand up together as a unified force. What seems like a battle between development and tradition is, essentially a battle to protect nature.

The leader of the All India Bishnoi Mahasabha, Devendra Budiya has compared the felling of Khejri, with the Bishnoi history of the fearless Amrita Devi in Khejarli village. Once again Khejri and other botanical wealth is being destroyed at a widespread scale, against which our struggle will continue (*Hindustan Times*, 2023).[145] The Mahasabha and Akhil Bhartiya Jeev Raksha Sansthan have taken the battle to the Rajasthan High Court.

In Bikaner, the Bishnoi Mahasabha orchestrated a massive *bandh* (shutdown), garnering widespread support from local businesses and residents.

Rampal Bhavad of BTF has repeatedly stated in all media reports that the Bishnois are not opposing renewable energy; they are opposing the reckless destruction of nature, and an amendment and revision of the Rajasthan Tenancy Act, which hardly imposes a deterrent for those who cut trees. This is a demand shared by all environmentalists. The Act imposes a mere ₹100 fine for cutting trees on non-forestry land, hardly a deterrence for any solar company not to cut trees.

While no one is forcing farmers to give their land to solar plants, it is believed that the collective lands of *orans* need protection. Rajasthan has a large number of unregistered *orans*, maintained not just by Bishnois, but by other communities as well. The locals also wish to protect unregistered *orans* from renewable energy companies.

On the other hand, the Supreme Court has come down heavily on NGOs challenging projects, saying not every project can be stalled citing environmental concerns. Even an environment-friendly solar power project was being questioned in the guise of saving the environment, when it is the government's policy to promote solar energy (*Times of India*, 2025).[146]

As India takes strides towards using renewable energy, integrating environmental assessments and community consultations into project planning is crucial.

How much is a tree worth anyway?
Once upon a time (not in a fairy tale) when the king's men came to cut trees, a woman stood in their way and proclaimed,

सर साटे रूंख रहे तो भी सस्ता जान
Even if my head must roll to save a tree, it is worth it.

And heads did roll, indeed. This woman didn't hold a degree in environmental science; neither did she have access to SDG goals. Her motivation didn't come from a fancy conference. What she did have was clarity and courage that came from her *dharma*.

Fast forward 300 years.

Today, if you want to cut down a tree, you don't need a sword, just one hundred rupees—the fine for cutting a tree under the Rajasthan Tenancy Act is less than a cup of cappuccino in an urban café. I cannot resist adding a sarcastic sentence, that this money is not even enough to buy a sugary muffin on the side. That's the legal value of a tree that may have taken a hundred years to grow, fixed nitrogen worth a hundred harvests, fed a hundred deer, protected groundwater, anchored soil and supported entire ecosystems, like a quiet sentinel.

One tree. One hundred rupees. Slaughtered in the name of modern-day progress.

How did we go from 'giving a head for a tree' to 'coffee for a tree'?

Since we like to put a price on everything, *The Compensatory Afforestation Report* by a seven-member expert committee[147], prescribes a formula, where a tree's value is not just in its timber, but also in the invisible services it provides, its special relevance, habitat of other living organisms, soil, protection and water retention. It is a good formula that calculates the value as follows:

Tree Value = trunk area × unit price × species rating × condition rating × location rating.

Using this calculation, a neem tree, with a modest 88 cm girth is worth ₹1,33,056, that is one lakh, thirty-three thousand and fifty-six rupees.

If a tree must be cut, then instead of paying that value or protecting that tree, authorities can substitute it by planting 33 tall seedlings, with tree guards, on land provided by the user.

The same report mentions that states like Maharashtra propose to classify trees over 50 years as heritage trees. If a 52-year-old heritage tree must be felled, then 52 trees must be planted.

No matter how sophisticated the spreadsheet, how noble the policy draft, there's an uncomfortable truth staring back at us, especially when we try to calculate the value of something we once revered. Humans are God's unique creations that need a price tag to understand the value of everything. Ironically, we cut down trees to build sophisticated car parking lots and then look for shade to park our cars, in the scorching summer.

We don't know how to put a real price on something that came without an invoice. Maybe one day, we'll learn what our ancestors already knew, that nature doesn't work against a card swipe.

The Last Flight
How One Bird Redefined Climate Law

Rajasthan is home to the endangered species like the Great Indian Bustard (GIB) incidentally, also the state bird of Rajasthan, that now faces an unusual predator; power lines strung high above solar farms. Environmentalists say that the dense network of uncovered, overhead power transmission lines from solar plants pose a significant threat to the critically endangered GIB, as these birds face the risk of colliding with power lines and getting electrocuted.

The GIB is not just colliding with powerlines in the fragile ecosystem of Rajasthan, it is now also colliding, quite literally, with India's march toward green energy.

In a striking convergence of species survival and climate ambition, the Supreme Court of India (in M K Ranjitsinh versus Union of India),[148] is scripting what could become a landmark chapter in India's environmental jurisprudence.

The petitioners approached the Court seeking protection for the GIB, whose population was being decimated by high-voltage transmission lines powering solar and wind projects. In a protective gesture, the Court's 2021 interim order mandated restrictions on overhead lines across 99,000 square kilometres and called for underground cabling in sensitive areas.

Yet, the legal narrative took a nuanced turn in April 2024. While reaffirming India's commitment to green solar energy, the Court stepped back from its underground order, acknowledging both the technical limitations and the potential climate costs of halting solar power expansion.

In a balanced approach, the Court called for the formation

of an expert committee to explore workable alternatives, such as bird diverters, and to evaluate the feasibility of targeted undergrounding. The question now is on how to balance the urgent need for decarbonisation while, at the same time, protecting endangered species and fragile ecosystems.

What makes this case especially significant is the evolving legal frame. Scholars and activists are urging the judiciary to interpret the case through the lens of—just *transition*—a principle that insists climate action must be equitable, inclusive, and fair to all affected parties. The concept of 'just transition' came about in the 1970s to protect people whose livelihoods were threatened by environmental regulations. Traditionally used to protect people displaced by climate policy, could the idea be expanded to include the non-human world?

By acknowledging the GIB not merely as an environmental concern but as a stakeholder in climate policy, the Court may have the opportunity to push legal boundaries. It could draw on its eco-centric jurisprudence, recognising animals as sentient beings and granting legal personhood to rivers and ecosystems, to anchor nature itself as a legitimate subject of constitutional protection in a climate transition framework.

With over twenty legal disputes already arising from renewable energy conflicts across India, this case might become a torchbearer. The final verdict, expected soon, could hold the potential to move climate litigation away from being a zero-sum game, toward a model where clean energy, social justice, and biodiversity will coexist.

Balancing sustainable development with ecological preservation will ensure that progress does not trample upon the very roots that sustain the land and its people. This is a tricky balance for our country, our government, communities, law makers and enforcers.

※ ※ ※

Image ©Anu Lall Bishnois and the Blackbuck

Chapter 13
Badopal Wildlife Habitat Case
How Activism Helps

श्रेयान्स्वधर्मो विगुण: परधर्मात्स्वनुष्ठितात्
स्वधर्मे निधनं श्रेय: परधर्मो भयावह:

It is far better to perform one's prescribed duty, even with faults, than to perform another's duty, perfectly. It is preferable to die in the discharge of one's duty, than to follow the path of another, fraught with danger.
—Bhagavad Gita 3:35

Environmental victories are never easy, and they rarely happen overnight. For years, activists and communities have fought relentless battles against the forces of unchecked development striving to protect India's fragile ecosystems.

A recent example of the power of legal perseverance and community resilience is the successful declaration of the Badopal Conservation Reserve—a landmark success that came after twelve years of unrelenting effort. This achievement represents the outcome of the intricate collaboration between the Bishnoi community, environmental advocates, legal experts, and governmental institutions.

In this chapter, I present this successful case study—how it all began, the years of quiet and active perseverance and the eventual triumph. For the benefit of a lay person, I have summarised twelve years of legal proceedings, omitting technicalities while retaining the essence, balancing details with readability.

As part of this book project, I will also publish a legal case study on the Badopal Wildlife Conservation Reserve, inviting law colleges, public policy teachers, and research scholars to teach it as part of their curriculum. While young adults may hold starry-eyed images of environmental law, picturing global summits and jet-setting across continents for COP events—this case study offers a grounding reminder of what a real-world fight for the environment looks like, and how difficult it is to change things at the grassroots.

How it Started
Every day Vinod Karwasra Ji, a resident of Badopal village and a teacher at the Government High School in Kajalheri, would pass through vast grasslands—the habitat of wildlife. Herds of blackbuck leapt and grazed freely across the horizon, a sight that never failed to fill him with awe. Although this area was not a notified national park or sanctuary, it remained a significant habitat for wildlife.

While Karwasra had often heard about national parks and wildlife sanctuaries, in Bishnoi-dominated areas, wild species didn't need the protection of fenced reserves; they thrived in harmony along with the farmers.

Badopal in Fatehabad, Haryana, is an area of Bishnoi dominance. Around 500 acres of its land serve as the critical habitat for the blackbuck, a Schedule I species under the Wildlife Protection Act of 1972. It is the State Animal of Haryana. The region is also home to other ecologically significant species—blue bulls, desert foxes, jackals, monitor lizards, rare snakes such as the black-headed royal snake, cobra, racer snake and porcupines.

But in 2009, whispers of a looming threat began to spread. Despite its ecological importance, the region was threatened by a developmental proposal from the Nuclear Power Corporation of India Limited (NPCIL). The corporation intended to convert 187 acres of this vibrant habitat into a township for its upcoming nuclear power project. Such a project would have devastated the fragile ecosystem, and posed a threat to the blackbuck. Environmental degradation, habitat loss, and the endangerment to blackbuck and displacement of other wildlife, were no longer distant possibilities—they were imminent.

Building Awareness and Initial Resistance (2011–2013)
Sensing the looming threat, Karwasra decided to act. What began as a quiet concern soon grew into a movement, uniting villagers, activists, and conservationists in their determination to protect the land they loved.

In November 2012, he contacted Maneka Gandhi, who intervened, then alerted authorities, who dispatched a team to assess the ground realities. The issue was widely reported in the print media, gaining public attention.

Local activists collaborated with Akhil Bhartiya Jeev Raksha Bishnoi Sabha (ABJRBS) and People for Animals (PFA) launching awareness campaigns at village *melas* especially at Kajalheri and during the annual Bishnoi *mela* at Badopal—to educate the public about the endangered species under threat from the proposed township.

The Resistance Intensifies (2013–2014)
The awareness drive gradually evolved into active resistance. The community argued that the project did not have clearance from the Environment Ministry which mandated the conservation plan for Schedule I species. They demanded a site inspection by the Wildlife Institute of India (WII).

In 2013, under pressure from the Bishnoi community, NPCIL and the Chief Wildlife Warden wrote to WII and to the Ministry of Environment, Forest and Climate Change (MoEFCC), requesting a team for a comprehensive Conservation Plan.

In July 2013, the Wildlife Institute of India (WII) conducted a survey in the area, and submitted its report in August 2013, recommending the site as a critical blackbuck habitat and the best lekking site for blackbuck, essential for long-term conservation in Haryana. They advised that the NPCIL Colony site is on the natural habitat of blackbuck and should be relocated.

Ideally, this should have been a win for the community, but who knew about the long battle that was to follow.

NPCIL did not agree with these findings and requested for a revisit. Meanwhile, without any conservation plan, NPCIL set up a factory to manufacture pillar structures at the site, using heavy machinery and labourers with the intention of disrupting wildlife presence. Worse still, NPCIL erected a metal net fencing to cordon off their area, without a conservation plan and without obtaining Environment Clearance.

Some local farmers too had been using blade wire fencing in their farms. This led to the death of several blackbuck, because the fence created an obstacle and blackbuck became an easy prey to stray dogs.

Known for their agility and speed, reaching up to 80 kilometres per hour (50 mph)—blackbuck are incredible runners. It is virtually impossible to outrun this beautiful creature. They can leap up to six metres in length and two metres in height. When faced with near invisible metal nets, this god-gifted speed becomes a curse. The nearly invisible metal nets and fencing by NPCIL became death traps for the blackbuck.

The blackbuck were unable to detect the fence at high speeds

Haryana

Annexure P-XII

NPCIL colony a threat to blackbucks

SUSHIL MANAV
TRIBUNE NEWS SERVICE

FATEHABAD, FEBRUARY 4

Animal rights activists are worried at the fate of hundreds of wildlife animals like blackbucks, blue bulls and rabbits, whose natural habitat near Baropal village in Fatehabad has been acquired for setting up a residential colony for officials of the Nuclear Power Corporation of India Limited (NPCIL).

The NPCIL is coming up with an atomic power plant at Gorakhpur village, about 10 km from Badopal, and the authorities have acquired 185 acres of land near Badopal for setting up a residential colony for its employees.

Though Fatehabad Deputy Commissioner M.L Kaushik had assured that a park for these animals would be set up in the land acquired for the colony, the idea was rejected both by the NPCIL as well as animal lovers.

"I have worked as a teacher in Kajalheri village for over three years. During my to and fro journey between my native Badopal village and Kajalheri, I used to enjoy watching these beautiful creatures (blackbucks) in the fields. Now, with the land acquired by the government for a residential colony, I wonder where these animals will go", said Vinod Kumar Bishnoi, president of the People for Animals at Fatehabad.

"Farmers protested for their lands and got handsome compensation from the government for their land, buildings and trees etc. But what about these speechless creatures, whose natural habitat is being snatched by the government? No one is thinking about them. The land does not merely belong to the persons who own it but also to the wildlife that live in it," he reasoned.

Bishnoi alleged that while preparing its environment impact assessment (EIA) report, the NPCIL said there was no wildlife sanctuary near the plant.

However, the NPCIL ignored the presence of hundreds of blackbucks in the area. He alleged that a number of blackbucks were being mauled by stray dogs and the authorities were doing nothing to protect them.

Shakti Singh, Divisional Forest Officer (Wildlife),

Deer roam freely in fields and a blackbuck mauled by stray dogs near Badopal in Fatehabad.
Photos: Sushil Manav

Hisar, said his department had sent a proposal that the NPCIL should allow these animals to live in its green belt fenced area, so that they could be saved from wild dogs.

Gorakhpur Atomic Project renamed

FATEHABAD, FEBRUARY 4

The atomic power project coming up at Gorakhpur village in Fatehabad has been rechristened Gorakhpur Haryana Anu Vidyut Pariyojana (GHAVP).

Earlier, the district authorities and the Nuclear Power Corporation of India Limited (NPCIL), the government agency setting up this project, had been writing its name as Gorakhpur Atomic Power Project (GAPP) in the official correspondence.

The Deputy Commissioner, M.L Kaushik, along with ADC Rajiv Rattan and NPCIL senior functionaries TR Arora and Sanjay Gumasta, launched the work of fencing of the project land. He said the project would now be written as GHAVP in the official correspondence. — TNS and crashed into their death. Even feral dogs would chase these magnificent fast animals to these fences and kill them.

Local newspapers carried reports about how the NPCIL Colony is a threat to blackbuck. In just a matter of ten days (5 July – 14 July 2013) three blackbuck died, with the number going up to seven (*The Tribune*, 2013).[149]

The community demanded legal action against both the government administration that allowed the fencing and the NPCIL, who acted without permission and set up the death traps for the animals.

In protest, the Bishnoi community and People for Animals (PFA) activists held a demonstration and threatened to block the National Highway 10 at Badopal, if the fencing was not dismantled immediately.

Facing pressure to show progress on the nuclear project, the district administration chose a superficial solution. Instead of removing the fencing that acted as death traps, the district administrator advised NPCIL to cover the fences with red reflectors so that the blackbuck could see it. They also suggested leaving small gaps to facilitate the escape of the animals to the other side in the case of danger. However, this did not help the case as the move was a mere eyewash, intended more to pacify public anger and built-up resentment due to the death of blackbuck, rather than as a measure to protect wildlife.

Animal rights activists, including members of Akhil Bhartiya Jeev Raksha Bishnoi Sabha and the PFA strongly opposed the recommendation to cover up the fencing, at the district office.

By now, Vinod Karwasra had recognised the need for a structured platform, rather than acting alone. Representing the Haryana state Akhil Bhartiya Jeev Raksha Bishnoi Sabha, he filed a case in the National Green Tribunal (NGT).

NGT ruled in favour of the environmental activists and ordered NPCIL to remove the illegal fencing though it maintained a status quo on other aspects of the dispute.

Soon after, the District Collector announced that blade wire fencing, commonly used by farmers, would also be banned, as it was responsible for the deaths of blackbuck and blue-bulls that get trapped in the fencing while fleeing wild dogs or poachers. Prohibitory orders were promulgated to impose the ban on the fencing (*Tribune India* 2015).[150]

This was the first victory—small but significant. However, the larger battle of having the land declared as a conservation site remained unfulfilled. So, the community escalated their appeals to the Prime Minister's Office (PMO) and MoEFCC.

Twelve Years of Perseverance, RTIs and PILs

The community filed a criminal complaint against the officers involved in the deaths of blackbuck. Awareness campaigns intensified. A special awareness week was organised by the Bishnoi community during the *Mad Bhagwat Katha* led by Shri Kripacharya Ji Maharaj.

Several RTIs were filed and numerous visits were made to the Special Environment Court, Kurukshetra, in connection with the case of the death of seven blackbuck.

In September 2014, the court finally booked a criminal case against key officials, including the Chief Wildlife Warden, Haryana, District Collector, Fatehabad, SDM Fatehabad, Divisional Wildlife Officer, Hisar, Inspector Wildlife Fatehabad and NPCIL project heads, for dereliction of duty. Under CrPC 197, government officials enjoy special protection against legal cases, so the cases against them were dropped. However, the NPCIL officers continued to face criminal charges.

In 2015, the Wildlife Institute of India (WII) team revisited the site. By then, thirty-four blackbuck had already died in the area. The team documented that 146 out of 458—roughly 32 per cent of the total blackbuck population—were living on NPCIL-acquired land. The WII team again reiterated relocation of the proposed NPCIL colony for long-term conservation of blackbuck in Haryana and also recommended sterilising wild feral dogs to protect the blackbuck population.

The scientific backing from WII legitimised the Bishnoi community's demands and created a strong foundation for legal arguments. It seemed there would be a decision on the NPCIL colony soon, but despite several representations, appeals to ministry and the government, there is still no clarity. In March 2014, Akhil Bhartiya Jeev Raksha Bishnoi Sabha Vs Union of India and Ors, an appeal was filed before the NGT, and then several review petitions, showing there was no conservation plan by NPCIL followed.

Over the years, the community continued with the legal process and awareness campaigns. On 5 June 2014, World Environment Day, an awareness camp was held at Delhi Bishnoi Dharamshala advocating conservation. The community continued their efforts at Badopal, in keeping the site habitable for the blackbuck, by de-weeding, preventing poaching and preserving habitat conditions.

In 2017, NGT ordered NPCIL to create a watering hole for the animals, an order the company complied with. Organisations like Paryavaran Jeev Raksha Bishnoi Sabha (PJRBS), Akhil Bhartiya Jeev Raksha Bishnoi Sabha and People for Animals (PFA) and several individuals continued to pursue the case with resilience, navigating countless bureaucratic and legal twists.

Vinod Karwasra Ji led this battle bringing transparency to

the issue and highlighting the systematic gaps in regulatory oversight. He also actively engaged with media outlets, ensuring that Badopal's ecological importance reached a wider audience, creating a formidable coalition advocating for the region's protection.

He also led numerous awareness campaigns including that of educating communities.

Through the utilisation of the Right to Information (RTI) Act and strategic legal actions, critical information was unearthed regarding environmental impact assessments, governmental deliberations, and corporate plans for the region.

Simultaneously, legal petitions invoked the constitutional duty to protect the environment under Article 48A and Article 51A(g), which further reinforced the community's claims. The follow up with government agencies was done relentlessly and the case continued for many years.

Role of Media

National and regional newspapers regularly covered the movement, highlighting the relentless struggle of the Bishnoi community, emphasising their long-standing tradition of environmental conservation. Student organisations and environmental NGOs collaborated to spread awareness through social media and public demonstrations, along with regional news outlets that became powerful tools in amplifying the voices of the activists.

This widespread media attention placed pressure on policymakers and corporate stakeholders, making it increasingly difficult to ignore the growing demand for environmental protection.

Government Intervention and Victory

Finally, after nearly twelve years, the campaign reached a critical milestone on 18 June 2023, when the Haryana Forest and Environment Minister formally visited the site and sent a proposal to the government to transfer 187 acres of land of Nuclear Power Corporation of India (NPCIL) in Badopal, Fatehabad to the Forest Department for the purpose of conservation of blackbuck in Haryana.

The Haryana Forest and Environment Minister formally declared:

> 187 acres of land of Nuclear Power Corporation of India (NPCIL) in Badopal, Fatehabad would soon be transferred to the Forest Department for the purpose of conservation of black bucks in Haryana. Badopal Blackbuck habitat would be the first owned habitat by the state government.
>
> He said that blackbuck is the state animal of Haryana and Badopal Village of Fatehabad is a natural habitat of blackbucks. He also appreciated the local Bishnoi community for conserving blackbucks (Haryana State Government order no. No IPRDH/2023).[151]

Finally, the DO (Demi-Official) letter written by the Chief Minister of Haryana on 12 June 2024, was a significant step toward the declaration of a Conservation Reserve in Badopal, Fatehabad. This letter was addressed to the Central Government and included consent from the Department of Atomic Energy (DAE), which was necessary because a portion of the land in Badopal had been acquired for the Nuclear Power Corporation of India Limited (NPCIL) township.

All leading newspapers reported the story of this victory (*Hindustan Times*, 2023).[152] Facing sustained public and legal pressure, NPCIL eventually consented to the land's conservation and relocated the colony to Agroha, which was a significant compromise that balanced developmental needs with ecological priorities. Government officials acknowledged the ecological value of Badopal, recognising that its designation as a Conservation Reserve would not only safeguard biodiversity but also contribute to regional ecological resilience.

The success of the Badopal conservation movement was deeply rooted in the active mobilisation of the Bishnoi community, with their historical reverence for nature, and played a central role in galvanising support. Through public meetings, awareness drives, utilising religious *melas* to create awareness about the impending threat, the Bishnoi community sustained the movement.

This short case summary does not do justice to the twelve years of hard work, blood, sweat and toil of the community, environmental activists, and legal professionals that ultimately led to the protection of this ecologically significant area.

Governments often act as intermediaries, tasked with balancing developmental goals and environmental responsibility. However, delayed decisions, action taken without keeping an eye on the ground, red tape and apathy can cause a lot of damage. We need watchful citizens, and relentless community advocacy to deal with the complexity of legal and administrative frameworks. This case also reflects the role that social movements and environmental justice campaigns play in shaping policy outcomes, and the importance of actively seeking scientific recommendations.

This success story exemplifies how perseverance, strategic legal action, and collective determination can safeguard biodiversity for future generations.

But beyond the legal triumph, I again circle back to the deeper question—one that has echoed through centuries of environmental struggles:

Who owns the Earth? And who are we protecting it from?

And who, ultimately will be held accountable for the deaths of so many innocent creatures—lives lost to delays, negligence and indifference?

The story of Badopal Conservation invites each of us to reflect on our collective responsibility towards our planet. It demonstrates that environmental justice can only be achieved when science, community law, and relentless will come together.

Karwasra is also the moving force behind establishing water bodies and restoring grasslands, and the creation of three community reserves in Fatehabad district in Haryana:

- Guru Jambheswar Community Reserve (focused on peacocks and black partridges)
- Guru Gorakhnath Community Reserve (Indian soft-shell turtles)
- Shaheed Amrita Devi Memorial Community Reserve (for preservation of blackbucks).

When I first set foot in Badopal, in 2024, twelve years of resilience and dedication had finally paid off. Years of struggle had led to victory, unlike several of the ongoing protests which I had previously attended.

Vinod Karwasra Ji welcomed me with warmth that mirrored the spirit of the land. As we drove to the conserve area, he pointed out areas once marked for the NPCIL colony, and said, '*Yahan aati ji buildings, colony ki*'—This is where the colony buildings would have come up.'

I was witnessing a reclaimed landscape, now thriving and resonant with the sounds of wildlife. Animals grazed freely and blackbuck jumped around gracefully. As we sat on the edge of the conserved area, Vinod Ji rattled off the case facts—the case history tumbling out at a pace I struggled to keep up with. I scribbled furiously into my notebook.

The morning passed quickly and soon, the blackbuck were already beginning to settle in for their afternoon siesta.

As we were preparing to leave, we walked by the food fields that the community had planted, ensured the waterholes were filled and the sanctuary of survival was alive.

At Karwasra Ji's home, a curious sight caught my eye: an ambulance parked right in middle of his driveway.

'Why an ambulance?' I asked.

He explained, matter-of-factly, 'When an animal is attacked or injured, our community WhatsApp group springs into action. The nearest team responds, ensuring the animal gets help.'

He explained that emotions about saving animals

can only take us that far. In today's world, it was about building a system of care. We need villagers who were not just passionate about saving animals, but trained in emergency response, knew how to lift an injured animal without causing further harm, equipped with knowledge of first-aid and drivers who could navigate rough terrain till the wounded animal reached a rescue centre.

Over lunch, Karwasra Ji showed me a room filled with files—endless RTIs, PILs and their copies of paperwork that could drive even the most resilient soul to despair, in a twelve-year-long battle.

'But he knows all these by heart,' his wife said with a chuckle, as we ate.

'Even if you wake him up at midnight, he can tell you the exact date of the appeal filed with the NGT and pull out the right document.'

We laughed, a laugh of victory, of relief, and the sheer absurdity of the bureaucratic maze he had navigated and won.

I discovered another side of Karwasra Ji—his passion for photography. I suggested we feature some of his photographs in the book and assured him that my publisher would contact him for the financial transactions for the images. His response was as simple as it was profound.

'*Main* petrol pump *ka* UPI *de deta hoon ji. Aap wahin hi transfer kar dena.* Hiran rescue ambulance *ke liye,* court *aur sarkaari daftar ke chhakkar lagte hain,* petrol *bahut lagta hai. Kaam toh hum kar lenge.*'

(I'll give you the petrol pump's UPI. Just transfer

some money there. Whether it's rescuing a deer, running the ambulance, or the countless trips to courts and government offices, all we need is fuel. The work, that we'll manage.)

How do you counter such honesty, such unwavering commitment to *nishkam karma*—selfless service? I asked him what kept him going. What gave him the strength to persevere all these years of struggle.

'I am only doing the duty assigned by Guru Ji. *Jeev daya palani,* is my Bishnoi *dharma*. I used to see those animals every day on my way to school. Couldn't see them die.'

There it was—the power of *swadharma*, the realisation of one's duty performed with pure intent. No recognition sought, no rewards expected. Just the quiet strength that comes from doing your personal *dharma*, your assigned duty, on a path of righteousness.

Image ©Anu Lall Bishnois and the Blackbuck

Chapter 14
Religious Roots of Ecological Crisis

ता नः प्रजाः सं दुहतां समग्रा वाचो मधु पृथिवी धेहि मह्यम् ॥
May we your children, together get the essence of the divine order (ritam) present everywhere in you, O mother earth, through the correct sweet speech.
—Bhumi Suktam, Atharva Veda, 12.1.16

I began this book with a mythical story from a movie and an existential question: *Who owns the earth?* After exploring several sacrifices, ancient wisdom, philosophy, traditions, and contemporary legal advocacy rooted in reverence for nature—spanning five centuries—we return to the same question. Who asserts dominance over nature, environment, earth and ecology?

Globally, a multitude of organisations and missions have been established to address environmental challenges. Billions are poured into international organisations and environmental summits. Yet the Earth continues to choke. We are flooded with sustainability jargon, environmental sustainability goals, net zero, green finance and biodiversity indices. The air grows heavier, forests thinner, and species vanish, while the so-called environmental missions dine in luxury under banners of 'green growth'. Corporate brochures are often greener than their practices. Nations take climate pledges. But beneath all this talk lies a deeper malaise, of *green washing*.

Sustainability has become a checkbox, a marketing strategy, a stage for moral performance, where sincerity is the first casualty. The hypocrisy of the political and capitalist elite about the environment is increasingly transparent, seen by all, yet their talk is not perceived as serious by most. Their extravagant lifestyles have led many to believe that the rich and powerful would rather use the environment as an opportunity to cement their own global leadership positions and enjoy the indulgence at the expense of nature, without creating systems for saving it.

The super-rich are plundering and polluting the planet to the point of destruction. It is those who can least afford it who are paying the highest price (*The Guardian*, 2023).[153] Oxfam and the Stockholm Environment Institute published a special investigation titled the *Great Carbon Divide*, which said, the richest 1 per cent of humanity is responsible for more carbon emissions than the poorest 66 per cent (Khalfan, Ashfaq, Nilsson Lewis et al, 2023).[154]

Every now and then, the duplicity of climate change events and their conflict with sustainability becomes evident.

For instance, the UN Climate Change Conference at Dubai was attended by a whopping 83,000 attendees. Countless commercial flights and 644 private flights landed for the event, emitting an estimated 4,800 tonnes of CO_2 (*Euro News*, 2024).[155]

A similar show in Egypt had led to public criticism and protests, and environmental activists blocked private jets at Amsterdam's Schiphol Airport, before COP 27 (*BBC*, 2022).[156]

In preparation for the upcoming COP 30 in 2025 at Belém, Brazil, Amazon rainforests have been deforested to build an eight-mile, four lane highway (*New York Post*, 2025).[157] Thirty such projects are underway, including a new city park, conference centres, hotels and the port preparing to hold cruise ships for the guests. The sounds of insect chirps and birdsongs has been replaced by a chorus of diesel engines and excavators gutting down the forest. Local environmentalists and communities have raised concerns about the ecological impact and the message it sends regarding conservation efforts (*BBC News,* 2025).[158]

Meanwhile, Sustainable Development Goal (SDG) frameworks are immaculate in compliance, but no one lays down their life citing SDG goals. Compliance cannot motivate people to sacrifice themselves protecting animals and trees.

Besides the logistics and private jets, environmentalists like Vandana Shiva have been critical of even the core intention of such conventions, especially the Convention on Biological Diversity, which she says was ironically created for the protection for biodiversity, but was distorted to exploit biodiversity, instead. Shiva contends that such initiatives started out primarily as initiatives to help the global North 'globalise' control over biological resources needed as raw material for the biotechnology industry. (Vandana Shiva, 2012).[159]

These contradictions are not accidental, but symptoms of a deeper malaise. The sterile rhetoric around the environment fails to resonate with the rhythm of the planet.

How did we come to a point where sustainability conversations have lost their soul?

To understand the present ecological crisis, we must go deeper, into the historical roots of our disconnection, and the forgotten philosophies that once treated nature as sacred.

What are the Roots of Our Ecological Crisis?

Some ideas are like sparks, they ignite conversations, fuel debates, and simply refuse to die down. One such idea is outlined in the thesis, *The Historical Roots of Our Ecological*

*Crisis (*Lynn White, 1967*).*[160] He opined that the roots of the ecology crisis were ideology, culture, and more particularly Christian religious beliefs.

This short essay sent shockwaves through academia, theology, and environmental circles. Widely discussed, fiercely criticised, yet undeniably influential, this thesis laid the foundation for modern debates on the role of religion in environmental conservation.

White's argument was bold and even provocative. At its core, he claimed that the root cause of the modern ecological crisis was not just industrialisation or technological advancements, but something far deeper.

I summarise his thesis in a short note below:

Lynn asserted: 'What people do about their ecology depends on what they think about themselves in relation to things around them.'

The human mind is deeply conditioned by beliefs about our nature and destiny by religion. According to White Christianity inherited from Judaism a linear view of time, and a belief in divine creation, where the world was made for man's benefit. An all-powerful God created light and darkness, heavenly bodies, the earth—its plants, animals, birds, and fishes. Finally, God created Adam, and as an afterthought, he created Eve to keep man from being lonely. God planned all this explicitly for man's benefit and rule. Nothing in the physical creation had any purpose save to serve man's purposes. Man named all the animals, thus establishing his dominance over them. White went on to say, Christianity not only established a dualism of man and nature, but also insisted that it is God's will that man exploit nature for his proper ends. Christianity, was in absolute contrast to ancient paganism and Asia's religions. The victory of

Christianity over paganism was the greatest psychic revolution in the history of our culture (Lynn White, 1967).

White says, that in ancient times, the pre-Christian era, every tree, every spring, every stream and hill had its own guardian spirit. Before one cut a tree, mined a mountain, or dammed a brook, it was important to placate the spirit in charge. By destroying pagan animism, Christianity made it possible to exploit nature in a mood of indifference to the feelings of natural objects (White, 1967).

Nobel laureate Wangari Maathai, pioneer of the Green Belt Movement, gave examples that supported this argument, from her ethnic community, the Kikuyu from south-central Kenya. She said Christianity weaved itself into colonisation and exploitation of many parts of the world. Colonisation used Christian practices to remove the idea of sacred groves from local tribes. Sacred groves were sacred no more. Colonial forces demonised and marginalised the religious practices of those they conquered and occupied. Ancient Kikuyu traditions and worldview were considered 'primitive' by Christian missionaries, who judged the native rituals and ceremonies, demonised them and eventually destroyed them. Now scientists are beginning to recognise that these traditional cultures and their lifestyle were responsible for the conservation of the rich biodiversity.

She writes about an incident from 1914 when British colonisers destroyed sacred groves in Kenya to stamp out resistance to a programme of taxation and recruitment the colonisers intended to impose. Tribes were told God was found only in buildings built for him, with an altar set up controlled by a priest whose authority had come not from the community but from another representative who lived many miles away.

Even today the government of Kenya has barred members

of the Kikuyu community from praying to God facing Mount Kenya or visiting the mountain on a spiritual pilgrimage because such practices are deemed unacceptable by the dominant form of Christianity (Wangari Maathai, 2010).[161]

Years have passed after White's thesis. Whether one likes it or not, one cannot ignore his arguments. It still inspires heated debates long after it has been published. The book, *Lynn White Thesis at Fifty* (ed Todd LeVasseur, Anna Peterson, 2018),[162] succinctly summarised his key assertions:

1. Religion, especially Western Christianity, has shaped the way humans interact with nature, which is often destructive and exploitative rather than reverential to nature.
2. Christianity places humans above nature, which fostered an attitude leading to environmental degradation. By positioning God as external to the world, it severed the spiritual bond between humanity and the Earth.
3. In contrast, pre-Christian animist and pagan traditions, rivers, trees, and mountains were inhabited by spirits, and offered a more ecologically sensitive ethos.
4. Taking this logic further, if religion caused the problem, only a religious or spiritual transformation could solve it.

White was among the first scholars to directly hold Western religious thought accountable for environmental destruction.

While White did not explicitly critique Islam, but later scholars such as Ahmed Afzaal have extended similar arguments, tracing how Islamic conquests often displaced animist and nature revering indigenous traditions (Afzaal, Ahmed 2012).[163]

Historian Arnold Toynbee echoed White's thesis. He traced environmental degradation and abuse of nature to the loss of nature worship in monotheist religions. In polytheistic religions, man's attitude towards nature was friendly, nature was a treasure-trove, a goddess, 'Mother Earth'. The whole of his environment was divine. Man's greedy impulse to exploit nature used to be held in check by his pious worship of nature (Toynbee, A, 1974).[164]

Toynbee was certain that the only way to overcome the ecological crisis and to avoid the destruction of our civilisation was to discard the monotheistic outlook and to adopt a pantheistic one (Sadowski, 2023).[165]

It may surprise you how religious beliefs and practices, impact our behaviour and even policies.

In ancient Greece and Rome, elites openly flaunted their privileged status. They paid for their sins by purchasing 'indulgences', and not punishment. When the Roman emperor Constantine converted to Christianity, the practice continued. Some argue that this practice is the predecessor to today's carbon credit offsets showcasing the hypocrisy of the elite (Forbes, 2023).[166]

One must add that selling 'indulgences', was not a form of retributive legal justice, but a remission of punishment for sins, which among many other things laid the foundation of the Protestant revolution.

There has been a relentless pushback against the idea that Christianity and other monotheistic religions removed the protection of nature by eliminating animistic religions. Many religious leaders and environmental scholars rose to the defence of Christianity. They argued that Asian countries have worse levels of pollution and environmental degradation.

One can agree that Christianity and Islam displaced animism, but one cannot agree that they weakened the precepts that guarded nature. For these two religions have introduced rules which, though for other reasons, preserve the creation (Sadowski RF, 2020).[167]

An overlooked aspect of Lynn White's thesis is that he not only captured the essence of loss of divinity, by diagnosing the problem; he pointed to a solution as well. He argued that science and technology alone could not resolve the crisis because they, too, were shaped by the same worldview, one that saw nature as something to be dominated and exploited. This mindset, deeply embedded in Western thought, positioned humans as rulers over the natural world rather than as participants in its delicate balance.

He highlighted the work of Saint Francis (1181—1226) of Assisi, Italy, associated with patronage of animals and the environment. He envisioned a 'democracy of all God's creatures', and saw every living being, animals, plants, even the elements, as having intrinsic value, existing not merely for human use but to glorify a transcendent Creator. Saint Francis largely kept the human soul and animal soul at the same level arguing for empathy and non-violence. White proposed that Saint Francis be considered the patron saint of ecologists, a symbol of a harmonious relationship with nature.

Interestingly, the Church viewed Saint Francis's ideas as heretic and worked systematically to prevent their transmission. Patrons of such syncretistic practices were continuously persecuted by the Church over the better part of a millennium. Sadly, in the early 1300s, the so-called spiritual Franciscan heretics were burned at the stake in Southern France. Religious conservatives applauded Pope Benedict XVI's actions restraining Franciscan ideas, regarding interfaith dialogue. Interestingly, the diffusion of Indic ethical and religious doctrines into Christian ascetic practices can be traced because of interaction with intermediaries. Examining several medieval hagiographies, it can be argued that

Saint Francis's inspiration may have originated in the Buddhist Jataka stories carried to Europe along the Silk Road. If Christian doctrines related to animals and nature ultimately originated in India, this should be acknowledged (Wilson, Joseph 2009).[168]

Religion and Ecology

Over time, Lynn's thesis catalysed a global exploration of the religious roots of ecological attitudes. Across the world, leaders, activists, and scholars are scrambling back to ancient wisdom, desperately mining sacred texts for a deeper, more lasting motivation to protect the environment.

In recent times, environmentalists have discovered the domain where religion and ecology intersect. *World Religion and Ecology* by John Grim and Mary Evelyn Tucker and other books like *Buddhism and Ecology* edited by Mary Evelyn Tucker and Duncan Ryuken Williams, *Confucianism and Ecology* edited by Tucker and Berthrong (1998), *Hinduism and Ecology* (Chapple and Tucker, 2000), *Christianity and Ecology* (Hessel and Ruether, 2000), and *Islam and Ecology* (Foltz et al., 2003) have put spotlight on this aspect (Bikku Rathod, 2019).[169]

The Yale Forum on Religion and Ecology (FORE), is an international multi-religious project contributing to the field of religion and ecology. In 2020, the United Nations Environment Program published a book, *Faith for Earth: A Call for Action* that imbibed the reverence of all faiths for life on Earth.

White's thesis was published in the 1960s, yet, for decades, prominent Indian thought leaders did not create a model or framework based on *Sanatan Dharma*, one of the world's oldest living traditions with profound ecological insights. Scholarly heavyweights did not exactly rush in to claim intellectual frameworks from *Dharma*.

Ramachandra Guha's *Speaking with Nature: The Origins of Indian Environmentalism* (2024)[170], is a master class in selective history. Guha dutifully traces the roots of Indian environmentalism, but only as far back as the early 20th century, to the times of Rabindranath Tagore and Mahatma Gandhi. His work, while thorough in its recounting of modern figures, fails to even acknowledge communities such as the Bishnois, who have practised environmental conservation as a sacred duty for centuries.

Yet, ironically, Guha finds space to reference the burning of the Khandava forest in the Mahabharata, a singular act of destruction, while conveniently overlooking the profound ecological reverence embedded throughout the Hindu scriptures, Vedas, numerous references to nature and ecology in the Mahabharata, Ramayana, and the broader *Sanatan Dharma* tradition, which enshrined the earth herself as *Bhu Devi*, the divine Mother Earth. It's almost impressive, the sheer talent required to miss an entire civilisation's ecological ethos while looking straight at it.

Dr Vandana Shiva worked on the ground and took on giant multinational corporations to counter the capitalist approach to agriculture, and the use of chemicals in food causing ecological destruction. It is not surprising that despite being a powerful voice, a prolific writer, and a champion of ecofeminism, she did not gain centrestage in the Indian framework of environmentalism.

While the world has been scrambling for thought leadership on this matter, one might observe that the guardians of an ancient ecological philosophy had to be reminded of its existence by scholars far away from Indian shores. Their understanding was limited to the narrow scope of their own study, and not necessarily interpreting the entire body of interconnected-ness outlined in the *dharmic* framework.

Francis Zimmerman traced the ecological theme in *Hindu Medicine* which can be termed as largely Ayurveda, where he analysed classical texts, to categorise flora and fauna as an ecological form of knowledge, essentially utilitarian medicinal properties of various foods (Zimmerman, 1987).[171]

Notable work was done by Christopher Chapple, a Western scholar, in his book *Hinduism and Ecology*, initiating a larger conversation that arguably should have emerged from within India itself.

Late Dr O P Dwivedi, from Canada had been championing the cause of Hinduism and ecology and published *Satyagraha for Conservation: Awakening the Spirit of Hinduism*[172], advocating for a revival of religious values that honour environmental stewardship. He explained how *Vedic* and *Puranic* heritage, can lead us to eco-spirituality and environmental conservation.

However, the entire interconnected-ness of *dharmic* framework eludes most studies. They barely scratch the surface.

We are standing atop a mountain of ecological heritage, and still manage to look elsewhere for thought leadership. Alternatively, one is left to conclude that overlooking a living tradition of ecological wisdom requires not a lack of information, but a deliberate narrowing of intellectual focus.

Charting a *Dharma* Framework

The persistent tendency to overlook indigenous frameworks or look at them like relics of the past, without understanding the vast knowledge they can have, the lived philosophy, is not merely an academic oversight; it reflects a deeper epistemological bias. Despite inheriting a living tradition where environmental stewardship is not a peripheral concern, but a sacred duty woven into the very fabric of *dharma*, modern Indian scholarship often exhibits a preference for reinterpreting environmentalism through Western frameworks.

The result is a curious inversion: while the world turns toward ancient traditions seeking ecological wisdom, those most intimately connected to these traditions appear determined to validate their environmental consciousness through modern secular figures and imported intellectual paradigms.

This selective vision not only distorts the historical record but also impoverishes contemporary discourse. By ignoring the organic evolution of environmental ethics within *Sanatan Dharma*—from the personification of Earth as *Bhu Devi*, to the forest hermitages (*ashramas*) revered in the epics, to communities like the Bishnois who institutionalised environmental sacrifice—Indian environmentalism risks becoming a project severed from its own cultural and spiritual roots. The cost is significant: without grounding it in civilisational consciousness, the environmental movement in India risks superficiality, lacking the moral and spiritual depth that sustained ecological practices over millennia.

Dr Bikku Rathod writes how academic discourse often neglects the vital role of local environmental practices and the perspectives of affected communities. We need to support integration of micro-level ethnographic studies, a case in point being the Bishnois, into global climate change dialogues, urging the recognition of local knowledge as an essential resource for addressing contemporary environmental challenges (Bikku Dr, 2025).[173]

Academic thought leadership, far from being an open and neutral process, remains deeply entrenched within Western frameworks. This could also be because the larger amount of research is conducted in the west. Unless this dominance is challenged with more academic work, it will create significant barriers for Indian scholars seeking to articulate an indigenous knowledge system rooted in *dharmic* worldviews.

In this context, academic thought leadership functions less as a platform for intellectual diversity and more as a mechanism of epistemic colonisation by the west. As a few scholars have started taking up this discourse around Hindu environmentalism, critiques have predictably emerged from within the Western academic tradition.

Scholars like Emma Tomalin question the compatibility of Hindu bio-divinity with modern environmentalist priorities, suggesting a disjunction between traditional religious cosmologies and contemporary ecological frameworks. She argues against the Hindu view of bio-divinity and religious environmentalism, saying that the concept of bio-divinity easily finds support from within the Hindu tradition, but there is difference in priorities and concerns of modern environmentalists and world views of Hindu sages.

One must question, to what extent the Hindus of modern India, many of whom have little or no knowledge of the language and concepts central to contemporary environmentalist thinking, actually share the religious environmentalist's goal of ecological sustainability (Emma Tomalin, 2004).[174]

It is almost an insult, lightly veiled in the garb of academic discourse, revealing a narrow, technocratic view of sustainability, and overlooks the lived ecological wisdom embedded in Hindu practice, community ethics, and inherited cultural memory.

In the conservation discourse, humans were long viewed as spoilers. It was said that even if people have successfully managed resources in some harmonious past, that past was long gone. Several current writings on management of resources champion the role of community in bringing about decentralisation, meaningful participation, cultural autonomy, and conservation. The Bishnois stand out for their commitment to ethics of conservation sustained by their faith (Neekee Chaturvedi, 2017).[175]

Most Bishnois are not aware of the Western scientific discourse about global warming or biodiversity. For them, their tradition based on the words and life of their guru is the main reason for their environmental activism (Jain, 2016).[176]

However, the *'Bishnoi Effect'* is for everyone to see. It is evident and proven in scientific studies and anecdotal accounts.

The failure to recognise alternate models of environmental care is a limitation of a western intellectual discourse that refuses to open itself to new ideas. Ultimately, the burden of translation should not fall solely on indigenous traditions to prove their relevance to modernity. Instead, academic inquiry must develop the humility to engage with plural philosophies and acknowledge that sustainability, reverence for nature, and ecological responsibility are not exclusive products of Western modernity but have long been integral to the *dharmic* civilisational ethos.

Modern Indian thought leaders, scholars and researchers, need to base their frameworks on the Indian thought rooted in *Sanatan Dharma*. Indian academia needs to push back an approach to environment that disregards lived traditions, where the models have neither any spiritual foundations, nor frameworks to bring about change. We possibly need a global south approach to counter the largely global north narrative on the environment.

Democracy of all God's Creatures

Lynn White's description of Saint Francis' approach resonates immensely with the essence of a *Sanatan Dharma* framework.

Keeping criticisms of specific religions aside, White's core proposition was that to address the ecological crisis, we must revisit our spiritual paradigms. Since we inherit our dominant mindset from religion, only a religious or spiritual transformation could solve the problem and not just scientific transformation. An overhaul of our spiritual thinking is needed to address an ecological crisis rooted in belief systems.

The solution to our environmental crisis isn't just scientific innovation or policy change, rather a profound shift in consciousness, taking us towards a 'democracy of all God's creatures, rather than human dominance. A consciousness that rekindles our lost reverence for the Earth, not as a resource to be plundered, but as a sacred entity deserving of respect and protection.

The cosmic vision of interconnectedness of self and environment is repeated in almost every *Sanatan Dharma* text, where all beings are a part of the Supreme Being, and to harm another is to harm oneself. This belief promotes ecological awareness, urging individuals to protect the natural world because it is part of their own spiritual identity. When humans and nature are seen as inseparable, the motivation to protect and conserve becomes not just a practical necessity but a spiritual duty. *Dharma* has an ecological code of conduct built on reverence for nature and all its creations. These philosophies provide timeless guidance on how to achieve this (Rawat and Vashishtha).[177]

> The question remains: Can humanity unlearn centuries of separation from nature and rediscover its sacred bond with the planet?

Chapter 15

Can Dharma save the Environment?

Jiyan nai jugati, muaan nai mugati
A philosophy that gives a way of life while we are alive;
A philosophy that ensures mukti, after we die.
—Jambho Darshan

When Jambho Ji laid the foundation of the Bishnoi panth, the land was being scorched by relentless, recurring droughts, that threatened the continuity of life. They ravaged crops, emptied wells, and caused countless deaths of humans and animals. In modern-day language, it was an ecological disaster, much that we are facing today. Jambhoji saw it as a warning, a call to realign our lives with the laws of *prakriti*, the natural world, responding with courage, clarity, and compassion. He was not just laying down a spiritual path, but responding to a civilisational crisis, that not only averted future disasters but also created a sustainable way of life.

Seeing the fragility of human existence when divorced from nature's rhythms, he did not predict a prophecy of doom, but showed a path of renewal—a way of life rooted in harmony with nature and reverence for all living beings—a path that was both deeply spiritual and profoundly ecological. It is a path that creates no confusion about our duties to humanity and duty to environment. As he proclaimed in a few unforgettable words:

> *Jiyan nai jugti, muan nai mugati.*
> *It is a way to live in balance while we are alive, and the promise of mukti or liberation after death.*

The Bishnois: Last Standing Eco-warriors

The Bishnois hold a luminous lesson of how true sustainability arises not from compliance and extravagant summits, but from devotion. What truly drives a human being to protect nature, not as a checklist, but as an article of faith? What inspires people to live and die for nature?

Sustainability is born out of *shraddha*. Ecology is not an ideology—it is *dharma*.

No one is immune to the pressures of modernity. Education and urbanisation increasingly sever our bond with nature. Young members of the Bishnoi community seeking employment in big cities may get disconnected from the land. They may not return to clean the water bodies to maintain the *orans*.

With reduced dependence, the sacredness of land automatically reduces. Such change of behaviour is not cultural—it is existential.

One can live and die for nature, when one's entire life depends on it, and it is evident to us. Erosion of belief and philosophy cannot be corrected by reinstituting rituals; it can only be done when our lives are designed around that philosophy.

Framework and thought processes become irrelevant when they don't sustain our livelihoods, when they don't help us in our daily life, when we don't see their value in maintaining food health, when they don't design our cities and life. If unused, even centuries-old wisdom can wither.

Today, there exists a gigantic wedge between us, our consciousness and nature. This disconnect manifests itself not just environmentally, but also within: between mind and body, between spirit and self.

This connection is a two-way street, and the reverse is also true. We have lost our spiritual connection, and that's why our relationship with the natural world, and everything around us, once sacred and integral to our existence, is getting fractured. This is leaning towards a life, that treats nature as a commodity rather than as a living, breathing entity deserving of our reverence.

What we witness as the environmental crisis is, at its core, a reflection of our own spiritual crisis, a failure to recognise that nature is not separate from us, but an extension of our being, and we are its offspring.

The relationship between humans and the Earth was never meant to be fragmented. Humans were entrusted with a unique role in this divine creation. Unlike animals, who act solely on instinct, humans are endowed with higher consciousness, with the power to choose their actions. This endowed them with a sacred responsibility, to be the *Guardians of Nature*.

Yet the disconnection with nature manifests in every aspect of life, in our cities, our health, and our collective well-being, or the lack of it.

If humanity is to overcome the environmental challenges and the crisis of disconnection, it must rediscover the spiritual connection that binds us to the natural world. Only then can we create a sustainable future, guided by principles that have stood the test of time. We need to look beyond compliance frameworks as technocratic solutions have failed to inspire and deliver results.

The Five Elements: Reimagining Sustainability

Sanatan Dharma has five important *dharmic* debts or *rin*, reminding us of our responsibilities beyond ourselves, guiding us towards a life of gratitude and responsibility.

Deva rin is the debt owed to the deities, material, divine and cosmic forces that sustain life. *Pitri rin* is the debt to our ancestors, gratitude for our life, body, *samskaras* and repaid by preserving lineage, culture, and traditions. *Rishi rin* is the debt to the sages and teachers who preserved and shared wisdom, which we repay by learning, living, and passing knowledge forward. *Nri rin* or *manushya rin* is the debt to humanity, fulfilled by contributing to society and treating people respectfully.

Finally, *bhuta rin* is the debt to all elements of *prakriti*, environment, plants, and animals. This is, perhaps, the most pressing today. It emphasises our interdependence with all living beings and the natural world, urging us to protect ecosystems, treat animals with compassion, and live sustainably. *Bhuta rin* transforms environmental care from rituals into a sacred duty, reminding us that ecological responsibility is not optional but a spiritual obligation. By honouring this *rin*, we not only repay what we have received from nature but also conserve the ecology for generations to come.

In the *Sanatan Dharma* framework, the foundation of the universe and everything in it, along with environment and human existence rests on, 'The Five Elements' or the *Panchmahabhuta—Akasha* (space), *Vayu* (air), *Agni* (fire), *Aapah* or *Jal* (water) and *Prithvi* (earth). This elemental framework is more than philosophy; it is a lived cosmology, a sacred design linking the macrocosm, the universe with the microcosm, the individual.

These elements are living forces, shaping and forming the basis of the entire universe and everything in it, including our physical body and environment. Their dominance is seen in different aspects of the body like bones (earth), blood (water), metabolism (fire), breath (air), and consciousness (space). The science of Ayurveda details how these elements combine in different ratios to give us different body types, our mindset, governing our metabolic functions, our emotions and thoughts. A disturbance in these elements reflects as disharmony in the self and in nature, revealing the deep interdependence between inner balance and environmental sustainability.

Alexis Reichert delves into the recurring themes of interconnectedness within *dharma* and ecology, exploring how the five elements are not only the building blocks of life but also represent the interdependence of humans, non-humans, and the divine. These elements are sacred and harming any one of them is tantamount to disrupting the balance of the universe (Reichert, 2015).[178]

Sustainability, therefore, is not just a policy. It is about living in alignment with the elements—honouring the rhythms of nature—and restoring harmony through conscious choices in lifestyle, food, and thought. It may sound esoteric, but when put into action, it makes absolute sense. Centuries of Indian wisdom about food, and agriculture have survived and thrived with this knowledge.

These concepts are very deep, but let us attempt to understand how this works as a cycle.

These elements were believed to form both the human body and the natural world. The classical system of health is deeply rooted in the concept of the five elements. In the human body, these five elements combine to form three basic body types or *doshas* called—*Vata*, *Pitta* and *Kapha*.

For instance: *Vata* is air and space-dominant, which governs movement and nerve function. *Vata* body types are usually people who are quick-thinking. *Pitta* is made up of fire and water, which governs digestion and metabolism, making the person passionate and prone to anger. *Kapha* is dominated by earth and water giving stability, weight and immunity.

The same elements apply to plants, food, trees and agriculture produce. The science is called *Vriksha Ayurveda*—the ancient treatise on plant health—and details how the elemental balance applies to trees, crops and herbs. It guides us on how to nourish plants, protect them from disease, and grow them in harmony with nature. Just as humans have *doshas*, the same five elements determine the health and constitution of plants. Plants also reflect elemental imbalances. A plant receiving too much *agni* (fire) may suffer leaf burn, excess *aapah* (water) may cause root rot, and lack of air or space can stunt growth.

And just as the elements shape plants, those plants shape us through the food chain. The foods we eat, grains, fruits, vegetables, legumes and even meat, inherit the elemental qualities of the land and climate they grow in. For example, millets grow in dry, arid, windy regions and naturally carry *Vata* properties which are dry, light, and rough. When a person with a dominant *Vata* constitution consumes too much millets, it can aggravate their *Vata* even more, leading to increase in *Vata* in the body. We are advised to consume foods that balance and not intensify our natural individual *dosha* to maintain well-being.

It's Elementary, Dear Watson!

Both these sciences have countless books with innumerable volumes devoted to the essence of wellbeing to balance these elemental energies and maintain health and harmony in the body and mind. Summarising them up in a couple of lines is, admittedly a disservice to both these great sciences.

Modern science is warming up to the idea, but is not

there yet. Few researchers like Francis Zimmermann explores the ecological depth of classical Hindu medicine, revealing a worldview where health, landscape, and cosmic balance are deeply intertwined (Francis Zimmerman, 1988).[179]

He says that far from being obsolete, this ancient framework resonates with contemporary concerns around ecology, holistic health, and alternative medicine. Drawing from Sanskrit texts and anthropology, Zimmermann shows how Ayurvedic thought linked human well-being to the qualities of the soil and the broader environment. He focuses on how land health shaped not just agricultural practices, but also medical theories. The environment, land, soil and air, its dryness or moisture, heat or cold, directly influenced the elemental balance within the body.

Zimmermann highlights how this worldview was structured around the cosmic duality of *Agni* and *Soma*, *Agni* representing heat, transformation, and digestion and *Soma* representing coolness, nourishment, and moisture. Just as land was drained, cultivated, and balanced, so too was the body managed through therapies, herbs, and rituals that guided the flow of saps, juices, and humours.

Zimmermann's work is invaluable for scholars trying to understand a system where medicine, environment, and spiritual philosophy meet, a vision that is relevant for today's efforts to live sustainably, in harmony with the Earth and ourselves.

Ayurveda and *Vriksha Ayurveda* are just two aspects of the grand elemental design that is so well explained in Indian thought. The body is like the land, both are *kshetras* or fields of elemental energies. Both must be nurtured, cultivated, cleared, and balanced.

In this paradigm, medicine, agriculture and ecology are inseparable. When we take care of our mind, body, food and plants, we automatically end up taking care of the environment and the earth. The human body is like ecological agriculture, and the maintenance of the environment is just as we would maintain the human body. Healing is a process of aligning the human microcosm with the rhythms of the universal macrocosm.

Justice S Vaidyanathan of the Madras High Court echoed this in a landmark judgement on the absence of open spaces and public parks, in the cramped city of Chennai. He delivered a deep message on the importance of open spaces, where he eloquently underscored the importance of the five elements or *Panchmahabhuta* in city planning.

Speaking about the *Panchmahabhuta* or five great elements, he highlighted the importance of each, voicing how a dismissal of reverence for nature may have contributed to worsening of environmental issues. The ancient reverence for nature, the veneration of *Panchmahabhuta* was not superstition but science in practice. These rituals were not empty gestures; they were safeguards, ensuring that the earth remained abundant for future generations.

I quote from the judgement:

> Environmental degradation and global warming are wreaking havoc in the world. At this juncture, the organs of the state should unite to serve the purpose.
>
> Our tradition and values passed down from our ancestors are not wrong beliefs, They are scientific, rational and logical. That is why they worshipped nature. Even now, many of them who follow our ancestral beliefs continue to do so as it has got abundant sanctity. They worshipped trees, *bhoomi* the soil, sun—the fire, rivers water, and sky—the space and Vayu, Air.

It is not at all irrational. Religious beliefs are rather protective of human civilisation and the environment. People will never alter their religious beliefs. Thus, nature was protected in those days.

In the name of rationality, the religious taboos were violated, the result of which we suffer these days. If all of us had followed our ancestors, we would not have been pushed to this disastrous situation.

As the concept of *panchabhootham* goes, all the elements which are present in the human body are present in our planet earth. Proper utilisation of all the elements is needed not only for a human body, so also for nature as well.

Earth, our *bhoomi,* the land reserved for open spaces, parks, etc. should not be dug for sand so that the land and soil can be protected. Open spaces serve a purpose of moving around freely, help promoting the health of the people by allowing them to walk freely. This in turn promotes oxygen inhalation, lessens pollution, and protects nature.

Parks protect nature, lessens pollution, prevents soil erosion, etc., thereby providing the vital element of *panchabhootham.*

We know the importance of something only if we are denied of it. All rivers were worshipped in earlier days. They knew its importance and hence did not pollute it.

Space is the secret of successful living in this planet. Without space, we are devoid of all the other four elements and hence the importance of space matters a lot. Development should not amount to degradation of the environment. Sustainable development is what is required (Vanitha Manickavasagam vs The Member Secretary). [180]

The Madras High Court reminded us that rationality and spirituality are not at odds, rather, they complement each other. The reverence our ancestors had for the natural world was not superstition; it was science wrapped in faith, ensuring nature's survival through devotion and discipline.

Involution: The Inner Works

Indic *dharmic* wisdom offers a powerful lens to reimagine health, conservation, and well-being, reminding us that to heal the planet, we must first heal ourselves from within, and repair our relationship with the environment. We need to design our lives around this wisdom, and change our our approach to health and wellness, agriculture, forests and trees, our cities, our spaces and everything else.

The solution to our environmental crisis isn't just scientific innovation or policy change; it's a profound shift in consciousness. We need to bring back our connection with ourselves. Before we bring back divinity in our discussions and lives, there is a need to end the dissonance in ourselves, that is so prevalent in the modern world. Everything outside reflects humanity's chaos inside—it's a two-way street. The first step of resolving the crisis begins from within, our inner selves—where we pause and take a deep look within, like an inner revolution—an involution, that works from within—the inner working towards the outside.

1. I–Me–Myself

Core insight: Disconnection from nature mirrors disconnection from self. When we maintain the elemental balance within us, we sustain bodily stability and emotional clarity. The Bishnoi principles and *dharmic* practices—eating clean food, doing *japa*, fasting on *Amavasya*—help us heal from within—heal our mind and body. This is the first step towards any meaningful change.

Daily reflection:
- How does my inner state feel?
- Do I have the energy for my daily work?
- Is there stress and anxiety?
- If your energy feels low, your elemental balance needs to be brought back into equilibrium.

Action:
- Practise mindful eating.
- Walk barefoot on Mother Earth to reconnect with nature.
- Maintain a healthy digestive fire, *Agni*, as digestion is like a daily *yagya*.

- If we depend on chemical digestives to digest food, it signals the fire element of the body is out of sync or there is overconsumption.
- Reduce chemical medicine intake by improving lifestyle choices.
- Fast occasionally.
- Choose natural sustainable clothing if possible.

2. **My family**
   Core insight:
- Family values shape our ethics.
- Teach children to share food and toys.
- Participate in *dana,* or *dasham.*
- Conserve water.
- Eat only what is needed.

Reflection:
- What is the basis of my engagement with my family?
- What values are we passing on to the next generation?

Action:
- Integrate sustainability in family life.
- Recycle.
- Conserve water.
- Celebrate birthdays in eco-friendly ways.
- Reduce wasteful gifting.
- Visit nature sanctuaries.
- If space permits, start a home garden.
- Track and reduce plastic waste, especially from packaged food.

3. **My Community**
   Core insight: Community grounds us.
   - It offers belonging, support, shared purpose and stability.
   - Activities taken as a community reward all of us. Like the Bishnoi villages which act as a collective steward of trees, water, and animals.
   - The Bishnoi principle of avoiding *ninda* or unnecessary gossip, works well in maintaining harmony in family and community.

Reflection: How does my community engage with and protect its natural surroundings?

Action:
- Join or organise clean-up drives.
- Desilt local ponds.
- Plant native trees.
- Initiate a community compost or green waste programme.
- Organise a children's programme to count trees in the neighbourhood.
- Besides action—cultivate clean speech—avoid violence of speech.
- Refrain from speaking ill against anyone.

4. **My country**
   Core insight:

National consciousness flows through the air—through our laws, ideas, collective values, and narratives. Maintain a model of ecological patriotism, through being a nation that values sacred groves, crafts, conservation laws, and supports sustainable living that embodies ecological *dharma*.

Reflection: How does my country embody ecological consciousness in its policies and cultural practices?

Action:
- Support green policies at local and national levels.
- Uphold indigenous traditions of environmental care.
- Engage in civic environmental campaigns.
- Work on laws that protect nature.
- Avoid processed foods to reduce impact on environment.

5. **My Earth**
   Core insight: The *Akash* element represents space, connectivity, and consciousness, while earth represents being grounded.

   Our earth and environment are both a mirror and matrix, and its degradation reflects inner dissonance. The planet is the great composition of all five elements—and it suffers when they fall out of balance. Global change begins with local action.

   When we violate one element (e.g., deforesting land), the rest spirals into imbalance.

Reflection: How am I contributing to the health or degradation of my environment?

Action:
- Support global conservation campaigns.
- Suggest centuries-old *dharma* framework, which can be adopted into global practices.
- This worldview is not anthropo-centric but Cosmo-centric, rooted in reciprocity and reverence.

6. **My Ishvar**
   Core insight: To see the divine in nature is to see every tree, river, and animal as a sacred space. Out of the five elements, *Akash* is not only space but also the spiritual realm—the vast, silent witness. The Bishnois remind us that any ecological action is not separate from spiritual practice. The *Sanatan Dharma* worldview treats trees, animals, and even water bodies as sacred. Worship without reverence for life is hollow. To live in awe of creation, to walk gently upon the Earth, and to protect even the smallest creature is to honour the divine within all.

Reflection: Can I perceive the divine in the natural world and act accordingly to preserve its sanctity?

Action:
- Meditate in nature.
- Offer gratitude to trees and rivers around you.
- Protect life in all forms as a sacred commitment.

This involution is not a new model. This reverence for all elements of nature, what is inside us and outside is precisely what Jambho Ji taught us: to live in balance while alive, and seek liberation after death. To be aligned with our family, community, country and Ishvar.

Jiya nia jugti, muan nai mugti

Reconnect with Earth through *Dharma*

In the modern world, the relationship between humans and nature has been aggressively 'secularised. In stripping away the spiritual and *dharmic* aspects of daily life, we have ruptured our sacred bond with nature. Mechanistic institutions have replaced meaning with metrics.

The real crisis, is not just environmental or political—it is spiritual.

The real crisis lies in our own individual fractured relationship with nature.

The real crisis is our own lack of faith in the sacred.

Before we restore our forests and oceans, we must repair our own inner ecology. Even before these become policy questions; they are questions of consciousness, and how to raise the consciousness of humans. We need to bring back a transformation in our daily lives, relationships, community, and policies.

For centuries, human beings have been portrayed as a catastrophe for the planet, the scourge of the environment. The idea that we are using too much of the earth, is not lost on anyone.

But today, amidst ecological despair, we need a counter-narrative. We cannot allow the status quo where one human driven by greed can cut down forests, destroy rivers, and entire ecosystems.

What we need is the belief that another human guided by *dharma,* principles of righteous conduct, can regenerate them. What we need is:

- The businessman who builds without destroying.
- The farmer who cultivates without exploiting.
- The leader who governs with an environmental conscience.

All these are manifestations of *dharma* in action. And they begin with ordinary humans, guided by their sense of righteousness that can bring about a change.

Transforming governance and policy seems ambitious, but transformation begins with thought, and thought begins with us, as individuals.

The path forward is not to wait for change, but to be the change that reclaims our connection with the Earth, again as individuals. The framework exists. The tradition endures. Now, we must find a way to live it.

Sanatan Dharma offers us a way back, not as dogma, but as *dharma*. *Dharma* is not rigid; it is contextual, dynamic, and rooted in balance. Dharma does not offer simplistic commandments, but a compass for navigating complexity. In a dharmic worldview, we are not masters of nature; instead, we are participants in a sacred cosmic dance.

Dharma offers a framework of responsibility, a higher purpose that transcends individual desires and connects people to a greater cause. In contemporary discussions about environmental conservation, the role of spiritually motivated environmentalism needs to be recognised.

We need to weave such values into the fabric of a community's spiritual and religious beliefs, otherwise living them every day would be nearly impossible. No one can lay down their life for a deer or tree to meet a performance metric, but as a principle.

Change will not come from carbon credits. It must come from *dharmic* consciousness.

Sustainability is not just a technological or policy challenge, it is a civilisational imperative that we create for ourselves. The answers we seek do not lie in reinventing the wheel or importing frameworks, but in reviving the timeless principles that have long guided harmonious coexistence with nature.

No one Owns *Prakriti* or Nature

In *Sanatan* thought, no one owns *Prakriti* or Nature.

Prakriti is an expression of divine consciousness, the *param brahm*, the divine creator and the protector of life—the sky, earth, oceans, people and animals. We have no authority over nature. We have only duties and obligations towards all aspects of creation.

The Hindu belief in the cycle of birth, death and rebirth requires Hindus to give all species equal respect and reverence, for they may be reborn as an animal, bird or insect in another life—not just as another human. Even Lord Vishnu's first four incarnations were animals: fish *(Matsya)*, tortoise *(Kurma)*, boar *(Varaha)* and man lion *(Narasimha)* (Nandita Krishnan, 2010).[181]

Sanatan Dharma offers a profound, integrated framework for ecological wisdom, rooted in reverence, balance, and interdependence. While much of the world scrambles to construct new environmental ideologies, India is uniquely positioned. We do not need to borrow a compass; we already possess one. What remains is the courage to align our personal lives, public consciousness, and policy decisions with this *dharmic* vision.

The answer lies in looking at *Sanatan Dharma*—the mother ship of sustainability. It rekindles our lost reverence for the Earth, not as a resource to be exploited, but as a sacred entity worthy of respect and protection. This is the *dharmic* framework that Bharat itself has largely forgotten.

The Earth is not a lifeless object; she is *Bhu Devi*, a living goddess. It is no coincidence that the *Bhumi Suktam* in the *Atharva Veda* has countless verses celebrating the Earth as a living, breathing divine entity—the nourisher of all life—the bearer of truth, strength, and patience. She is the foundation of *dharma*, of rituals, growth, and human aspiration. She holds mountains and rivers, supports the mighty and the meek alike, and gives equally to all who dwell on her.

Bhumi Suktam calls for harmony with trees, herbs, animals, and all beings. It prays that human activity be rooted in balance and respect, not greed. It calls upon the Earth to forgive our trespasses and to accept our offerings, even as she endures our weight and misdeeds. The *Bhumi Suktam* is not just a prayer—it is a reminder of our sacred contract with nature: to live gently, gratefully, and in deep connection with the land that sustains us.

Each verse encapsulates the belief that Earth is not just a physical realm but a divine force that nourishes and sustains all life. It reflects the intimate relationship that ancient cultures maintained with the natural world, seeing the Earth as a living, sentient being deserving of reverence.

May the Earth that bears the weight of all life, of the forests, mountains, rivers, and oceans, be kind to us.

This prayer highlights the Earth's incredible capacity to hold and sustain every form of life, from the smallest insect to the tallest tree, from the deepest ocean to the highest peak. It emphasises that the Earth is a delicate balance of interconnected systems, and when humans disrespect this balance, we invite disaster—not only for the planet but for ourselves. When we pollute the air, destroy forests, or harm animals, we disrupt this natural harmony, and sever our bond with nature. The Earth is not an object to be exploited but a deity to be revered. Every element—soil, water, wind, fire, and space—is sacred.

The Bishnois, through their devotion to nature, have demonstrated that this reverence and responsibility go hand in hand. At its core, conservation is not merely a policy—it is *dharma*. It is the natural order, the eternal duty of every living being. The Bishnoi legacy offers a powerful blueprint for the future. Their villages are greener. Their lands shelter more wildlife. Their customs have preserved life where others have destroyed it. This is not folklore; it is a living, breathing testament to what is possible when human beings see themselves as caretakers, not conquerors.

The question we must ask ourselves is: are we willing to learn from them?

Last Word

If everything written in this book, can be distilled into a single verse, then it is Jambho Ji's *Sabadvaani* which says: to reap good crops, one needs not only water, fertile land and labour—but also good seeds. The deeper meaning is clear: we need good *karmas*.

This resonates strongly with the message from the *Bhagavad Gita*:

अन्नाद्भवन्ति भूतानि पर्जन्यादन्नसम्भवः |
यज्ञाद्भवति पर्जन्यो यज्ञः कर्मसमुद्भवः ||

(*Bhagavad Gita* 3.14)

All living beings subsist on food; food is dependent on rain. Rain is born of sacrifice, and sacrifice arises from the performance of duty.

Life depends on food. Food depends on rain. Rain depends on sacrifice. And sacrifice is born of duty. The story of life has always been cyclical. Seasons change, rivers flow, forests rise and fall—everything moves in harmony.

The survival of our planet depends on whether we choose to honour this sacred cycle—or break it beyond repair. We must return to values, to reverence, to simplicity. We must return to a state where we see not just the planet as alive, but ourselves as part of that aliveness.

Yes, *dharma* can save the environment. But only if we allow it to save us first.

Appendix

Chronology: Salman Khan Vs State of Rajasthan
The details and case chronology are based on the following judgements/orders of Court(s) and newspaper sources, which are freely accessible on the internet:
a. 'State vs Salman Khan' dated 25.07.2016 by the Rajasthan High Court; https://indiankanoon.org/doc/118428326/
b. 'Salman Khan vs State' dated 12.11.2013 by the Rajasthan High Court; https://indiankanoon.org/doc/34001335/
c. 'State of Rajasthan vs Salman Khan' dated 14.01.2015 by the Supreme Court; https://indiankanoon.org/doc/82050546/
d. 'Salman Khan vs State of Rajasthan' dated 21.03.2022 by the Rajasthan High Court; https://indiankanoon.org/doc/159412414/
e. 'Poor enforcement, weak laws make poaching an easy game' dated 05.01.2012 published in the *Down to Earth* website; https://www.downtoearth.org.in/environment/poor-enforcement-weak-laws-make-poaching-an-easy-game-6547

f. A timeline of Salman Khan's blackbuck/chinkara poaching cases' dated 07.04.2018 published on *The Hindu* website; https://www.thehindu.com/news/national/other-states/a-timeline-of-salman-khans-blackbuck-poaching-cases/article23441405.ece

For the shooting of the film *Hum Saath Saath Hain,* actors Salman Khan, Saif Ali Khan, Tabu, Sonali Bendre, Neelam and others were present in Jodhpur in September-October 1998. During their stay in Jodhpur, 3 FIRs were filed against them for 3 incidents of hunting Blackbuck and Chinkaras, the details of which are as follows: There were 4 FIRs filed, the last one was for not having a gun license. Later a license was produced in the court

First Case: Alleged killing of two Chinkaras at Bhavad on 26.09.1998, for which FIR (No.162/1998) was registered on 11.10.1998 at Police Station Mathania, Jodhpur. It resulted in Criminal Case No. 207/1999.

Second Case: Alleged killing of one Chinkara at Ghoda Farms on 28.09.1998, for which FIR (No.163/1998) was registered on 11.10.1998 at P S Mathania, Jodhpur. It resulted in Criminal Case No. 206/1999.

Third Case: Alleged killing of two Blackbuck on the intervening night of 01.10.1998 and 02.10.1998, for which FIR (No.93(26)/1998) was registered on 02.10.1998 with the Forest Department. It resulted in Criminal Case No. 66/2011.

Fourth Case: A fourth FIR (No.180/1998) was filed under The Arms Act, 1959 at P S Luni for using two firearms with expired licenses. It resulted in Criminal Case No. 68/2011. But we will restrict ourselves to the three cases of wildlife crime.

All the evidence was collected during the investigation of

FIR No. 93(26)/1998, the third case. The same was used against the accused in all the 3 cases.

Case Outcome: First Case No. 207/1999

a. Facts as per the FIR and the statement of the sole eyewitness (Harish Dulani) under Section 164, CrPC: Harish Dulani was the driver of the Gypsy on 26.09.1998 but the same was driven by Salman Khan. Satish Shah was sitting next to Salman. One Yashpal and four others were sitting at the back. Salman, on seeing the deer, fired three rounds. He missed the aim twice and managed to hit the deer in the third round. Thereafter, Salman got down and cut the throat of the deer with his knife. On the same night, Salman shot another deer and he cut its throat in the same manner. Both the deer were put into the Gypsy. Thereafter, Salman and Satish were dropped at Ummed Bhawan Palace, while the others went to Hotel Ashirwad. Since everyone was sleeping at Hotel Ashirwad, they went to the house of one Bhanwar Singh, but Bhanwar refused to chop the deer at his house. Thereafter, they came back to Hotel Ashirwad where the killed deer were unloaded and the Gypsy was washed and cleaned the next morning.
b. Trial Court: Accused Salman Khan was convicted for offence under Section 51 of the Wildlife Protection Act, 1972 and sentenced to undergo one year's simple imprisonment, along with a fine of Rs 5,000/- vide judgement and order dated 17.02.2006 passed by Chief Judicial Magistrate, Jodhpur. The Court acquitted the other co-accused.
c. Appeal: Three appeals by (Salman as well as State of Rajasthan) arose out of the above judgement, which were heard together by the Rajasthan High Court (Jodhpur

Bench). The High Court set aside the conviction and sentence awarded to Salman Khan by the Trial Court vide judgement and order dated 25.07.2016.

d. The High Court, bound by the confines of law, arrived at this conclusion based on the following factors, as noted by the High Court in the judgement itself:

- Hurried investigation by the investigating agency due to the pressure to solve the case as quickly as possible.
- Prime witnesses of the prosecution turned hostile.
- Major procedural lapses on part of the prosecution, like not examining the eye-witness Harish Dulani (the sole direct evidence) in Court. As a result, his statement to the Magistrate, under S.164, CrPC, was not considered by the Court as evidence.
- Due to the above-mentioned lapse, the prosecution was left to prove the case only on circumstantial evidence. In cases resting on circumstantial evidence, the prosecution must prove that all the evidences lead 'only' to 'one conclusion' that it was the accused (and no other person) who committed the crime.
- The Court took note of the following lacunae in the chain of evidence adduced by the Prosecution, such as:
- Recovery of blood stains from Gypsy on 07.10.1998, though the Gypsy had been washed before that.
- As per the FSL (Forensic) Report, the blood stains found in the Gypsy were of deer. However, the prosecution failed to prove that the blood stains were of the deer hunted on 26.10.1998.
- Recovery of hair and pellets from Gypsy on 12.10.1998, though the Gypsy was seized and searched on 07.10.1998 itself.

- The Gypsy was sent for FSL examination as late as on 24.10.1998. Also, the Gypsy, itself, was sent for FSL examination instead of just sending the piece of matting where the blood stains were found.
- No documentary evidence (like Malkhana Register) produced to prove the proper custody of Gypsy from 07.10.1998 to 24.10.1998 before it was sent for FSL examination.

Recovery of Weapons and Pellets

Salman Khan's room: Air Rifle/Gun (.22 bore) (Not Firearm); Uday Raghavan: (a) Revolver (.32 bore), (b) Rifle (.22 bore) (Firearm); Saif Ali Khan: Air Rifle/Gun (.22 bore) (Not Firearm).

A .22 Air Gun is not a firearm, and is used for hunting small game like birds, rabbits, squirrels, etc. For killing wild pigs, deer, normally and Air Rifle like .45 and .50 calibre are used.

There was no evidence of the use of either of the weapons recovered from Uday Raghavan. Air Gun .177 pellets recovered from Gypsy could not be used in .22 Air Rifles. Air Gun .22 pellets recovered from Gypsy could be used in either of the 2 Air Guns. So, it could not be established as to which Air Gun was used, whether one belonging to Salman Khan or Saif Ali Khan. 'Single head' pellets were recovered from Gypsy, while 'Double head' pellets were recovered from Salman's room.

- The carcass of the deer was not recovered in this case (but in the third case, where the deer were not loaded in the Gypsy but left at the spot). And hence, there is no medical evidence as to the cause of killing.
- Recovery of blood stains from Hotel Ashirwad: Dried blood stains found on 13.10.1998 (17 days after the hunt) despite the hotel being regularly cleaned during the said period (as

stated by the Hotel sweeper). Also, the person giving the chemical report of blood samples was not examined.
- Staff of the above hotel turned hostile, leaving no evidence of whether the killed deer were brought to the hotel and cooked.
- The only witness produced by the prosecution to prove that cooked meat was brought from Hotel Ashirwad to Ummed Bhawan Palace (Bhanwar Singh) turned hostile in court.

Outcome of Second Case (No. 206/1999):
Trial Court: Accused Salman Khan was convicted under Section 51 of Wildlife Protection Act, 1972 and sentenced to five years' simple imprisonment along with a fine of Rs. 25,000/-vide judgement and order dated 10.04.2006. Appeal to Sessions Court was dismissed. Revision Petition (No. 905/2007) filed before the High Court: The same was admitted by the High Court.

Vide order dated 31.08.2007, the High Court suspended the sentence of Salman and granted bail to him. However, while suspending the sentence, one of the restrictions imposed on him was that he will not leave the country without prior permission of the Court. But the above condition was deleted vide order dated 21.02.2011, passed on an application moved by Salman. The High Court permitted him to travel abroad during the pendency of the Revision Petition.

In the meanwhile, Salman's application for a visa for travelling to the United Kingdom was rejected. As a result, he filed an application for suspension of the order of conviction before the High Court.

Vide order dated 12.11.2013, the High Court allowed the above application of Salman and suspended the order of conviction. The High Court reasoned that his profession requires him to travel abroad, and that he is neither a public servant, nor has he been convicted of any corruption charges.

The State of Rajasthan appealed before the Supreme Court against the above order. The Supreme Court, vide order dated 14.01.2015, set aside the impugned order, as the High Court had not given any finding that if the conviction is not stayed, irreparable harm or irreversible consequences or injustice would be caused to Salman which could not be restored.

Outcome of Third Case (No. 66/2011)

Trial Court: Accused Salman Khan was convicted under Section 9/51 of the Wildlife Protection Act, 1972 and sentenced to five years' imprisonment along with a fine of Rs.10,000/-, vide judgement and order dated 05.04.2018. The co-accused were acquitted of all charges.

Appeal: Two appeals against the above judgement were filed before the Sessions Judge and one Criminal Leave to Appeal was filed before the High Court. The Sessions Judge suspended the sentence during the pendency of the appeal. The High Court, vide order dated 21.03.2022, has transferred all the above appeals before itself to ensure that there is a comprehensive picture of the facts while making the necessary adjudication. The proceedings are ongoing.

Difficulties in Case

1. Witnesses to a wildlife crime are hard to find in the first place. On top of that, the limited number of witnesses turned hostile or absconded in this case. An investigation official said that the cross-examination of witnesses was a mere farce as they denied their own statements given during investigation.

2. Harish Dulani's testimony was a clinching piece of evidence for the Prosecution. The Defence even refused to cross-examine him. But adding to the woes of the Prosecution, he disappeared after his testimony. He did not reply to Court summons, nor could he be traced when a warrant was issued against him. He had written to the Court before his testimony, saying that Khan and his associates were threatening his family.
3. Forest Officials claim that Dulani and others succumbed to either money or muscle. Surprisingly, the first post-mortem report said that the blackbuck died of overeating. It was only when the State Veterinarian examining the carcass was suspended, that the new veterinary team confirmed that the animals had been shot.

363 Martyrs of Khejarli

The massacre that would define Bishnoi history. This list of 363 martyrs, along with their names, name of village and *gotra* was received from the Jambhani Sahitya Akademi, Bikaner. These 363 martyrs laid their lives protecting the Khejri trees. Their names are available on stone edicts at the Khejarli massacre site.

S.No	Name	Family Details	Village
1	Smt Amritadevi Beniwal	W/o Shri Ramoji	Khejarli
2	Kumari Ratni Bai	D/o Shri Ramoji	Khejarli
3	Kumari Asi Bai	D/o Shri Ramoji	Khejarli
4	Kumari Bhagu Bai	D/o Shri Ramoji	Khejarli
5	Shri Ramoji	Unknown	Khejarli
6	Shri Girdhari Ji	S/o Shri Simbhuji	Khejarli
7	Shri Jivanji	S/o Shri Simbhuji	Khejarli
8	Smt Jiyan Baniyal	W/o Shri Girdhari	Khejarli
9	Shri Pithoji	S/o Shri Girdhari	Khejarli
10	Shri Andoji	S/o Shri Girdhari	Khejarli
11	Smt Kani Kalirani	W/o Shri Andoji	Khejarli
12	Kumari Dami	D/o Shri Andoji	Khejarli
13	Kumari Chima	D/o Shri Andoji	Khejarli

14	Kumari Imarti	D/o Shri Andoji	Khejarli
15	Shri Harnathji	S/o Shri Andoji	Khejarli
16	Smt Ladu	W/o Shri Harnathji	Khejarli
17	Shri Samvatji	S/o Shri Harnathji	Khejarli
18	Shri Idoji	S/o Shri Harnathji	Khejarli
19	Shri Khivji	S/o Shri Harnathji	Khejarli
20	Smt Manba Kasvi	W/o Shri Khivji	Khejarli
21	Shri Barjangji	S/o Shri Binjaji	Khejarli
22	Kumari Bhagibai	D/o Shri Barjangji	Khejarli
23	Kumari Sabiyan Bai	D/o Shri Barjangji	Khejarli
24	Shri Chachaji	S/o Shri Barjangji	Khejarli
25	Shri Hariji	S/o Shri Mukanaji	Khejarli
26	Smt Mai Doodan	W/o Shri Mukanaji	Khejarli
27	Shri Akhji	S/o Shri Barjangji	Khejarli
28	Shri Umoji	Unknown	Khejarli
29	Shri Bherji	S/o Shri Durgaji	Khejarli
30	Shri Kalyanji	S/o Shri Motoji	Khejarli
31	Shri Kishanaji	S/o Shri Pemji	Khejarli
32	Shri Shukji	S/o Shri Pemji	Khejarli
33	Shri Isarji	S/o Shri Pemji	Khejarli
34	Shri Magji	S/o Shri Isarji	Khejarli
35	Shri Avoji	S/o Shri Isarji	Khejarli
36	Shri Sunderoji	S/o Shri Isarji	Khejarli
37	Kumari Hirabai	D/o Shri Isarji	Khejarli
38	Shri Hardasji	S/o Shri Kharjoji	Khejarli
39	Smt Kasumbi Khod	W/o Shri Hardasji	Khejarli
40	Shri Karamsingh	S/o Shri Hardasji	Khejarli
41	Shri Kisanji	S/o Shri Dhanji	Khejarli
42	Shri Dedaramji	S/o Shri Bhimji	Khejarli
43	Shri Binjoji	S/o Shri Hiroji	Rasidora
44	Shri Ridmalji	S/o Shri Binjoji	Rasidora
45	Shri Tejoji	S/o Shri Binjoji	Rasidora
46	Shri Keshoji	S/o Shri Kumbhaji	Rasidora
47	Smt Haria Godari	W/o Shri Keshoji	Rasidora

48	Shri Bhagwanji	S/o Shri Keshoji	Rasidora
49	Shri Rasoji	S/o Shri Kaluji	Rasidora
50	Smt Nanra Nain	W/o Shri Rasoji	Rasidora
51	Shri Keshoji	S/o Shri Rasoji	Rasidora
52	Shri Jeshoji	S/o Shri Akoji	Hoon
53	Shri Udoji	S/o Shri Akoji	Hoon
54	Shri Keshoji	S/o Shri Hardasji	Hoon
55	Shri Hemaji	S/o Shri Hardasji	Hoon
56	Shri Loonoji	S/o Shri Natho ji	Hoon
57	Shri Andoji	S/o Shri Natho ji	Hoon
58	Shri Manroopji	S/o Shri Khetaji	Hoon
59	Shri Genoji	S/o Shri Kherajji	Hoon
60	Shri Gokalji	S/o Shri Kherajji	Hoon
61	Shri Pemoji	S/o Shri Jesoji	Hoon
62	Lai Bai	D/o Shri Jesoji	Hoon
63	Shri Sunderoji	S/o Shri Malji	Netada
64	Shri Sajananji	S/o Shri Malji	Netada
65	Shri Biramji	S/o Shri Malji	Netada
66	Shri Dauji	S/o Shri Rupoji	Netada
67	Shri Keshoji	S/o Shri Ramoji	Netada
68	Binji Lol	W/o Shri Samoji	Netada
69	Shri Sadarji	S/o Shri Manoharji	Birani
70	Shri Andoji	S/o Shri Manoharji	Birani
71	Kumari Andubai	D/o Shri Manoharji	Birani
72	Kumari Jiman Bai	D/o Shri Sujoji	Birani
73	Kumari Sukhiya Bai	D/o Shri Manoharji	Birani
74	Shri Jesaji	S/o Shri Dhanoji	Birani
75	Shri Nothoji	S/o Shri Jaswantji	Birani
76	Smt Seri Dhattarwal	W/o Shri Natho ji	Birani
77	Shri Motaji	S/o Shri Natho ji	Birani
78	Shri Kachroji	S/o Shri Karamchandji	Lamba
79	Shri Madmoji	S/o Shri Karamchandji	Lamba
80	Shri Bhojoji	S/o Shri Surjanji	Lamba
81	Shri Panchoji	S/o Shri Surjanji	Fitkasani

82	Shri Rupoji	S/o Shri Panchoji	Fitkasani
83	Shri Budhoji	S/o Shri Asoji	Fitkasani
84	Shri Rugoji	S/o Shri Ladhuji	Fitkasani
85	Shri Bhiyoji	S/o Shri Natho ji	Fitkasani
86	Shri Pithoji	S/o Shri Jasji	Fitkasani
87	Shri Tejoji	S/o Shri Jasji	Fitkasani
88	Shri Lakhoji	S/o Shri Ajoji	Fitkasani
89	Shri Rauji	S/o Shri Ajoji	Fitkasani
90	Shri Sujaan	S/o Shri Ajoji	Fitkasani
91	Shri Jetoji	S/o Shri Gordhanji	Fitkasani
92	Shri Narsingh ji	S/o Shri Gordhanji	Fitkasani
93	Shri Bhiyoji	S/o Shri Kachreji	Fitkasani
94	Shri Pithoji	S/o Shri Bhiyoji	Fitkasani
95	Smt Padma Khod	W/o Shri Pithoji	Fitkasani
96	Shri Nathoji	S/o Shri Bhiyaji	Fitkasani
97	Shri Manoharji	S/o Shri Andoji	Fitkasani
98	Shri Rupoji	S/o Shri Jiyaji	Fitkasani
99	Shri Sabloji	S/o Shri Jiyaji	Fitkasani
100	Shri Bhanwarji	S/o Shri Sujoji	Fitkasani
101	Shri Netiram	S/o Shri Bhanwarji	Fitkasani
102	Shri Manoharji	S/o Shri Bhanwarji	Fitkasani
103	Shri Nohitasji	S/o Shri Jasji	Fitkasani
104	Shri Jetoji	S/o Shri Jasji	Fitkasani
105	Smt Soni Godara	W/o Shri Jetoji	Fitkasani
106	Shri Jagoji	S/o Shri Ramoji	Fitkasani
107	Shri Damoji	S/o Shri Motalji	Guda Bishnoiyan
108	Shri Amroji	S/o Shri Puranji	Guda Bishnoiyan
109	Shri Panchoji	S/o Shri Karamoji	Guda Bishnoiyan
110	Shri Bharmalji	S/o Shri Hariramji	Guda Bishnoiyan
111	Shri Jivrajji	S/o Shri Hariramji	Guda Bishnoiyan
112	Shri Panchoji	S/o Shri Hariramji	Guda Bishnoiyan
113	Shri Lakhoji	S/o Shri Vishnoji	Guda Bishnoiyan
114	Shri Ramoji	S/o Shri Keshoji	Guda Bishnoiyan
115	Shri Karamsingh	Ji S/o Shri Keshoji	Guda Bishnoiyan

116	Shri Narbadji	S/o Shri Saluji	Guda Bishnoiyan
117	Shri Hero	S/o Shri Saluji	Guda Bishnoiyan
118	Shri Keshoji	S/o Shri Saluji	Guda Bishnoiyan
119	Shri Sandu Das ji	S/o Tejoji	Guda Bishnoiyan
120	Shri Devoji	S/o Shri Karamsingh	Guda Bishnoiyan
121	Shri Kuboji	S/o Shri Bhagwanji	Guda Bishnoiyan
122	Shri Lakhoji	S/o Shri Asuji	Guda Bishnoiyan
123	Shri Raymalji	S/o Shri Asuji	Guda Bishnoiyan
124	Shri Hemrajji	S/o Shri Asuji	Guda Bishnoiyan
125	Shri Saindasji	S/o Shri Sadeji	Guda Bishnoiyan
126	Shri Gangaramji	S/o Shri Kherajji	Guda Bishnoiyan
127	Shri Suratannji	S/o Shri Champji	Guda Bishnoiyan
128	Shri Andoji	S/o Shri Champji	Guda Bishnoiyan
129	Chasoda Godara	W/o Shri Chandji	Guda Bishnoiyan
130	Shri Devaraj	S/o Shri Amaraji	Guda Bishnoiyan
131	Shri Jiyogi	S/o Shri Amaraji	Guda Bishnoiyan
132	Smt Keshi Degiyal	W/o Shri Amaraji	Guda Bishnoiyan
133	Shri Champoji	S/o Shri Udoji	Guda Bishnoiyan
134	Shri Rupoji	S/o Shri Netoji	Guda Bishnoiyan
135	Shri Achaloji	S/o Shri Bhojoji	Guda Bishnoiyan
136	Smt Lunga Siyag	W/o Shri Achaloji	Guda Bishnoiyan
137	Smt Binji Siyag	W/o Shri Devaraj	Guda Bishnoiyan
138	Shri Kanwarji	S/o Shri Gordhanji	Guda Bishnoiyan
139	Kumari Hirabai	D/o Shri Gordhanji	Guda Bishnoiyan
140	Shri Danoji	S/o Shri Rugoji	Bhagatsani
141	Shri Baluji	S/o Shri Rugoji	Bhagatsani
142	Shri Harko ji	S/o Shri Viramji	Bhagatsani
143	Shri Lakhoji	S/o Shri Kanwarji	Rudakali
144	Shri Ramji	S/o Shri Akhji	Rudakali
145	Shri Manoji	S/o Shri Akhji	Rudakali
146	Shri Jivrajji	S/o Shri Akhji	Rudakali
147	Shri Kharatoji	S/o Shri Akhji	Rudakali
148	Shri Dasonji	S/o Shri Jagmalji	Rudakali
149	Shri Ramoji	S/o Shri Andoji	Rudakali

150	Shri Sonagji	S/o Shri Khirajji	Rudakali
151	Shri Khumonji	S/o Shri Khirajji	Rudakali
152	Shri Mukanoji	S/o Shri Ratnaji	Rudakali
153	Shri Karamoji	S/o Shri Asoji	Rudakali
154	Shri Manoharji	S/o Shri Khamoja	Rudakali
155	Shri Devji	S/o Shri Asuji	Rudakali
156	Shri Jivanji	S/o Shri Asuji	Rudakali
157	Shri Nagarajji	S/o Shri Bharmal	Rudakali
158	Shri Narsinghji	S/o Shri Madhoji	Rudakali
159	Shri Kishnoji	S/o Shri Kalji	Peethawas
160	Shri Karamsingh	Ji S/o Shri Kalji	Peethawas
161	Shri Damoji	S/o Shri Raichandji	Peethawas
162	Shri Daoji	Shri Jesaji	Peethawas
163	S/o Shri Manoji	S/o Shri Keshoji	Peethawas
164	Smt Kesuji Siyag	W/o Shri Manoji	Ramadawas
165	Shri Devji	S/o Shri Isharji	Ramadawas
166	Shri Jaimalji	S/o Shri Harnathji	Ramadawas
167	Shri Karamchandji	S/o Shri Surtaanji	Ramadawas
168	Shri Suratannji	S/o Shri Hemrajji	Ramadawas
169	Shri Panchoji	S/o Shri Motoji	Ramadawas
170	Shri Kalji	S/o Shri Motoji	Ramadawas
171	Shri Gordhanji	S/o Shri Chokji	Ramadawas
172	Shri Harkoji	S/o Shri Siyanji	Ramadawas
173	Shri Manoji	S/o Shri Rajuji	Ramadawas
174	Shri Meyoji	S/o Shri Hemji	Ramadawas
175	Shri Chokji	S/o Shri Manoharji	Ramadawas
176	Smt Deepa Chahar	W/o Shri Chokji	Ramadawas
177	Shri Jodhramji	Unknown	Ramadawas
178	Shri Dhanrajji	S/o Shri Manoharji	Ramadawas
179	Shri Oopoji	S/o Shri Gordhanji	Feech
180	Smt Rami Godara	W/o Shri Asoji	Feech
181	Shri Sujanji	S/o Shri Sirdarji	Feech
182	Shri Jagtrathji	S/o Shri Simbhuji	Feech
183	Smt Deu Devi	Shri Jagannathji	Feech

184	Shri TejoJi	S/o Shri Dauji	Feech
185	Shri Ugroji	S/o Shri Polaji	Feech
186	Smt Seru Janwar	W/o Shri Polaji	Feech
187	Shri Panchanji	S/o Shri Polaji	Feech
188	Shri Udoji	Shri Keshoji	Feech
189	Smt Ganga	W/o Shri Khetoji	Feech
190	Shri Andoji	S/o Shri Khetoji	Feech
191	Smt Somi Panwar	W/o Shri Khetoji	Feech
192	Shri Sunderoji	S/o Shri Kishnoji	Feech
193	Smt Ida Kaswan	W/o Shri Sunderoji	Feech
194	Shri Jagmalji	S/o Shri Sunderoji	Feech
195	Shri Hemrajji	S/o Shri Sunderoji	Feech
196	Shri Andoji	S/o Shri Sunderoji	Feech
197	Shri Jivrajji	S/o Shri Fatehji	Feech
198	Shri Sanwalji	S/o Shri Bogoji	Feech
199	Shri Sanvatji	S/o Shri Bogoji	Feech
200	Shri Pithoji	Unknown	Dhava
201	Smt Bali Baniyal	W/o Shri Pithoji	Dhava
202	Shri Raichand	Ji S/o Shri Pithoji	Dhava
203	Shri Rupoji	S/o Shri Andoji	Dhava
204	Shri Motoji	S/o Shri Fatehji	Dhava
205	Shri Girdhariji	S/o Shri Jivanji	Dhava
206	Shri Bhaguji	S/o Shri Hemoji	Dhava
207	Shri Andoji	S/o Shri Manji	Dhava
208	Shri Kherajji	S/o Shri Hemji	Doli
209	Shri Devarajji	S/o Shri Hemji	Doli
210	Shri Jiyoji	S/o Shri Andoji	Doli
211	Smt Deepa Khod	W/o Shri Jiyoji	Doli
212	Shri Ratnnoji	S/o Shri Harji	Doli
213	Shri Samelji	S/o Shri Harji	Doli
214	Smt Lado Saharan	W/o Shri Samelji	Doli
215	Shri Harji	S/o Shri Bharmalji	Doli
216	Shri Divrajji	S/o Shri Bharmalji	Doli
217	Shri Khimji	S/o Shri Hirji	Doli

218	Smt Kali Saharan	W/o Shri Khivji	Doli
219	Shri Karamoji	S/o Shri Khivji	Doli
220	Shri Mahesji	S/o Shri Harchandji	Doli
221	Shri Laluji	S/o Shri Bithalji	Doli
222	Shri Ratnoji	S/o Shri Tetaji	Doli
223	Shri Ratnoji	S/o Shri Jitoji	Khadolo
224	Shri Rajuji	S/o Shri Jitoji	Khadolo
225	Shri Magoji	Unknown	Bhavad
226	Shri Savaiji	S/o Shri Mangoji	Bhavad
227	Shri Ajoji	S/o Shri Motoji	Bhavad
228	Smt Sundar Godari	W/o Shri Ajoji	Bhavad
229	Shri Sunderoji	S/o Shri Ajoji	Bhavad
230	Shri Harji	S/o Shri Chaikji	Kosana
231	Shri Bhikhji	S/o Shri Chaikji	Kosana
232	Smt Nabhi Panwar	W/o Shri Bhikhji	Kosana
233	Shri Tikuji	S/o Shri Chaikji	Kosana
234	Shri Dhanji	S/o Shri Bhagwanji	Kosana
235	Shri Tikuji	S/o Shri Bastiji	Kosana
236	Shri Narayanji	S/o Shri Motoji	Kosana
237	Smt Hira Rahad	W/o Shri Narayanji	Kosana
238	Shri Kishnoji	S/o Shri Sajanji	Kosana
239	Shri Sajanji	Unknown	Kosana
240	Shri Gahadji	Unknown	Kosana
241	Shri Shyamji	S/o Shri Simbhuji	Dhoru
242	Smt Nara Dhayanl	W/o Shri Simbhuji	Dhoru
243	Shri Saidas	S/o Shri Rasoji	Dhoru
244	Shri Nathojal	S/o Shri Simrathji	Dhoru
245	Shri Redoji	S/o Shri Simrathji	Dhoru
246	Shri Durgoji	S/o Shri Simrathji	Dhoru
247	Shri Udoji	S/o Shri Hirji	Dohoriyon
248	Shri Jiyaramji	S/o Shri Andoji	Dohoriyon
249	Shri Laloji	S/o Shri Andoji	Dohoriyon
250	Shri Bhauji	S/o Shri Magji	Jalimliya
251	Shri Dedaji	S/o Shri Sujanji	Danwro

252	Smt Bira Dudi	W/o Shri Sujanji	Danwro
253	Shri Sajanji	S/o Shri Asoji	Danwro
254	Shri Kishnoji	S/o Shri Dariyanji	Danwro
255	Shri Bastiji	S/o Shri Champeji	Nandiyan
256	Shri Harchandji	S/o Shri Manoji	Nandiyan
257	Shri Thakarji	S/o Shri Manoji	Nandiyan
258	Shri Ramoji	S/o Shri Amroji	Honguniyan
259	Shri Motoji	S/o Shri Aloji	Tilwasani
260	Shri Karnoji	S/o Shri Aloji	Tilwasani
261	Smt Khinvadevi	Patni Shri Motoji Nain	Tilwasani
262	Shri Panchoji	S/o Shri Binjaji	Tilwasani
263	Smt Damu Nain	W/o Shri Panchoji	Tilwasani
264	Shri Keshoji	S/o Shri Binjaji	Tilwasani
265	Nathi Nain	W/o Keshoji	Tilwasani
266	Shri Khumanji	Unknown	Tilwasani
267	Shri Kirpoji	Unknown	Tilwasani
268	Smt Khivnibai	Unknown	Tilwasani
269	Shri Gopaldasji	Unknown	Tilwasani
270	Thanibai Khokhar	Unknown	Tilwasani
271	Shri Tejoji	S/o Shri Gohadji	Tilwasani
272	Smt Sajni Thalod	W/o Shri Jetoji	Tilwasani
273	Shri Laloji	S/o Shri Dedoji	Tilwasani
274	Shri Hardasji	S/o Shri Dhanji	Tilwasani
275	Shri Amroji	S/o Shri Jibanji	Loowana
276	Shri Dedoji	S/o Shri Narsinghji	Loowana
277	Shri Narayanji	S/o Shri Devarajji	Loowana
278	Shri Durgaji	S/o Shri Motoji	Loowana
279	Shri Ugroji	S/o Shri Nagarajji	Baalle
280	Shri Sadulji	S/o Shri Savji	Baalle
281	Shri Devoji	S/o Shri Ramoji	Baalle
282	Shri Bastiji	S/o Shri Isharji	Joon
283	Shri Birmiji	S/o Shri Isharji	Joon
284	Shri Boroji	S/o Shri Kushaloji	Joon
285	Shri Karnoji	S/o Shri Kushaloji	Joon

286	Shri Mahoji	S/o Shri Kushaloji	Joon
287	Shri Rohitasji	S/o Shri Jasoji	Joon
288	Shri Siyoji	S/o Shri Jasoji	Joon
289	Shri Raichandji	S/o Shri Pithoji	Joon
290	Shri Rupoji	S/o Shri Pithoji	Joon
291	Shri Danoji	S/o Shri Paramchandji	Olvi
292	Shri Choodji	S/o Shri Pujwanji	Olvi
293	Shri Devaraj	S/o Shri Natho ji	Olvi
294	Shri Harichandji	S/o Shri Durgaji	Balla
295	Shri Narsingh	Ji S/o Shri Kumbhoji	Balla
296	Smt Deepa Ravavi	W/o Shri Narsinghji	Balle
297	Shri Choloji	S/o Shri Bharmalji	Joliyali
298	Smt Rekhi Saharan	W/o Rajuji	Joliyali
299	Shri Jagannathji	S/o Shri Ramchandji	Joliyali
300	Smt Asi Visu	W/o Shri Ramchandji	Joliyali
301	Shri Panchanji	Unknown	Joliyali
302	Smt Khemi Saharan	W/o Shri Panchanji	Joliyali
303	Shri Hemrajji	S/o Shri Sameji	Joliyali
304	Shri Madji	S/o Shri Hamrajji	Bisalpur
305	Smt Suwat Dhaki	W/o Shri Hemraj	Bisalpur
306	Shri Sadoji	S/o Shri Gopal	Matoda
307	Shri Bharmal	Ji S/o Shri Champoji	Matoda
308	Shri Badariji	S/o Shri Champoji	Matoda
309	Smt Suji Nain	W/o Shri Bharmalji	Matoda
310	Shri Jesoji	S/o Shri Biramji	Matoda
311	Shri Keshoji	S/o Shri Biramji	Matoda
312	Shri Kishnoji	S/o Shri Sajanji	Badde
313	Shri Ratnoji	S/o Shri Sajanji	Badde
314	Shri Netoji	S/o Shri Rajeji	Hingoli
315	Smt Asi Badiyani	W/o Shri Netoji	Hingoli
316	Shri Motoji	S/o Shri Bharmalji	Hingoli
317	Shri Kushaloji	S/o Shri Jiyoji	Hingoli
318	Shri Dedoji	S/o Shri Keshoji	Hingoli
319	Shri Natho ji	S/o Shri Keshoji	Hingoli

320	Shri Kushaloji	S/o Shri Andoji	Artiya
321	Shri Baluji	S/o Shri Bhagchandji	Artiya
322	Shri Ratnoji	S/o Shri Ganeshji	Artiya
323	Smt Hira Panwar	W/o Shri Ratnoji	Artiya
324	Shri Lakhoji	S/o Shri Harkhoji	Artiya
325	Shri Kanwarji	S/o Shri Ganeshji	Beru
326	Smt Rupa Khod	W/o Shri Kanwarji	Beru
327	Shri Laduji	S/o Shri Guneji	Beru
328	Shri Magoji	S/o Shri Gohadji	Beru
329	Shri Dharajji	Unknown	Jaanglu
330	Shri Hardasji	S/o Shri Davadji	Jaanglu
331	Shri Kishnoji	S/o Shri Hardasji	Jaanglu
332	Shri Ramchandji	S/o Shri Tejoji	Jaanglu
333	Smt Jati	W/o Shri Tejoji	Jaanglu
334	Shri Deidasji	S/o Shri Nathuji	Begariya
335	Shri Akhji	S/o Shri Nathuji	Begariya
336	Shri Natho ji	S/o Shri Karamchandji	Haaniya
337	Shri Natho ji	Unknown	Sirmandi
338	Shri Karamsingh	Unknown	Sirmandi
339	Shri Narsingh	Unknown	Saanwdau
340	Shri Rupoji	S/o Shri Bhagwanji	Pancholi
341	Shri Durgoji	S/o Shri Bhagwanji	Pancholi
342	Shri Ruponji	S/o Shri Dhanji	Burcha
343	Shri Redoji	S/o Shri Poloji	Tabdiya
344	Shri Bhojoji	S/o Shri Poloji	Tabdiya
345	Shri Motoji	S/o Shri Dhanrajji	Tabdiya
346	Shri Maheshji	S/o Shri Ramchandji	Tapoo
347	Shri Andoji	S/o Shri Shankar	Tapoo
348	Shri Keshoji	Unknown	Kudi
349	Shri Tejoji	Unknown	Kudi
350	Shri Champoji	S/o Shri Barjangji	Bhaksarani
351	Shri Motoji	Unknown	Unknown
352	Shri Panchoji	Unknown	Unknown
353	Shri Pithoji	Unknown	Unknown

354	Smt Harkubai	Unknown	Unknown
355	Smt Sundar Bai	Unknown	Unknown
356	Smt Karmi Bai	Unknown	Unknown
357	Smt Gora Bai	Unknown	Unknown
358	Shri Harji	Unknown	Unknown
359	Shri Haroopji	Unknown	Unknown
360	Shri Gugutji	Unknown	Unknown
361	Shri Tejoji	Unknown	Unknown
362	Shri Udoji	Unknown	Unknown
363	Shri Kanoji	Unknown	Unknown

Census of Marwar 1891

Report on the Census of 1891. Volume II, The castes of Marwar. Published by the order of the Marwar Darbar, Jodhpore, 1894. Bishnois are mentioned in Chapter II, on pages 41–42 as a minor agricultural community. The population is estimated to be 40,023 people, largely in the area of Marwar. It is stated that Bishnois were originally Jats, who became Bishnois, under the foundation of their sect by Jambho Ji, who was regarded as an incarnation of Vishnu Ji.

BISHNOI.

The Bishnois have been returned as 40,023 in Marwar. They were originally Jats, and owe the foundation of their sect to Jambhaji, a Punwar Rajput who was born in 1451 A. D. and led the life of an ascetic and a

(42)

celibate. He is said to have performed many miracles. In 1487 when a famine broke-out in Nagor and about 800 Jats were emigrating, he arrived there and with a maund of grain he fed them for three years. This led the conversion of the Jats to Vishnuism, Jambhaji being regarded by them as an incarnation of Vishnu, and hence the origin of the name Bishnoi. Another interpretation of the word is that as the doctrines of the new creed numbered 29 or in other words *bis* (twenty) and *nau* (nine), the adherents of the sect, therefore came to be called as Bishnois.

They are numerous in Marwar only, and have the same clans or subdivisions among them as the Jats. Widows are also allowed to contract *Nata*. Their chief occupation is cultivation and they also keep large number of camels. In their rites and ceremonies they partake of both Hindu and Musalman religion.

The following extract from the Punjab census report of 1881 will fully explain the tenet and practice of the Bishnois:—

"They (Bishnois) abstain entirely from animal food, and have a peculiarly strong regard fo animal life, refusing as a rule to accompany a sporting party, they look upon tobacco as unclean in all its form; they bury their dead at full length, usually at the threshold of the house itself or in adjoining cattle-shed, or in a sitting posture like the Hindu Sanyasis; they shave off the *choti* or scalp-lock; and they usually clothe themselves in wool as being at all times pure. They are more particular about ceremonial purity than even the strictest Hindu, and there is a saying that if a Bishnoi's food is on the first of a string of 20 camels and a man of another caste touch the last camel, the former will throw away his meal. In their marriage ceremonies they mingle Mohamedan with Hindu forms, verses of the Quran being read as well as passages of the *Shastras*, and the *pheras* or circumambulation of the sacred fire being apparently omitted."

References

1. Kumar, S. C. (2024). *From folklore to film: The politics of storytelling and ecological agency in the film Kantara.* Rupkatha Journal, *16*(1). https://doi.org/10.21659/rupkatha.v16n1.17
2. Shiva, V. (2015, September 10). *The food dharma.* Common Dreams. https://www.commondreams.org/views/2015/09/10/food-dharma
3. Guha, R. (2024). *Speaking with nature: The origins of Indian environmentalism.* HarperCollins.
4. Guha, R., & Gadgil, M. (1989). State forestry and social conflict in British India. *Past & Present, 123*(1), 141–177. https://doi.org/10.1093/past/123.1.141
5. Jones, G. (2022). Capitalism and the environment. In C. Casson & P. R. Rössner (Eds.), *Evolutions of capitalism: Historical perspectives, 1200–2000* (pp. 187–211). Bristol University Press.
6. Shiva, V. (Ed.). (1994). *Close to home: Women reconnect ecology, health, and development worldwide.* New Society Publishers.

7. Poor enforcement, weak laws make poaching an easy game. (2012, January 5). *Down to Earth*. https://www.downtoearth.org.in/environment/poor-enforcement-weak-laws-make-poaching-an-easy-game-6547
8. Saini, M. (2015, January 31). *Six convicted in Pataudi blackbuck poaching case*. The Times of India. https://timesofindia.indiatimes.com/india/6-convicted-in-pataudi-blackbuck-poaching-case/articleshow/46073719.cms
9. *Salman convicted: Saif Ali Khan's father Mansur Pataudi had too killed blackbuck using daughter Soha's gun*. (2018, April 5). India Today. https://www.indiatoday.in/india/story/salman-convicted-saif-ali-khan-s-father-mansur-pataudi-had-too-killed-blackbuck-using-daughter-soha-s-gun-1205340-2018-04-05
10. Salman Khan death threat: Notorious gangster Lawrence Bishnoi says will kill Bollywood actor https://www.financialexpress.com/india-news/salman-khan-death-threat-notorious-gangster-lawrence-bishnoi-says-will-kill-bollywood-actor/1005159/
11. Who is Lawrence Bishnoi, the gangster at the centre of India-Canada spat? https://www.aljazeera.com/news/2024/10/16/who-is-lawrence-bishnoi-the-gangster-at-the-centre-of-india-canada-spat
12. Kashyap, H. (2016, November 24). *You are a blackbuck horn away from jail*. Bangalore Mirror. https://bangaloremirror.indiatimes.com/bangalore/others/you-are-a-blackbuck-horn-away-from-jail/articleshow/55588356.cms
13. *Hiran ka maans, 150 rupees mein*. (2017, November 15). Rajasthan Patrika.

14. Chaudhry, P. (2011). *Prosopis cineraria (L.) Druce: A life line tree species of the Thar Desert in danger. Journal of Biodiversity and Ecological Sciences, 1*, 289–293.
15. Chaudrary, R. (2024, September). *Barmer deer hunting case: Venison meat demand reason explained. Dainik Bhaskar.* https://www.bhaskar.com/local/rajasthan/jaipur/news/hotel-owners-buy-deer-meat-at-three-times-the-profit-133482568.html
16. *This nature-loving sect in India dragged one of the world's biggest movie stars to court—and won.* (2018, May 17). *Los Angeles Times.* https://www.latimes.com/world/asia/la-fg-india-conservationist-sect-20180517-htmlstory.html
17. Ghose, I. (2025, March 23). *History & wildlife meet @ Nara's Deer Park. Deccan Herald.* https://www.deccanherald.com/lifestyle/travel/history-wildlife-meet-naras-deer-park-3456360
18. Choudhary, N., & Chisty, N. (2022). Behavioural biology and ecology of blackbuck (*Antelope cervicapra*): A review. *Flora and Fauna, 28.* https://doi.org/10.33451/florafauna.v28i2pp355-361
19. Sarita, Dave, S., & Parihar, G. R. (2021). Ecological assemblage and behavioural patterns by blackbuck in semi-arid areas of Thar. *Bulletin of Environment, Pharmacology and Life Sciences, 10*(5), 10–14.
20. Ahmad, Z., Bashir, M., Fahid, A., Khan, A., & Bibi, A. (2023). Feeding ecology of reintroduced blackbucks in Lal Suhanra National Park. *Journal of Bioresource Management, 10*(2), 175–190.
21. Ranjitsinh, M. K. (1997). *Beyond the tiger: Portraits of Asian wildlife.* Brijbasi.
22. Gehlot, H., & Moolaram. (2017). Involvement of

Bishnoi community for biodiversity conservation in desert landscape of Rajasthan (India).

23. Sinha, B. L. (n.d.). *The Bishnois of Western Rajasthan.* Sahapedia. https://www.sahapedia.org/the-bishnois-of-western-rajasthan

24. Wadhawan, D. A. (2025, March 3). *Protesters demand arrested deer hunters' parading, throw stones at police station.* India Today. https://www.indiatoday.in/india/story/deer-hunters-arrested-protesters-parading-stones-bajju-police-station-bikaner-rajasthan-bishnois-2687943-2025-03-03

25. Parmar, A. (2014, January 31). *Five lakh reward for kin of Bishnoi who fought poachers.* The Times of India. https://timesofindia.indiatimes.com/city/jaipur/rs-5-lakh-for-kin-of-bishnoi-who-fought-poachers/articleshow/29632406.cms

26. Gehlot, Hemsingh & Moolaram. (2017). Involvement of Bishnoi Community for Biodiversity Conservation in Desert landscape of Rajasthan (India)

27. *Press Information Bureau (PIB).* (2001, August 24). *Shaurya Chakra Award (posthumously) to wildlife lover Late Shri Ganga Ram Bishnoi.* Government of India. https://archive.pib.gov.in/archive/releases98/lyr2001/raug2001/24082001/r2408200117.html

28. Pankaj Jain, 2016, *Dharma and Ecology of Hindu Communities: Sustenance and Sustainability,* Routledge

29. Ayers Butler, R. (2025, May 24). *Radheshyam Bishnoi, protector of India's wildlife, died on May 24, 2025, aged 28. Mongabay News.* https://news.mongabay.com/short-article/2025/05/radheshyam-bishnoi-protector-of-indias-wildlife-died-on-may-24-2025-aged-28

30. *Sanctuary Wildlife Awards 2021.* (2021). *Sanctuary Nature Foundation.* https://sanctuarynaturefoundation.org/article/the-sanctuary-wildlife-awards-2021
31. *Radheshyam Bishnoi leaves behind legacy of Great Indian Bustard conservation: Jaisalmer won't forget.* (2025, May 26). *The Print.* https://theprint.in/environment/radheshyam-bishnoi-leaves-behind-legacy-of-great-indian-bustard-conservation-jaisalmer-wont-forget/2637925/
32. Sohel, A., & Naz, F. (2024). The Bishnoi: Revisiting religious environmentalism and traditional forest and wildlife management in the Thar Desert. *Environment & Society Portal, Arcadia (Summer 2024),* no. 10. Rachel Carson Center for Environment and Society.
33. Bikku, D. (2018). *Climate change and culture of conservation among the Bishnois of Rajasthan, India.*
34. Pankaj Jain, 2016, *Dharma and Ecology of Hindu Communities: Sustenance and Sustainability,* Routledge, Pp 65
35. Mangilal. (2020). Bishnoi movement of Khejarli: A socio-cultural analysis. *International Journal of Advanced Research,* 8, 381–383. https://doi.org/10.21474/IJAR01/11109
36. Sunderlal Bahuguna: The man who taught India to hug trees. *BBC World News Asia.* 21 May 2021 Soutik Biswas India. https://www.bbc.com/news/world-asia-india-57171363
37. Vandana Shiva, *Staying Alive Women, Ecology and Survival in India,* 2009 Women Unlimited pp 67
38. Wangari Maathai, *Replenishing the Earth: Spiritual Values for Healing Ourselves and the World.* Deckle Edge, 14 September 2010 pp75

39. Bishnoi - Green Warriors of Thar, Prasar Bharti Archives, Premiered on 24 Jul 2022, https://youtu.be/x0294sOtHfw
40. Willing To Sacrifice, documentary by Yamini Films. Directed by Papa Rao Biyyala. Screened at Indian Panorama 1999. https://youtu.be/xlZxMNmFm1Q
41. Neekee Chaturvedi, *Cultural Tourism and Bishnois of Rajasthan,* 2018 pp 34-35
42. *Faunal Heritage of Rajasthan: General Background and Ecological Vertebrae.* Ed. Dr B.K. Sharma et al. Springer New York 2013
43. Film to be made on 363 Bishnoi community members, martyred 282 years ago. *Times of India,* June 6, 2013. https://timesofindia.indiatimes.com/city/jaipur/film-to-be-made-on-363-bishnoi-community-members-martyred-283-years-ago/articleshow/20452952.cms
44. 9 दसिंबर को रिलीज मूवी साको 363 का पहला टीजर पीपासर में दिखाया. *Dainik Bhaskar,* Nagor, Rajasthan. https://www.bhaskar.com/local/rajasthan/nagaur/news/the-first-teaser-of-the-movie-sako-363-releasing-on-9-december-was-shown-in-pipasar-134144704.html
45. Karmakar, G., Pal, P. Examining (in)justice, environmental activism and indigenous knowledge systems in the Indian film Kantara (Mystical Forest). *Socio Ecol Pract Res* 6, 117–130 (2024). https://doi.org/10.1007/s42532-024-00180-2
46. Forest Religion vs Desert Religion | Wisdom Sutra EP 3 with Rajiv Malhotra. Infinity Foundation Official, Premiered on 18 Jul 2022. https://youtu.be/pML4y-wB9HI?si=6b8ftwdneiM9bNA2

47. Biswas, S., & Rao, L. (2022). The guru, the community and environmental ethics. *The Review of Contemporary Scientific and Academic Studies*, 2. https://doi.org/10.55454/rcsas.2.5.2022.006
48. Bishnoi, P. R. (2018). *Guru Jambhoji and Sabadvaani*. Jambhani Sahitya Akademi.
49. Bikku, Dr (2018). *Climate change and culture of conservation among the Bishnois of Rajasthan,* India
50. Bishnoi, K. R., & Bishnoi, N. R. (Eds.). (2002). *Religion and environment* (Vol. II). Arihant Prakashan Pvt. Ltd.
51. Chaudhary, M. (2022). Jambhoji and environment protection. In O. P. Jai Narain (Ed.), *Jambhani darshan avam paryavarn* (pp. 23–28). Jai Narain Vyas University.
52. Mangilal 2020, *Bishnoi movement of Khejarli,* a socio-cultural analysis. International Journal of Advanced Research. 381-383. Doi 10.21474/IJAR01/11109
53. Alam, Khabirul & Halder, Ujjwal, 2018, *A Pioneer of Environmental Movements in India: Bishnoi Movement.* 8. 283-287.
54. Mishra, S. A. (2022). Human relationship with nature, technology, and importance of Jambhani philosophy for environmental protection. In O. P. Jai Narain (Ed.), *Jambhani darshan avam paryavarn* (pp. 198–200). Jai Narain Vyas University.
55. Bikku, Dr (2018). Climate change and culture of conservation among the Bishnois of Rajasthan, India
56. Acharya, S. B. (n.d.). *Shabadwaani.* Shri Jambeshwar Jajiwaal Dhora, Bishnoi Printing Press.
57. Prithwi Raj Bishnoi, *Guru Jambhoji and Sabadvaani,* Jambhani Sahitya Akademi, Bikaner, 2018, p. 29

58. *World Giving Index 2024.* (2024). Charities Aid Foundation. https://www.cafonline.org/home/world-giving-index
59. *How the world's richest Hindu temple earns and spends money.* (2024, April 26). *The Economic Times.* https://economictimes.indiatimes.com/news/india/how-the-worlds-richest-hindu-temple-earns-and-spends-money/articleshow/109629750.cms
60. Raghvan, S. (2024, April 16). *TTD receives 1031 kgs of gold worth ₹773 crore as donations in 2023. The Times of India.* https://timesofindia.indiatimes.com/city/amaravati/ttd-receives-1031-kg-gold-worth-rs-773-crore-as-donations-in-2023/articleshow/109351731.cms
61. *Ayodhya Ram Mandir: The cost and the funding.* (2024, January 25). *The Hindu Business Line.* https://www.thehindubusinessline.com/data-stories/data-focus/ayodhya-ram-mandir-the-cost-and-the-funding/article67748796.ece
62. *Hindu temple in India receives record one-day donations.* (2012, April 2). *BBC News.*
63. *Ram Temple Trust pays ₹400 crore in taxes over past five years.* (2025, March 16). *The Economic Times.* https://economictimes.indiatimes.com/news/india/ram-temple-trust-pays-rs-400-crore-in-taxes-over-past-five-years/articleshow/119081199.cms
64. Bharti, J., Sahota, R., Parveen, S., & Sharma, A. (2023). From tradition to troubles: Evaluating the consumption of opium as social practice in Western Rajasthan. *Journal of Drug and Alcohol Research, 12,* Article ID 236236. https://doi.org/10.4303/JDAR/236236

65. Maheshwari, H. (2011). *Shri Jambhoji aur Jambhvaani Mimamsa.* Shri Guru Jambheshwar Sahitya Sabha. ISBN 978-81-921682-0-3
66. *Agony of Indigo Cultivators.* (2017). National Council for Science Museums. https://indianculture.gov.in/video/agony-indigo-cultivators
67. Bhattacharya, S. (1977). The Indigo Revolt of Bengal. *Social Scientist, 5*(12), 13–23. https://doi.org/10.2307/3516809
68. Le, N. (2020, July 20). *The impact of fast fashion on the environment.* Princeton Student Climate Initiative. https://psci.princeton.edu/tips/2020/7/20/the-impact-of-fast-fashion-on-the-environment
69. *The story of India's gold.* (2020, December 13). *Al Jazeera.* https://www.aljazeera.com/features/2020/12/13/indigo-and-the-story-of-indias-blue-gold
70. Prithwi Raj Bishnoi, Guru Jambhoji and Sabadvaani, Jambhani Sahitya Akademi, Bikaner, 2018, p. 29
71. *Shabadwaani,* Swami Bhagirathdas Acharya, Shri Jambeshwar Jajiwaal Dhora, Bishnoi Printing Press. Jodhpur
72. Beck, G. L. (2012). *Sonic liturgy: Ritual and music in Hindu tradition.* University of South Carolina Press.
73. Rastogi, V., Krishnanand, S., & Panwar, R. B. (2022). Quality analysis, antibacterial activity, and chemical characterization of ethnobotanical (Hawan) medicinal fumes. *Interdisciplinary Journal of Yagya Research, 5*(1).
74. Kapoor, V., Belk, R., & Goulding, C. (2022). Ritual revision during a crisis: The case of Indian religious rituals during the COVID-19 pandemic. *Journal of Public Policy & Marketing, 41*(3), 277–297. https://doi.org/10.1177/07439156221081485

75. Sanu, U. S., & Vernekar, S. S. (2023). Role of Agnihotra in maternal and child healthcare: A narrative review. *Indian Journal of Ayurveda and Integrative Medicine (KLEU)*, 4(2), 41–46. https://doi.org/10.4103/ijaim.ijaim_30_23
76. Bansal P, Kaur R, Gupta V, Kumar S, Kaur R. Is There Any Scientific Basis of Hawan to be used in Epilepsy-Prevention/Cure? *Journal of Epilepsy Res.* 2015 Dec 31;5(2):33-45. doi: 10.14581/jer.15009. PMID: 26819935; PMCID: PMC4724851.
77. Nilachal N, Trivedi P. A case study of the effect of Yagya on the level of stress and anxiety. *Interdisciplinary Journal of Yagya Research.* 2019;2(2). doi:10.36018/ijyr.v2i2.44
78. Golechha GR, Deshpande M, Sethi IC, Singh RA. Agnihotra - a useful adjunct in recovery of a resistant demotivated smack addict. *Indian Journal of Psychiatry.* 1987 Jul;29(3):247-52. PMID: 21927247; PMCID: PMC3172482.
79. Dwivedi, O. P. (2003). *"Satyagraha for conservation: Awakening the spirit of Hinduism."*
80. Russell, R. V. (1873-1915). *The tribes and castes of the Central Provinces of India.* Pp. 34.
81. Pankaj Jain, *2016, Dharma and Ecology of Hindu Communities: Sustenance and Sustainability Routledge, Pp 53*
82. Khan, Conversions and Shifting Identities: Ramdev Pir and the Ismailies in Rajasthan, 1997, Dominique-Sila Khan. Manohar Publishing pp187
83. Kumar, U. (2025). *Eminent historians: Twists and truths in Bharat's history.* Blue One Ink.
84. Khan, Conversions and Shifting Identities: Ramdev Pir

and the Ismailies in Rajasthan, 1997, Dominique-Sila Khan. Manohar Publishing pp204
85. *Tribute: Dominique Sila-Khan.* (2016, November). *Islamic Voice.* https://islamicvoice.com/people/tribute-dominique-sila-khan
86. Oommen, M. A. (2021). Beasts in the garden: Human–wildlife coexistence in India's past and present. *Frontiers in Conservation Science, 2*, 703432. https://doi.org/10.3389/fcosc.2021.703432
87. Pankaj Jain, 2016, *Dharma and Ecology of Hindu Communities: Sustenance and Sustainability,* Routledge, Pp 56
88. Khan, Conversions and Shifting Identities: Ramdev Pir and the Ismailies in Rajasthan, 1997, Dominique-Sila Khan. Manohar Publishing pp204
89. Khan, Conversions and Shifting Identities: Ramdev Pir and the Ismailies in Rajasthan, 1997, Dominique-Sila Khan. Manohar Publishing pp204
90. Hall, J. C., & Chhangani, A. K. (2015). Cultural tradition and wildlife conservation in the human-dominated landscape of rural Western Rajasthan, India. Indian Forester, vol. 141, no. 10, pp. 1011–1019, Oct. 2015
91. Hall, J. (2010). *Distribution of Prosopis cineraria on agricultural farmland in Western Rajasthan: Ecological and economic impacts of Bishnoi community-based conservation.*
92. Hall, J. C., & Hamilton, I. M. (2014). Religious tradition of conservation associated with greater abundance of a keystone tree species in rural Western Rajasthan, India, *Journal of Arid Environments, 103*, 11-

16. https://doi.org/10.1016/j.jaridenv.2013.12.007
93. Chaturvedi, N. (2018). *Cultural tourism and Bishnois of Rajasthan.* Rajasthani Granthagar.
94. Reichert, A. (n.d.). *Sacred trees, sacred deer, sacred duty to protect: Exploring relationships between humans and nonhumans in the Bishnoi community.* (Master's thesis). University of Ottawa.
95. Pankaj Jain, 2016, *Dharma and Ecology of Hindu Communities: Sustenance and Sustainability,* Routledge, Pp 61
96. M.K Ranjitsinh, *Beyond the Tiger, Portraits of Asian Wildlife, Brijbasi,* 1997, pp 54
97. Mukul, S. (2024, October 15). Why blackbucks are so dear to Bishnoi community. *India Today.* https://www.indiatoday.in/india/story/lawrence-bishnoi-rajasthan-bollywood-salmankhan-why-blackbucks-chinkara-important-for-bishnoi-community-2616720-2024-10-15
98. Khan, H. (2018, August 20). Till the last deer is saved. *The Indian Express.* https://indianexpress.com/article/india/india-news-india/till-the-last-deer-is-saved-2974563/
99. *Bishnois worship the blackbuck like JambhaJi.* (2006, February 22). *The Times of India.* https://timesofindia.indiatimes.com/india/bishnois-worship-black-bucks-as-jambaji/articleshow/1423823.cms
100. Hall, J. C. (2011). *Ecological dynamics of vultures, blackbuck antelope, khejri trees, and the Bishnoi people in Western Rajasthan, India* [Doctoral dissertation, Ohio State University]. OhioLink Electronic Theses and Dissertations Center.

101. Hall, J. (2010). *Distribution of Prosopis cineraria on agricultural farmland in Western Rajasthan: Ecological and economic impacts of Bishnoi community-based conservation.*
102. Jambhani Darshan Avam Paryavarn, 2022. Editor Dr Om Prakash. Chapter: Prosopis the 'Kalpvriksha of desert' and its role in sustainable development. pp 179-182 Monika Sharma and Rachana Dinesh. Jai Narain Vyas University (Ed.). (2022). *Jambhani darshan avam paryavarn.* Jai Narain Vyas University.
103. Shiva, V. (2012). *Monocultures of the mind.* Natraj Publishers.
104. Veena, A., Singh, A., & Bathla, N. (2021). *Territories of life: 2021 report.* ICCA Consortium. https://report.territoriesoflife.org
105. Gehlot, H., & Moolaram. (2017). *Involvement of Bishnoi community for biodiversity conservation in desert landscape of Rajasthan (India).*
106. Pankaj Jain, *2016, Dharma and Ecology of Hindu Communities: Sustenance and Sustainability,* Routledge, Pp 53
107. Shougrakpam, D. et al. (2024). Sacred groves of Rajasthan through folkloric beliefs: An overview. *International Journal for Multidisciplinary Research.* E-ISSN: 2582-2160.
108. Murugesan, A. (2016). *Sacred groves of India: An overview.* 3, 64-74.
109. Malhotra, K. C. (1998). Anthropological dimensions of sacred groves in India: In P. S. Ramakrishnan, K. G. Saxena & U. M. Chandrashekara (Eds.), *Conserving the sacred for biodiversity management* (pp. 423-438).

Oxford & IBH Publishing Co.
110. Deshmukh, S. (1999). *Conservation and development of sacred groves in Maharashtra – Final report of the World Bank aided Maharashtra Forestry Project* (289 pp.). BNHS, Mumbai.
111. Jamir, S. A., & Pandey, H. N. (2003). Vascular plant diversity in the sacred groves of Jaintia Hills in Northeast India. *Biodiversity and Conservation, 12*, 1497-1510. http://dx.doi.org/10.1023/A:1023682228549
112. Kandari, L. S., Bisht, V. K., Bhardwaj, M., et al. (2014). Conservation and management of sacred groves, myths and beliefs of tribal communities: A case study from North India. *Environmental Systems Research, 3*(1), 16. https://doi.org/10.1186/s40068-014-0016-
113. Murugesan, A. (2016). *Sacred groves of India: An overview.* 3, 64-74.
114. Barik, S., Gogoi, R., Kharbih, S. H., Roy Suchiang, B., Nonghuloo, I., Adhikari, D., Upadhaya, K., Malhotra, K., & Tripathi, R. (2018). Assessment of ecosystem services from sacred groves of India.
115. Murugesan, Amirthalingam. (2016). Sacred groves of India - An Overview. 3. 64 - 74
116. Murugesan, A. (2019). *Plant and animal diversity in Valmiki's Ramayana.*
117. Rock shelters of Bhimbetka: Continuity through antiquity, art & environment. (2003). Excerpt from the report of the 27th Session of the World Heritage Committee, Archaeological Survey of India.
118. Lutgendorf, P. (2001). *City, forest and cosmos: Ecological perspectives from the Sanskrit epics.* In C. Chapple & M. E. Key (Eds.), *Hinduism and ecology* (pp. ...). Oxford

119. Murugesan, Amirthalingam. (2019). Plant and Animal Diversity in Valmiki's Ramayan
120. Rawat, S. K., & Vashishtha, A. (2019). Philosophy of some hymns of Vedas and Puranas in relation to environmental status. *International Journal of Advanced Academic Studies, 1*(1), 222-224.
121. Jain, S., & Kapoor, S. (2007). *Divine botany – universal and useful but under-explored traditions.*
122. Debroy, B. (2011). *The Mahabharata: Volume 3.* Penguin Books.
123. Krishna, N. (Ed.). (2005). *Ecological traditions of Tamil Nadu.* CPR Publications.
124. Ghai, R. (2024, October). Iralai Maan: How blackbuck featured in Sangam literature. *Down to Earth.* https://www.downtoearth.org.in/wildlife-biodiversity/iralai-maan-how-blackbuck-featured-in-sangam-literature
125. Supreme Court of India. (2024, December 18). T.N. Godavarman Thirumulpad vs. Union of India. https://indiankanoon.org/doc/94069814/
126. *Sharad Krishi Magazine.* (2017, January).
127. RFI. (2012, March 3). *Khamu Ram Bishnoi: A Bishnoi in Paris.* https://www.rfi.fr/fr/emission/20120303-1-reportage-khamu-ram-bishnoi-bishnoi-paris-rediffusion
128. *7 साल की बच्ची का योग.* (2022, June 20). *Dainik Bhaskar.* https://www.bhaskar.com/local/rajasthan/jodhpur/news/fatherscolded-when-i-saw-yoga-learned-from-youtube-in-theroom-129961434.html
129. ABP Live. (2024, June 15). 9-year-old Parineeti becomes yoga guru at the age of 9 and gave tips to CM Bhajanlal

Sharma. https://www.abplive.com/photo-gallery/states/rajasthan-jodhpur-parineeti-bishnoi-became-a-yoga-guru-at-the-age-of-9-also-gave-tips-to-cm-bhajanlal-sharma-ann-2715531

130. The Better India. (2018, December 18). This roadside mechanic from Rajasthan has rescued over 1,180 injured wild animals. https://thebetterindia-com.translate.goog/167113/rajasthan-hero-animal-rescue-wildlife-inspiring-india/

131. *Vice President of India, Shree Venkaiah Naidu felicitates 'RBS Earth Heroes'.* (2018, November 1). *Business This Week.* https://businessnewsthisweek.com/national/vice-president-of-india-shree-venkaiah-naidu-felicitates-rbs-earth-heroes/

132. Luthra, S., & Sinha (n.d.). *Conservation politics in the Thar: The case of the Bishnoi Tiger Force.* (2014, 2016).

133. Budhnagar, R. N. (2018, November 12). In conversation with Ram Niwas Budhnagar of the Bishnoi Tiger Force (BTF) *Sahapedia.* https://www.youtube.com/watch?v=zJl5_OI6axA

134. Luthra, Sinha 2020. *In defence of the endangered black buck: Bishnois of India raise the stakes for hunters and poachers.* (n.d.). Paper presented at the Inter-Congress of the International Union for Anthropological and Ethnographic Sciences (IUAES).

135. *SC/ST act being used for blackmail, says Supreme Court.* (2018, March 21). *The Hindu.* https://www.thehindu.com/news/national/scst-atrocities-act-has-become-a-means-to-blackmail-citizens-public-servants-sc/article23303970.ece

136. Anand, S. (2023, December 20). India attracts $6.1

billion FDI in renewable sector, boosting green power drive. *ET Energy World.* https://energy.economictimes.indiatimes.com/news/renewable/india-attracts-6-1-billion-fdi-in-renewable-sector-boosting-green-power-drive/106138553

137. *Rajasthan shines as India's solar power hub.* (2024, October 20). *The Financial Express.* https://www.financialexpress.com/business/industry/rajasthan-shines-as-indias-solar-power-hub/3644887/

138. Iqbal, M. (2022, July 11). Villagers stir against solar plants, protect khejri trees. *The Hindu.* https://www.thehindu.com/news/states/villagers-stir-against-solar-plants-protects-khejri-trees/article65625082.ece

139. *NGT asks solar firm to plant 10 times trees cut by them for Rajasthan plant.* (2022, October 24). *The Economic Times.* https://energy.economictimes.indiatimes.com/news/renewable/ngt-asks-solar-firm-to-plant-10-times-trees-cut-by-them-for-rajasthan-plant/95064709

140. *Locals protest govt decision to cut down 100 000 trees for power plant in Rajasthan's Baran.* (2024, October 9). *ETV Bharat.* https://www.etvbharat.com/en/!state/locals-protest-govt-decision-to-cut-down-1-lakh-trees-for-power-plant-in-rajasthan-s-baran-enn24100900663

141. *HC directs Rajasthan Govt and Centre to decide on Baran project.* (2025, May 1). *The Times of India.* https://timesofindia.indiatimes.com/city/jaipur/hc-directs-centre-raj-to-decide-on-baran-pumped-storage-project/articleshow/120774707.cms

142. Dookia, S. (n.d.). Interview with Dr Sumit Dookia, Associate Professor, University School of Environment Management at GGS Indraprastha University.

143. Aggarwal, M. (2017, August 23). Govt eases environment-clearance rules for solar projects. *The Mint*. https://www.livemint.com/Politics/QW4cJ9yjhmvUtOZCPyOt3J/Govt-eases-environment-clearance-rules-for-solar-projects.html
144. Ranjitsingh, M. K. (n.d.). Speech by Dr M K Ranjitsingh (IAS, Retd.), Former Director, Wildlife Preservation of India: International Conference at SCDR, JNU with Jambhani Sahitya Academy II Inaugural Session, Part 5 https://www.youtube.com/watch?v=n4cXBl0CQ6Y
145. Bothra, D. (2023, April 12). Bishnois raise concern over felling of khejri trees. *Hindustan Times*. https://www.hindustantimes.com/cities/jaipur-news/protests-erupt-as-solar-companies-destroy-thousands-of-trees-in-rajasthan-including-state-tree-khejri-for-renewable-energy-projects-101681309991923.html
146. Mahapatra, D. (2025, April 2). NGOs can't stall every project citing ecological concern. *The Times of India*. http://timesofindia.indiatimes.com/articleshow/119888896.cms
147. Expert Committee. (2021). *Compensatory conservation in India: An analysis of the science, policy and practice report submitted to the Hon'ble Supreme Court by the 7-Member Expert Committee pursuant to the directions dated 25 March 2021 in Special Leave Petition (Civil) No. 25047 of 2018*. (Report).
148. *M.K. Ranjitsinh vs Union of India* (2024, March 21). Supreme Court of India. https://indiankanoon.org/doc/128036238/
149. Manav, S. (2013, July 7). Death of three blackbucks sparks protests in Fatehabad. *The Tribune*. https://www.

tribuneindia.com/2013/20130708/haryana.htm#1
150. *Blade-wire fencing, blackbuck death trap, banned in Fatehabad.* (2015, January 9). *The Tribune.* https://www.tribuneindia.com/news/archive/governance/blade-wire-fencing-blackbuck-death-trap-banned-in-fatehabad-27837/
151. *Badopal blackbuck habitat would be the first owned habitat by the state government.* (n.d.). https://prharyana.gov.in/en/haryana-forest-and-environment-minister-sh-kanwar-pal-said-that-187-acres-of-land-of-nuclear-power-No-IPRDH/2023
152. *Haryana to transfer 187 acres to forest dept for blackbuck conservation.* (2023, July 27). *Hindustan Times.* https://www.hindustantimes.com/cities/chandigarh-news/haryana-forest-minister-transfers-land-for-blackbuck-conservation-plans-forest-research-institute-in-yamunanagar-101690402288990.html
153. *Richest 1 % account for more carbon emissions than poorest 66 %.* (2023, November 20). *The Guardian.* https://www.theguardian.com/environment/2023/nov/20/richest-1-account-for-more-carbon-emissions-than-poorest-66-report-says
154. Khalfan, A., Nilsson, L., Aguilar, A., Lawson, C., Jayoussi, M., Persson, S., Dabi, J., & Acharya, S. (2023). *Climate equality: A planet for the 99 %. Oxfam International.* https://doi.org/10.21201/2023.000001
155. *Did people have to fly to COP29? Private jet use soared, but one group got to Baku overland.* (2024, November 15). *Euronews.* https://www.euronews.com/green/2024/11/15/did-people-have-to-fly-to-cop29-private-jet-use-soared-but-one-group-got-to-baku-overland

156. *How many private jets were at COP27?* (2022, November 9). BBC News. https://www.bbc.com/news/63544995?
157. Massive stretch of Amazon rainforest destroyed for upcoming COP30 climate summit. (2025, March 12). *New York Post*. https://nypost.com/2025/03/12/world-news/amazon-rainforest-destroyed-to-build-road-for-climate-summit/
158. Amazon forest felled to build road for climate summit. (2025). BBC News. https://www.youtube.com/watch?v=DYtmc2JPIfM
159. Shiva, V. (2012). *Monocultures of the mind*. Natraj Publishers. (p. 151)
160. White, L., Jr. (1967). The historical roots of our ecological crisis. *Science, 155*, 1203-1207.
161. Maathai, W. (2010, September 14). *Replenishing the Earth: Spiritual values for healing ourselves and the world*. Deckle Edge. (pp. 95-96)
162. LeVasseur, T., & Peterson, A. (Eds.). (2018). *Religion and ecological crisis: The 'Lynn White Thesis' at fifty*. Routledge.
163. Afzaal, A. (2012). Disenchantment and the environmental crisis: Lynn White Jr., Max Weber, and Muhammad Iqbal. *Worldviews: Global Religions, Culture and Ecology, 16*, 239-262. https://doi.org/10.1163/15685357-01603004
164. Toynbee, A. J. (1974). The religious background of the present environmental crisis. In *Ecology and religion in history* (pp. 137-149). Harper & Row.
165. Sadowski, R. F. (2024). Roots of (and solutions to) our ecological crisis: A humanistic perspective. *Ecological Civilization, 1*(1), 10001. https://doi.org/10.35534/

ecolciviliz.2023.10001

166. Shellenberger, M. (2019, August 20). The real reason they behave hypocritically on climate change is because they want to. *Forbes.* https://www.forbes.com/sites/michaelshellenberger/2019/08/20/the-real-reason-they-behave-hypocritically-on-climate-change-is-because-they-want-to/

167. Sadowski, R. F. (2020). On religious and cultural principles of environmental protection. *Problems of Sustainable Development, 15*, 75–81.

168. Wilson, J. (2009). The life of the saint and the animal: Asian religious influence in the medieval Christian West. *Journal for the Study of Religion, Nature and Culture, 3*(2), 169–188. https://doi.org/10.1558/jsrnc.v3i2.169

169. Bikku, D. (2019). Religion and ecological sustainability among the Bishnois of Western Rajasthan. *Unpublished manuscript.*

170. Guha, R. (2024, October). *Speaking with nature.* Fourth Estate India.

171. Zimmermann, F. (1987). *The jungle and the aroma of meats: An ecological theme in Hindu medicine.* University of California Press.

172. Satyagraha for Conservation: Awakening the Spirit of Hinduism, by O. P. Dwivedi in *This Sacred Earth,* 2003, Routledge.

173. Bikku, D. (2025). Religion and ecology: A study on the religious beliefs and practices in conserving ecology and adapting to climate change among the Bishnois of the Thar Desert in Rajasthan, India. *Religions, 16*(3), 380. https://doi.org/10.3390/rel16030380

174. Tomalin, E. (2004). Bio-divinity and biodiversity:

Perspectives on religion and environmental conservation in India. *Numen, 51*(3), 265–395.

175. Chaturvedi, N. (2017). Bishnois: The eco-warriors of Rajasthan. *Proceedings of the Rajasthan History Congress, XXXII*, 2321-1288. Department of History, J.N.V. University, Jodhpur.

176. Pankaj Jain, 2016, *Dharma and Ecology of Hindu Communities: Sustenance and Sustainability,* Routledge, pp 77

177. Rawat, S. K., & Vashishtha, A. (2019). Philosophy of some hymns of Vedas and Purāṇas in relation to environmental status. *International Journal of Advanced Academic Studies, 1*(1), 222–224.*

178. Reichert, A. (2015). *Sacred trees, sacred deer, sacred duty to protect: Exploring relationships between humans and non-humans in the Bishnoi community* (Master's thesis, University of Ottawa, Department of Classics and Religious Studies).

179. *Zimmerman, Francis. The Jungle and the Aroma of Meats: An Ecological Theme in Hindu Medicine, (Comparative Studies of Health Systems & Medical Care), Motilal Banarsidass Publishers, 2011ecological theme in Hindu medicine.* (Comparative Studies of Health Systems & Medical Care). University of California Press

180. Madras High Court. (2017, July 25). *Vanitha Manickavasagam v. The Member Secretary*, W.P. No. 4995 of 2012. https://indiankanoon.org/doc/76600959/

181. Krishna, N. (2010). *Sacred animals of India* (pp. 6, 15–16). Penguin Books India.

Index

A

Advaita	156
afeem	94
Amavasya	82, 104–106, 167, 239
Ayurveda	223, 233–235, 282

B

Badopal	viii, 197–199, 202, 204–208, 290
Barmer	42, 44, 46, 94, 143, 168, 275
Bhagwan	76
Bhimbetka	151, 286
Bhumi Suktam	11, 141, 213, 246, 247
Bishnoi, Amrita Devi	38, 46–47, 55, 57–58, 67–69, 71, 106, 135
Bishnoi, Dhookalaram	42
Bishnoi Effect	viii, 127–129, 139, 226
Bishnoi, Ganga Ram	37–38, 276
Bishnoi, Nihal Chand	36
Bishnoi, Radheshyam	50, 276–277

Bishnoi, Shaitan Singh	36, 48
Blackbuck	ix, x, xvi, xix, 11–13, 17–22, 26–28, 31–33, 47, 127, 130–136, 161–162, 166–167, 172, 198–200, 202–204, 206, 209, 252, 258, 274, 275, 284, 287, 290–291
Brahm	70, 86, 87
Buddhist	151, 221

C

Capitalism	3, 6, 98, 273
Chaturvedi, Neeke	61
Chinkara	x, 13, 37–38, 40–42, 44–47, 49, 130–131, 166, 172, 252, 284
Chipko movement	59, 69
Chitrakuta	150–151
Christianity	xxiii, xxiv, 74, 216–219, 221

D

Dandakaranya	150–151
deer	xix, 11, 13–15, 21, 23, 26–27, 30, 39, 44–46, 48, 62, 65, 92, 104, 130–131, 133, 167, 176, 185, 193, 211, 245, 253–256, 275–276, 283–284, 294
desert	13, 48, 50–53, 58, 65, 70, 73–74, 77, 96, 102, 104, 120, 124, 128–130, 135–137, 141–144, 157, 166, 168, 172–173, 181, 187–190, 198, 276, 284–285
desert ecology	135
dhani	31

dharma	xix, xx, xxi, xxiii, xxv, xxvi, 3–5, 31, 35, 40, 53, 70, 73–76, 95, 130, 132–133, 139, 141, 158, 192, 211, 223, 230, 233, 241–242, 244–246, 248–249, 273, 300
dharmic tourism	102
Dhora	xv, 77–78, 86, 103, 129, 132, 143, 163, 279, 281
Dwivedi, O P	xxiv, 110, 223

E

Earth	vi, vii, xx, xxii, xxiii, 1–3, 8–9, 11, 17, 31, 59, 69, 89, 157, 161, 172, 208, 213, 218–219, 221–222, 224, 227, 231, 235, 237, 239, 242–243, 245–247, 251, 274, 277, 287, 292–293
ecological crisis	215–216, 219, 227, 292

F

forensic	14, 15, 17

G

Gandhi, Indira	69
Great Indian Bustard (GIB)	49, 144, 194, 277
Guha, Ramchandra	5
Guru Jambeshwar	64, 76, 169

H

havan	78, 80, 95, 107–111, 132
Hindu	xxiv, xxv, 25, 87, 91, 105–107, 109, 113–116, 118–119, 121, 123, 147, 184, 189, 222–223, 225, 235, 246, 252, 276, 277, 280–283, 285, 288, 293–294
Hinduism	xxiv, 73, 113, 116, 118–119, 221, 223, 282, 286, 293
Hindustan Times	191, 207, 290–291
Hiran	183, 186, 210, 274

I

indigo	82, 96–98, 281

J

Jain, Pankaj	42, 57, 116, 119, 130, 144, 153–154, 226, 276–277, 282–283, 285, 293
Jambhoji	76, 85, 104, 229, 279, 281
Jodhpur	11, 13, 29, 32, 37, 44, 45, 47–49, 55–57, 59–63, 67, 94, 131, 134, 142–143, 163, 172, 183, 188–189, 252–254, 281, 293
Judaism	74, 216

K

Kantara	1–4, 141, 273, 278
Khejarli Massacre	vii, 55, 67, 174
Khejri tree	21, 57, 61, 135, 137, 142, 149, 188
Krishna Jinka	26

M

Mahabharata	xxii, 35, 127, 149, 150, 154–155, 179, 222, 286
Malhotra, Rajiv	73–74, 278
martyrdom	33, 36, 42, 56, 59
Martyrs	vii, viii, 35, 37, 53, 68, 259
Marwar	viii, ix, 40, 44, 114, 116–117, 271
melas	90, 101, 103, 105–107, 111, 179, 199, 207
Mukkam	105
Muslim	87, 113–114, 117–119, 121–123

N

Neem	144, 173

O

opium	82, 92–94, 167, 280
Oran	141, 143

P

Panchavati	150–151
Panchmahabhuta	232, 236
Panjurli	1–2, 4
panth	xxv, 43, 75–78, 86, 105, 229
philanthropy	89–90, 92
poaching	xvi, xix, 12–13, 17–18, 21, 27, 29–32, 39, 40, 44, 49–50, 66, 130, 161, 166, 181–182, 184–185, 204, 251–252, 274

policy	xvi, xxvi, 99, 139, 159, 179–180, 187, 190, 192–193, 195, 198, 207, 227, 233, 239, 244–247, 290
Prahlad Panthi	78
prakriti	xxi, 141, 229, 232
Prasar Bharati	59
Puranas	152, 155, 286

R

Ramayana	xxi, 96, 149–152, 154, 222, 286
Rathod, Bikku	221, 224

S

Sabadvaani	25, 73, 80, 86–88, 107, 248, 279, 281
sacred forests	xxiv, 2, 146–147
sacred groves	xxii, 4, 67, 141–145, 147–149, 156–158, 217, 241, 285–286
Sakas	60–62
Sampradaya	25, 75
Sanatan Dharma	xx, xxi, xxiv, xxvi, 7, 20, 33, 75, 91–92, 96, 123, 221–222, 224, 226–227, 231–232, 243, 245–246
SDG (Sustainable Development Goal)	192, 215
shaheed	35–36, 39
shila-lekhs	43
Shiva, Vandana	xxiv, 4, 58, 137, 215, 222, 277
Sikhism	73
smark	43
solar plants	50, 186–191, 194, 288
superstar	xix, 11, 32
sustainability	xx, xxiii, xxvii, 78, 98–99, 127, 163,

	213–215, 225–226, 230–231, 233, 240, 246, 293
sustainable	vi, xx, xxvi, 5, 77–78, 81, 86, 98–99, 195, 229, 231, 240–241, 284
syncretic	114, 118

T

Tamarapatra	56
temple	65, 71, 90–93, 103–105, 107, 111, 120–121, 129, 131–133, 146, 280
Thar Desert	49, 113, 180, 189, 275, 277, 293
The Hindu	184, 246, 252, 280, 288
The Tribune	202, 290
Times of India	19, 30, 36, 63, 91, 131, 189, 192, 274, 276, 278, 280, 284, 289–290
Trithankars	153

U

Upanishads	150, 155
Uttarakhand	68–69, 147

V

Vana Parva	xxii, 150, 155
Varaha 2, 246	
Vedas	1, 11, 86, 95, 123–124, 141, 152, 213, 246, 222, 286, 293
Vishnoi	38
Vishnu	2, 37, 73, 78–79, 81–82, 88, 119, 123, 167, 169, 246, 271

W
White, Lynn   xxiii, 216–218, 220, 226, 292

Y
yagya   108–110, 239

About the Author

Anu Lall holds a Master's in business administration (MBA) from XLRI Jamshedpur and is a Bachelor of law (LLB) from Delhi University. She has had a career in the pharmaceutical and technology industries, working in India, US, Europe and Singapore for over twenty-five years.

She is a trained yoga asana and pranayama teacher. Anu's immensely viral videos about current issues, *dharma* and law resonate with audiences worldwide and are widely shared across platforms.

Anu is a popular face on television debates, besides being an author and a regular contributor of opinions and articles to national and international newspapers.